ECONOMIES:
IN SEARCH OF GREATER EFFECTIVENESS

EQUAL PAY PROTECTION IN INDUSTRIALISED MARKET ECONOMIES: IN SEARCH OF GREATER EFFECTIVENESS

F. Eyraud et al.

INTERNATIONAL LABOUR OFFICE GENEVA

First published 1993

Eyraud, F., et al.
Equal pay protection in industrialized market economies: In search of greater effectiveness
Geneva, International Labour Office, 1993
/Case study/s, /Equal pay/, /Work of comparable worth/, /Sex discrimination/, /Woman worker/s, /Labour legislation/, /Comment/s, /Application/, /Australia/, /Canada/, /Finland/, /France/, /Japan/, /Netherlands/, /Spain/, /UK/, /USA/. 13.07
ISBN 92-2-108254-7

ILO Cataloguing in Publication Data

ILO publications can be obtained through major booksellers or ILO local offices in many countries, or direct from ILO Publications, International Labour Office, CH-1211 Geneva 22, Switzerland. A catalogue or list of new publications will be sent free of charge from the above address.

Printed in Switzerland PCL

Preface

During the last three decades, major progress has been made in the area of equal pay between men and women. Since the adoption in 1951 of international labour Convention No. 100 and Recommendation No. 90 on equal remuneration for work of equal value, the ILO has played a major role in prompting countries to take equal pay measures. The last ILO comprehensive report on the situation of those countries which had ratified Convention No. 100 was produced in 1985.[1]

As pointed out in the conclusion to that report, the progress made in this area does not by any means signify the complete eradication of pay discrimination. Not only does direct pay discrimination still exist but what progress was made in this area threw light, by contrast, on what is called indirect pay discrimination, which is much more difficult to prove before a tribunal and therefore much more difficult to eradicate. Indirect pay discrimination arises from the fact that wage determination and the composition of pay at the plant level is a very intricate matter. Wages do not only correspond to the requirements of the job undertaken, a factor to which the equal pay principle applies directly, but are also determined by many other aspects of work such as performance, seniority, attitude towards work, and so on. This complexity gives room for discriminatory pay practices which are rather difficult to prove, in turn demonstrating the need for appropriate institutional devices to help prevent and redress discrimination.

It therefore seems appropriate at this juncture to reconsider equal pay, limiting the geographical scope of the study in order to make a more systematic analysis of the legislation and the practice of selected industrialised countries. Each chapter considers, for each country examined, the essential provisions regarding equal pay legislation as well as the enforcement arrangements for implementing them, and their relative effectiveness in helping to solve equal pay problems. Summaries of significant equal pay cases highlight the practical difficulties linked to the implementation of equal pay legislation. Lastly, the role of the social partners in the area of equal pay is analysed and evaluated.

The introductory comparative chapter examines basic equal pay provisions, their evolution and the questions they raise. Its main conclusion is that significant progress in implementing equal pay has been achieved using the lever of legislation. However, while further improvements could still be made, for instance in the areas of scope of comparison and burden of proof, the legislative approach has its limits. In fact, taking into account that pay discrimination is often a matter of day-to-day informal practices at the plant level which are difficult to overcome through legal means alone, significant new breakthroughs could only be made by a greater involvement of the social partners. Thus, the dynamic development of collective bargaining both at branch and plant level would have a more far-reaching effect in terms of implementing the equal pay principle.

This study was originally based on 15 national monographs. Because of editorial constraints, only nine could be published: Australia, Canada, Finland, France, Japan, the Netherlands, Spain, the United Kingdom and the United States.

The ILO would like to thank all the national collaborators for their contributions to this project, as well as Caroline Hartnell for the invaluable work she did in editing the country monographs published in this book.

Notes

Throughout this text, the pronoun "he" is used to refer to employers, labour inspectors, judges, and so on. This is not intended to imply that such occupations are performed exclusively by men, and the text applies equally to women in such occupations. At the same time, the pronoun "she" is used to refer to claimants in equal pay cases. Although claimants in such cases are more likely to be women, this need not be the case.

[1] ILO: *Equal Remuneration: General Survey by the Committee of Experts on the Application of Conventions and Recommendations,* Report III (Part 4B), International Labour Conference, 72nd Session, Geneva, 1986.

Contents

2. Equal pay in Australia *(Margaret Thornton)*

3. Equal pay in Canada (*Dr. Patricia C. McDermott*)

4. Equal pay in Finland ***(Jukka Heikkerö, Pirkko K. Koskinen and Paavo Nikula)***

5. Equal pay in France ***(Christophe Pettiti)***

9. Equal pay in the United Kingdom *(Christopher McCrudden)*

10. Equal pay in the United States *(Janice R. Bellace)*

1

Equal pay: An international overview

*François Eyraud**

1. Introduction

1.1 The importance of legislation in the campaign for equal pay

In the field of worker protection, it has often been a combination of economic and social forces that has constituted the instrument of change. The intervention of national laws and regulations, especially in countries with systems based on Roman law, has in many cases had the effect of consolidating and generalising "social benefits"[1] already accepted in practice. Admittedly, this is not a hard-and-fast rule, and the issue of equal pay is, in fact, one of the exceptions. Legislation in this field appears rather to be ahead of both business practice and collective bargaining.

This is especially true of international Conventions. Thus, in the 1950s and 1960s, the Equal Remuneration Convention, 1951 (No. 100), adopted by the International Labour Conference, facilitated the implementation of measures designed to improve the treatment of women in terms of pay, particularly in those countries that had ratified the Convention. To be sure, these effects vary from one country to another. In countries such as France, where the Convention was introduced in the form of a law, its practical effects have been somewhat watered down, whereas in Italy, Sweden and Finland, where the Convention was taken up in collective bargaining, it has played an important role in the implementation of the principle of equal pay. One of its immediate effects was the abolition of separate wage rates for women in collective agreements.

Even though in the majority of countries, with the passing of time, these results may appear relatively meagre, bearing in mind that women are still in the lowest wage brackets, the Convention was a decisive first step in the campaign against wage discrimination. Later, in the European countries, the 1975 Directive of the European Economic Community (Equal Pay Directive 75/117/EEC) played an essential role in inducing these countries to improve their legislation in this field.

* International Labour Office, Geneva.

The pioneering role of legislation is also the cause of considerable difficulty: it must not only try to combat the inertia of the social partners, an inertia that is not necessarily intentional, but it is also faced with the practical difficulty of trying to define discriminatory actions that have not yet been clarified by social practice with sufficient precision. This is particularly obvious, as we shall see, when it comes to the question of comparing the value of different jobs. This problem is difficult to explain in theory; it is even more complicated to solve in practical, concrete terms.

It is not the purpose of this synthesis to provide a detailed analysis of the various legislations, as this has already been done in the national monographs. Thus, for example, we shall not dwell at length on the protection provided by each law or regulation, which may vary according to whether it applies to the public or the private sector, or according to state or region in countries with a federal system of government. We shall concentrate entirely upon the main problems and trends of these laws and regulations in an attempt to glean, from the national experiences of the nine industrialised market economy countries included in this volume, the factors that might constitute the most effective and realistic means of combating wage discrimination. We also refer in our discussion to a number of other such countries.

This study differs, therefore, from the study conducted by the ILO on equal remuneration in 1985,[2] which provided a general review of all the countries and their overall legislation with a view to evaluating the implementation of the Equal Remuneration Convention, 1951 (No. 100), and Recommendation, 1951 (No. 90) It also differs from the 1986 reports of the Commission of European Communities concerning the application of the directives on equal pay (Directive 75/117/EEC) and equal treatment (Directive 76/209/EEC). These latter covered only the Community countries and concerned itself primarily with compatibility between European directives and national laws and regulations. These studies nevertheless have a number of points in common with the present one, and this publication is intended to update them to the beginning of 1990.

1.2 Problems associated with equal pay

The campaign for equal pay is confronted with two major questions: that of establishing job comparisons, in other words comparing the value of the work performed by different people, and that of finding a more realistic and at the same time more effective procedure for promoting the principle of equality. The answers to these questions have evolved in a very pronounced manner at legislative level.

As regards the question of comparing the value of different jobs, the main development here has been the change from the concept of equal work to that of work of equal value. We shall enlarge on this in section 3, and confine ourselves here to specifying the problems associated with this change. The principle of equal pay for equal work implies no more than equal treatment where jobs are identical in content but are referred to under different titles. In this case, the object is to eliminate flagrant discrimination, but this is far from sufficient to eliminate all the aspects of inequality to which women may be subject in the matter of pay. Indeed, since women are often employed in predominantly female occupations, there may well be no male comparator to supply the evidence of inequality of treatment. Generally speaking, the segregation between male and female jobs can easily lead to *de facto* pay discrimination, since the greater value attributed to strictly male qualities of predominantly male occupations is likely to result in higher pay for men than for women.

In view of these considerations, it was deemed preferable to adopt the principle of equal pay for work of equal value, assessed on the basis of common criteria (such as complexity, responsibility, etc.). The main problem is of course that of establishing criteria for assessing the value of this or that occupation. We shall not dwell here on the theoretical dimensions of this question, which is a particularly controversial one, especially from the economic point of view. As an illustration of the difficulties, we would merely point out that the value can be assessed from the point of view of work content (complexity, responsibility, etc.) or from the point of view of the market (relative shortage of certain types of jobs). These two criteria can undoutedly be combined, bearing in mind that the more complex the job the rarer it will be on the market. But they can also conflict. Take, for example, the case of an enterprise in which certain secretarial jobs mainly performed by women and technical jobs in which men pre- dominate have been assessed as being of comparable value. They should, from the point of view of work content, be paid at the same rate. However, if there is a shortage of one or other of these types of job on the market, they should, from the market point of view, be paid differently. This is one of the problems raised by the application of the principle of equal pay for work of equal value, which we shall examine in greater detail in section 12.

The adoption of the principle of equal pay for work of equal value also raises the question of indirect discrimination. This appears when there is inequality of treatment, based not on gender as such, but on the criteria that are used in relation to work typically performed by women and work typically performed by men. Thus, the criteria for promotion may be such that women, or workers in jobs in which women predominate, are less likely to be promoted than men. The skills associated with female-dominated occupations may be systematically downgraded, or, conversely, certain benefits or bonuses may be paid only in the case of male-dominated occupations. Similarly, part-time jobs, in which women predominate, are underrated and underpaid. This type of discrimination, which is largely attributable to the fact that women are concentrated in certain occupations or sectors of activity, explains why the average wage for women is lower than that for men. It does, however, go beyond the scope of this study, to the extent that it refers to the wider problem of equality in employment and occupation, whereas we are more concerned here with the question of equal pay. It is, none the less, of considerable importance in procedures for settling disputes when the question of supplying proof of discrimination arises. This brings us to the second major question regarding equal pay: how to promote the principle of equality.

The advantages of a collective labour dispute settlement procedure are well known. It avoids the individual confrontation between worker and employer, in which the former may well be in a weaker position, and where personal tensions can build up and jeopardise the future employment relationship. This is obviously the case with disputes over wage discrimination. In the countries reviewed, such disputes are generally dealt with by courts or tribunals. The current trend is to try to remedy the situation by encouraging what are known as "proactive" measures, where the employer takes positive steps to combat discrimination by revising the wage grid, or by what are referred to as "affirmative" or "positive" measures, where the social partners enter into negotiations with a view to eliminating discrimination, especially in its indirect forms. The question that arises here is how to develop collective procedures for settling cases of discrimination, and how to involve the social partners. We shall elaborate on these two aspects in sections 3 and 4 respectively. But first we shall, in the next section, give a brief outline of the principal stages of legislative development.

2. Principal stages of legislative development

Leaving aside the general statement of the principle of equality to be found in most constitutions, from the legislative point of view we find a set of laws and regulations on equal pay dating from the 1970s. Admittedly, there are some outstanding exceptions such as the Federal Equal Pay Act of 1963 in the United States and provincial laws in Canada dating back to the 1950s (in the collective bargaining field, we might add to the above exceptions the movement to abolish separate women's wage rates in collective agreements in Sweden and Italy, for example). By and large, however, the 1970s can be labelled as the period of the first major breakthrough towards equal pay in the industrialised market economy countries.

The 1980s saw another movement to intensify measures to combat gender-based discrimination in matters of remuneration. There were two distinct trends. The first involved broadening the basis of comparison from the concept of equal, identical work to that of work of equal value. The second involved providing a more precise definition of the concept of equal value. A third trend, which also appears to be emerging, is to give more concrete expression to the principle of equal pay for work of equal value, mainly through improving implementation procedures. In this latter field, however, there have been no more than a few ripples. It is scarcely necessary to mention that not all countries have reached the same level of development in respect of the general trends. Let us now look at the different phases.

2.1 From the concept of equal work to that of work of equal value

The United Kingdom provides us with one example of the broadening of the basis of comparison, with the 1983 Equal Pay Amendment Regulations amending the 1970 Equal Pay Act, with a view to extending the scope of job comparison, hitherto restricted to identical jobs or jobs previously graded as equivalent. From 1983 on, the comparison was to be based on the criterion of equal value, even in the enterprises that did not have a standard job classification system. In Canada, until the mid-1970s, comparison was limited to jobs that were virtually identical, but this is no longer the case. In Spain, on the other hand, the law concerning the status of employees still refers only to the concept of "equal work". And in the United States, the 1963 Equal Pay Act is still considered to apply only to "substantially equal" work. However, a number of states have adopted laws based on the concept of equal value. This is the concept that is today most widely accepted among the countries under review.

2.2 *Towards a more general definition of equal value*

The general principle of equality of treatment between men and women is frequently stated in the constitutions of a large number of countries. In their efforts to give practical effect to this principle, many governments, while broadening the basis of job comparisons, have tried to make the concept more operational by giving a more precise definition of the elements to be compared. This has been done either using specific laws concerning equal pay or in the context of more general laws concerning equality in employment and occupation (thus including general questions of discrimination in employment as well as questions of pay). France, for example, amended its 1972 law, which stated the general principle of non-discrimination in wages, by a law on equality in employment and occupation enacted in 1983, specifying the criteria to be applied in comparing jobs. Many legislations have established similar criteria for comparison. In general, they are skill, responsibility, effort and conditions of work. Some laws also refer to job evaluation methods as a means of establishing equality. Such references can be quite useful in avoiding a restrictive interpretation of the concept of equal value, which might lead to its being equated with being of identical value. In fact, the application of aggregated skills evaluation criteria can promote a more general acceptance of the idea of equal value.

2.3 *New developments: Towards a broader interpretation of discrimination and a greater involvement of the social partners*

Here we ought to mention the fact, even though it goes beyond the scope of this study, that it was in this period too that legislators, taking advantage of reports and analyses emphasising the need to take account of indirect discrimination if wage discrimination was to be combated effectively, devoted their efforts to the promotion of women's employment, in what are referred to as affirmative measures. Thus, in 1985 Japan promulgated its Equal Employment Opportunity Act with a view to combating indirect discrimination, while in France the 1983 law, referred to earlier, endeavoured, among other things, to promote vocational training for women to further their promotion opportunities. It was also during this period that some of the countries that had hitherto relied on collective bargaining, for example Sweden and Finland, began to enact laws specifically designed to promote women's employment.

If we look at the matter from the point of view of procedures, the general movement, which is as yet very much in its infancy, is towards placing greater responsibility on the employer in the fight against discrimination, and advocating collective rather than individual action in this respect. Certain Canadian provincial laws, described as "proactive", provide a good example of this two-pronged movement. These laws place employers under an obligation to investigate discriminatory practices in their enterprise and apply a collective remedy. However, such laws are the exception rather than the rule. And yet, as we shall see, the inadequacy of the available procedures constitutes the most serious obstacle to the implementation of the principle of non-discrimination. This is probably the area most in need of progressive measures.

* * *

Today, we can point to three distinct stages in the evolution of regulations on equal pay. The first is the statement of the general principle, to be found for the most part in national constitutions and laws, aimed at eliminating blatant inequalities, in particular unequal pay for identical work. The second is an enlargement of the concept of equal pay, broadening the basis of comparison to work of equal value. The third stage, currently in progress, involves finding means of overcoming "structural" inequalities resulting from the patterns of women's integration in the labour market and the work-place (for example, the confinement of women workers to low-paid job categories with no career prospects). From this point of view, the question of equal pay in the strict sense tends to be subsumed under the broader concept of equality in employment and occupation. While it makes the problem all the more complex, this trend is probably the most realistic in its approach to an effective campaign against discrimination. Another feature of this third stage is the attempt to overcome procedural difficulties in disputes over equal pay.

In the course of this chapter, we shall attempt to evaluate the limitations of current legislation and, in so doing, to suggest the elements of future progress in this field.

3. The difficulties of providing an operational definition of the principle of comparability

We have seen that, with one or two exceptions, national laws and regulations have accepted as a principle of comparison that of work of equal value, the comparison to be based on general job evaluation criteria. This makes it possible to insist on equal pay, not only when the job titles are different but their content similar, but also when the job content is dissimilar but has been assessed as being of the same value. While it seems necessary and desirable to use a general concept of this sort, the problems of applying it, owing to the difficulty of measuring the value of work, can easily be imagined. This value can, in fact, be assessed according to different criteria, which can lead to divergent results. National experiences enable us to identify three general interacting criteria, divergent interpretations of which are the main cause of disputes: the value of the job content, the market value, and the value produced by the workers.

3.1 Comparability based on the value of the job content

This is the main criterion found in all the national laws and regulations referred to in this study. As already indicated, it is generally based on four major elements: skill (training and experience), responsibility, physical and mental effort, and the conditions under which the work is performed.

We find that these are the principal criteria applied in job evaluation schemes. However, not all laws refer explicitly to such schemes; this mainly occurs in the United

Kingdom and the Netherlands. While a job evaluation scheme has the advantage of rationalising the comparison rather than relying on the inevitably subjective statements of employees and employers, as happens in a number of countries, it also involves well-known dangers. There is a considerable amount of literature on the evasions and subterfuges that such methods can entail, in particular the implicit upgrading of certain criteria specific to male jobs. Among the most glaring examples are the higher ratings attributed to physical effort than to mental stress, to strength than to dexterity, to economic accountability than to moral responsibility. Moreover, if the procedure is presented as a scientific method, it becomes very difficult to contest it. This is why some trade unions reject it out of hand, as in Italy. Sweden has adopted a different approach: there the law requires the schemes to be negotiated. In the light of cases dealt with by the tribunals, it is difficult to pass a definitive judgement on the advantage of job evaluation schemes. They are probably useful so long as the evaluation criteria are not biased, which might be a very good reason for combining systems in order to limit the dangers.

Meanwhile, the problem becomes more complicated as new forms of work organisation call in question the whole concept of the job description, with the introduction of greater flexibility as regards job content making it more difficult to describe specific jobs. In this respect, Japan offers a good example, inasmuch as the Japanese worker is not assigned to a job as such, but to a series of activities within a working group. In this case, the concept of job evaluation or classification becomes meaningless.

Finally, even if work content is admitted as the criterion of value, the problem of the comparator still arises, especially when the occupational category in question consists for the most part of women. Most national laws and regulations remain silent on this subject. Those of Ontario and Nova Scotia in Canada require that employers group their employees in “employment categories” on the basis of skills, responsibilities, duties and remuneration. They must then identify the groups in which women predominate (either 60 or 70 per cent women) and, if necessary, increase their wages to the level of the lowest wage paid in all comparable male-dominated categories. Manitoba’s and Prince Edward Island’s legislations allow female job classes to receive an average of the wages of possible comparators. This is probably the most satisfactory solution, so long as the field of comparison is confined to the same enterprise. This raises the basic question of the area in which the principle of equal pay should apply, which we shall examine in greater detail later. One aspect of this question is the relationship between equal pay and market value, which we shall deal with in the following paragraphs.

3.2 Comparability based on market value

No legislation explicitly admits of different pay for two jobs of equivalent content, for the sole reason that there is a relative shortage of a certain type of skill. This is undoubtedly where the contradiction between purely economic logic and the logic of social protection, embodied in labour law, is at its most glaring. If one thinks in terms of equal value and not just of equal work, one can equate different skills: for

NEW FORM WORK ORG.

example, dexterity with physical strength. This equation is based on a scale agreed by employer and workers. This scale will not necessarily be the same as one established by the market if there is a momentary shortage of certain skills or qualifications. In this case, market mechanisms will raise the price of the rarer qualification.

The discrepancy between the evaluation given within the enterprise and the market evaluation is likely to be intensified and perpetuated with the existence of internal markets, which are not uncommon, especially in the case of large enterprises. The internal patterns which develop in such enterprises may be at odds with market logic, which makes it very difficult to recruit highly skilled or qualified personnel from outside. Similarly, if a job that is traditionally paid at the same level as another were to become rare within such an internal market, it would be very difficult to modify the internal wage hierarchy without risking conflict. If the market criterion (rarity) were applied, this would mean that, within the one enterprise, two jobs, which are different but classed as equivalent by a job evaluation system or by usage, could be paid at different levels if there were a change in supply and demand as regards the skills or qualifications in question. But work is not a commodity like other goods on the market, so legislators are justified in rejecting, in principle, the criterion of market value.

In practice, however, the principle has sometimes been admitted. Thus, in the United Kingdom in 1986, in the case of *Fletcher* v. *Clay Cross,* the House of Lords conceded that an employer might introduce a pay disparity based on a material difference other than the individual's skill or qualification. This could include economic factors such as the comparative shortage of a given type of manpower. Similarly, in Sweden in 1990, the labour tribunal upheld the defence of an employer, not covered by a negotiated wage scale, who had paid a male journalist a higher salary than a female journalist on the grounds that he had been recruited six months later at a time when there was a shortage of qualified journalists.[3]

The principle has also been adopted in a less direct manner in the United States, where a tendency has been observed to adapt the job classification system to market requirements. For example, physical strength will be rated more highly if it is in short supply. A detailed analysis of classification scheme and the corresponding wage scales undertaken in a number of countries would undoubtedly show that this phenomenon is not confined to the United States. We know that several such schemes are based on job evaluation methods. However, the discriminatory nature of certain evaluation criteria applied has been widely debated, and such criteria probably affect the classification systems in use today.

More generally speaking, when legislation limits the comparison of jobs to the enterprise, or even to the establishment (in cases where the establishments are scattered through the national territory), as is often the case, the constraints of local markets must, in fact, be taken into account.

3.3 Comparability based on the value produced by the employees

It is hard to see how one can assess the value produced by employees in complex production organisations where the workers' relation to the end product is very indirect.

However, most countries do admit merit or points systems which make it possible to pay different wages to workers with the same level of skill or qualification. The principle of non-discrimination is not called in question by this type of system so long as it applies to all workers. However, it is important that the criteria for awarding the bonuses involved should not in themselves be discriminatory. Here again the question of control arises, and it is rendered all the more difficult in this case, as the bonuses are multiple and non-transparent, and thus far more difficult to identify than the basic wage. The case of a Spanish company provides a good example in this respect. A "staff bonus" is paid, but it is paid at a much higher rate to a specific, highly qualified category comprising men only. Discrimination is difficult to prove in this case, inasmuch as women are not directly discriminated against as such, but only the skill levels in which they predominate. The situation is further aggravated by the fact that the periodical wage increases are largely based on this "staff bonus".

There is also the particular problem of seniority bonuses and overtime pay, which, in conjunction with productivity, are the main criteria generally recognised by national legislations as justifying wage differentiation in jobs where the work content is of equivalent value, thus implying that they actually produce different values.

As far as seniority is concerned, bearing in mind that women are far more subject than men to career interruptions, this criterion is, in fact, discriminatory. It is even more discriminatory when seniority plays a major role in wage-fixing, as is the case in a large number of countries. This is especially true of Japan, where it is an essential criterion for wage increments, and in countries where internal markets tend to predominate. The problem cannot be solved by parental leave, which, despite the benefits it confers in terms of allowances and the obligation to reinstate, does not make up the loss of seniority.

As regards overtime, while it appears perfectly legitimate that longer working hours should be more highly paid, it is a well-known fact that statistically overtime is one of the major sources of wage differentiation to the disadvantage of women. To a considerable extent, this reflects the fact that women tend to undertake such an unfairly large share of work in the home, and so have no time to work overtime, a subject which goes beyond the scope of this study. On the other hand, in certain cases, and in certain countries such as the United Kingdom, for example, fictitious overtime has been used as a supplement to wages. This might be the case where an employer wants to satisfy a wage claim for one category of workers but wishes to avoid other worker groups demanding the same increase. In other words, overtime in this case enables the employer to prevent a comparison which would give rise to wage increases for all worker categories. Such a practice could prove to be indirectly discriminatory if it involved wage discrepancies which were not justified by actual work, and if it benefited men only.

These comments on bonuses can also be applied to the other elements of remuneration as defined in the laws and regulations concerning equal pay. With very few exceptions, the definition of the elements to be taken into account when comparing pay is a very broad one in the countries under review. It includes not only the basic wage, but also in several countries all supplementary payments including bonuses and voluntary social insurance schemes (retirement, sickness, etc.). The few cases brought before the tribunals, in a small number of countries, usually concern the issue of family allowances being paid to men, who are regarded as the principal breadwinners. On the other hand, there have been complaints from men demanding certain benefits to which women are entitled, such as child-care allowances and maternity leave, obviously considered as parental leave. From the legislative point of view, protection against discrimination is fairly well guaranteed. However, difficulties arise as soon as one considers the growing complexity of remuneration systems.

On the one hand, it is sometimes difficult to obtain a clear idea of the total remuneration paid to employees. This can be made more difficult by the confidential nature of this type of information in a number of countries. Even in the case of complaints, the tribunals cannot be of much help in this area. In fact, even when they are in a position to obtain very detailed information in order to reach their decisions, as is the case in the United States in particular, tribunals are often reluctant, when prescribing redress, to interfere in wage policy at enterprise level, as this is considered to be a matter of management for which the employer alone is responsible.

On the other hand, as suggested earlier, the criteria for determining bonuses can involve implicit discrimination. The most blatant instance of this is in the matter of physical strength, but it can also apply to bonuses granted to certain worker categories consisting mainly of men (as in the case of the Spanish company referred to above). All this bears out the need for a precise analysis of remuneration systems, which would make it possible to assess actual discriminatory practices, irrespective of any overall statistical indicator, such as the average wage. From the legal point of view, these few examples underline the importance of investigation methods, and reflect therefore the essential role that appeals procedures have to play, which we shall discuss in the next section.

3.4 The fight against discrimination and restrictions on management freedom

The complex and frequently contradictory interaction between the three work evaluation criteria that we have just examined can to a certain extent explain the practical difficulties encountered in the fight against wage discrimination. In a large number of cases, the defence of women against wage discrimination imposes certain restrictions on employers' freedom of management. This gives rise to the question of the extent to which wage-fixing systems can be monitored in order to limit discriminatory tendencies, without depriving employers of the margin of independence and ability to react to circumstances needed if they are to adapt to economic and social changes and to maintain and increase their efficiency and productivity. Bearing this question in mind, certain legislations have limited the possibilities of comparing jobs to one employer, and sometimes even to one establishment. It is easy to imagine that a group will, intentionally or unintentionally, specialise production in its companies and establishments in such a way that the female workforce will be concentrated in the establishments paying the lowest wages, and there will thus be no possibility of comparison. Understandably, legislating in this area is a delicate matter, inasmuch as it is diffuclt to distinguish between a company's economic growth strategy, which is indispensable in a market economy, and the actual intention to discriminate, which legislation must try to combat.

In this situation, other things being equal, a centralised wage-fixing system with a broader field of comparison might seem to be the best guarantee against the social injustice of discrimination. A policy of upgrading low wages can also help to improve women's wages, to the extent that women tend to be concentrated in low-paid job categories. From this latter point of view, the anti-discrimination campaign is part of the campaign against low wages in general. These two aspects are combined in such countries as Sweden and Australia, where the differences between men's and women's earnings are least among the countries under review.

The Australian system of wage-fixing by tribunals has, up to now, restricted consideration of the specific characteristics of companies in favour of comparability between awards (which cover an entire industry or certain worker categories regardless of employer). This has made it possible to limit the discriminatory practices that might otherwise have been perpetrated at the workplace. Moreover, since the wage increases under the "award" obtained by the higher-paid employees are used as a basis of comparison for the determination of other "awards" the lower-paid workers, most of whom tend to be women, gain here too. These characteristics will have been reinforced as a result of the introduction in 1987 of a two-tier wage system, involving an absolute increase in favour of the lowest-paid workers, and a second increase designed to introduce greater flexibility into the wage-fixing system. This has also been used to upgrade the lowest wages. Although different in form, the Swedish system has so far produced similar results by means of centralised bargaining in conjunction with a policy of freezing wages, which brings about a decrease in wage differentials.

Systems such as these imply major restrictions on employers' autonomy as regards wage policy, restrictions that might be difficult to impose in the majority of the countries under review. Besides, in both Australia and Sweden there is now a movement towards decentralisation. This is giving employers more and more freedom of action and bringing Australia and Sweden into line with other countries. In these circumstances other ways will probably have to be found to combat sex discrimination over wages.

The most realistic approach is probably to define discriminatory criteria more explicitly in the laws and regulations. Considerable progress has been made in this field as regards the comparison of job content. Further progress could be made if, in the job evaluation exercise, more emphasis were placed on the importance of not downgrading the characteristics of types of work performed mainly by women. On the other hand, there is very little protection as far as wage-fixing systems are concerned. For example, as mentioned earlier, while the principle of wages based on merit is widely accepted, the relevant laws are silent on the subject of the criteria to be applied. However, any action taken in this area would presuppose an analysis of these systems to detect dangers of discrimination. Although analyses of discrimination in job evaluation schemes are legion, there are very few studies on the discriminatory aspects of various types of wage system. The fact remains that, as far as measures against discrimination are concerned, the law, in a market economy, can realistically do no more than prescribe general restrictive principles, and these, as we have seen, should be improved. On the other hand, a considerable amount of work still needs to be done in the matter of implementation procedures, which are the Achilles' heel of a number of national legislations.

4. Procedures to give effect to the principle of equal pay: From individual complaint to systematic collective action

Procedures for combating wage discrimination vary considerably from one country to another. Moreover, each country offers several alternative procedures. These tend to be of three types:

(a) the classic procedure in which the court or tribunal deals with individual and/or collective complaints;

(b) parallel to this procedure, intervention by a specialised commission which assists in the settlement of the dispute, be it individual or collective; and

(c) a systematic collective procedure.

This classification is based on three variables:

(a) the individual or collective nature of the complaint;

(b) the type of institution that deals with the complaint; and

(c) the existence of machinery that automatically takes the antidiscriminatory issue into account in wage policy at enterprise level.

It is essential to take these three variables into account when evaluating the efficiency of legislation or wage-fixing systems in respect of equal pay, because the two main obstacles to effective action against discrimination are the employee's fear of entering into an individual dispute with the employer (which is removed if the action is collective and/or goes through a conciliation body) and the difficulty not only of proving but also of identifying discrimination (which is partly overcome with the help of a specialised body or if employers are themselves obliged to implement anti-discriminatory measures). From this point of view, the three types referred to above are in an ascending order of effectiveness as regards combating wage discrimination based on sex. Such characteristics obviously do not remove all other difficulties: for example, the difficulties mentioned in earlier paragraphs concerning the application of the principle of equal value, as well as indirect discrimination.

4.1 Traditional procedures involving tribunals: Limitations

All countries we have studied have a complaints procedure involving the courts. However, they vary as to the numbers of complaints submitted to courts and according to whether or not this is an alternative to another type of procedure. In many countries, including France, Italy, Japan and the United Kingdom, the court or tribunal is the main forum for the settlement of complaints. This raises two major difficulties: discrimination and the fear of reprisals on the part of the employer.

4.1.1 Proof of discrimination and the need for information

The difficulty of proving wage discrimination, not to mention indirect discrimination, is obviously even greater when looked at from the point of view of work of "equal value" rather than "equal work". The employee can be helped in this by two types of measure: placing the burden of proof on the employer, and requiring the employer to supply comprehensive information on job classification and wage-fixing systems.

As far as the burden of proof is concerned, the traditional principle is that the burden of proof lies with the claimant. That is still the case in a number of countries. However, there has been a marked development in this field: the European Community Commission has proposed that the burden of proof should be reversed or, rather, where it is presumed that there has been discrimination, that the employer should be required to prove that there has not been. So far this stage has not been reached in all European, or indeed other, countries. Nonetheless, there is a growing tendency for courts to insist that employers should substantiate their denial of discrimination once the claimant has supplied initial proof that discrimination has occurred. This tendency to place employers under a greater obligation to defend themselves, which is usually at the discretion of the court, gives employees the advantage of a greater insight into job classification and wage-fixing criteria, inasmuch as they obtain more information.

As far as information is concerned, the general rule is that once a complaint has been filed, the court may insist that the employer supply all information necessary for the examination of the complaint. In the United Kingdom, in cases of complaints concerning work of equal value (as distinct from wage differentiation for identical work), the tribunal is required to select an independent expert to analyse the case and submit a report to the tribunal. This ensures that even more information is made available, and that the employee's case is adequately presented, though the difficulties of assessing whether work is of equal value still remain.

However, there is still the question of recognising discrimination before bringing the case to court. This raises the problem of promoting awareness and providing advice on how to file a complaint. In this respect, various countries impose on employers some obligation to provide information, though this information is not necessarily specific to wage discrimination. For example, information must be supplied to the trade unions in the United Kingdom or to the works council in Germany, France, Italy and other countries to enable them to negotiate fair collective agreements. This creates possibilities of action on equal pay issues, but the extent to which they are exploited will depend on the capacities and priorities of the workers' organisations and management. Such provisions are not systematic in the way that the procedures existing in certain Canadian provinces are (cf. 4.3.1) but, if properly implemented, they could provide an alternative to a dynamic anti-discrimination policy. They would be carried out in the context of collective bargaining, the various elements of which will be discussed later.

4.1.2 Damages, reprisals and costs in individual actions

When a complaint is successful, the remedy in all countries is the removal of the discriminatory practice and the awarding of back pay, the amount of the latter varying from one country to another.

In most countries, back pay is limited to the two years preceding the filing of the complaint. This is the case in Japan, the Netherlands, the United States and the United Kingdom. In both France and Greece pay can be backdated by as much as five years. But the most favourable terms exist in Belgium, Finland and Italy, where pay may be backdated to the beginning of the discriminatory act.

Simultaneously, the law in general bans all forms of reprisal. In all the countries under review this ban concerns dismissal in particular, but could also be extended to all forms of reprisal. This is not necessarily a measure associated with wage discrimination, but comes under the terms of legislation on unfair dismissal. It is also true that in some countries, such as Finland, compensation for unfair dismissal takes the form of financial payment only, without any reinstatement obligation. As for other forms of indirect reprisal, such as the refusal of promotion, the law is usually silent on this subject. Besides, it would be difficult to draw up an effective means of redress other than that already in existence, that is, filing another complaint concerning discrimination.

In addition to the fear of reprisals from the employer, employees may also be worried about the costs of litigation, though these may, in fact, be quite moderate.[4] These different factors cause a number of employees to hesitate about taking individual action.

Admittedly, in a number of countries it is possible to bring a collective or class action before a tribunal, often with the help of a trade union. This possibility ought to be more widespread, though, like any other collective action, it is difficult to organise and presupposes a strong union presence. Moreoever, it would be particularly problematic in small and medium-scale enterprises where the union presence is not likely to be strong and personal relationships with the employer are closer. For this reason intermediary agencies between the employee, the court and the employer are absolutely essential.

4.2 Settlement of disputes through intermediary agencies other than the tribunal

4.2.1 Non-specialised intermediary agencies

In countries where the complaints procedure mainly takes the form of an action before a court or tribunal, as in Belgium, France, Italy or Japan, there are also other intermediary agencies, which are less costly from the psychological point of view. A typical example of this would be the labour inspectors, found in Belgium, Italy and Japan. The problem with these, however, is their lack of time, due to the extent of their duties, and their lack of specialisation in questions of wage discrimination. Expertise is particularly necessary in this field, which can be extremely complex, as we have already seen, especially when it comes to evaluating different jobs or pay structures. Even when there is a degree of specialisation in the subject of pay equality, as in Belgium for example, it is too marginal to give the labour inspectors the necessary effectiveness.

Special mention should be made here of certain conciliation procedures that exist in Italy and Japan. In Italy, there are local tripartite commissions responsible for conciliation in work-related disputes. In some regions, these commissions are the most commonly used mechanisms for settling labour disputes over wage discrimination. Unfortunately there is no available analysis to enable us to assess this sytem. In Japan, too, there are local government agencies that settle labour disputes informally, including those over equal pay. Here, too, there is a lack of information for assessment purposes, but they would appear to play a not inconsiderable role.

4.2.2 Specialised intermediary agencies

While retaining the possibility of using the traditional tribunal procedure, some countries also have specialised agencies that deal with matters of discrimination, including wage discrimination. Though their titles and procedures may differ, their functions in all cases are to assist in investigation and to attempt conciliation. Canada and the United States, especially at federal level, have specialised commissions which, in practice, virtually compete with the traditional court procedure, even though, legally speaking, they are complementary procedures, since only the court can pronounce a binding verdict.

Thus, in the United States, though a complaint about discrimination may be dealt with by a court or by a local fair employment practices agency, it is usually filed with the Equal Employment Opportunity Commission (EEOC), a federal agency well known to the public. At the claimant's request, this Commission may conduct a preliminary inquiry to evaluate the case and authorise proceedings. Although this is not required by law, the Commission attempts to conciliate and, in all cases, conducts a thorough investigation. Unfortunately, it only has sufficient resources to deal with a minority of cases. None the less, the private attorneys, at the request of their clients, attach great importance to its conclusions when making their decisions as to whether or not to pursue a case. The case is then settled by a civil action before the federal district court.

The Canadian Human Rights Commission and the Dutch Equal Treatment Committee fulfil a similar function in their respective countries, and can also initiate complaints in their own right.

The intermediary agency in Finland and Sweden is the Ombudsman. At the request of a claimant, the Ombudsman can attempt to settle a case of discrimination by conciliation. His opinion has no binding force, however. For this, he would have to request the intervention of the labour tribunal. Finland offers an alternative solution in that the Ombudsman can request the intervention of the Equality Board. In Sweden, the intervention of the Equal Opportunity Commission at the request of the Ombudsman applies only to affirmative action against discrimination (see below). It should be noted that the Swedish Ombudsman only intervenes concerning employees who are not represented by, or do not belong to, a trade union and, in the case of affirmative action, are not covered by an agreement in this respect.

The British Equal Opportunities Commission might also be placed in the above category. However, in view of the small number of complaints that it has defended so far, it seems rather to resemble the occupational equality institutions to be found in other countries, the main function of which is to promote equality in general. One possible explanation for this is undoubtedly the conciliation function of the Advisory, Conciliation and Arbitration Service (ACAS) in certain cases of discrimination, which tends to compete with that of the Commission. We might add that the British trade unions are increasingly active in the campaign against discrimination, as we shall see later, although the issue should be given still greater importance. Obviously the trade unions can act as a "natural" intermediary agency in this field.

Intermediary agencies have several advantages for the employee. In the first place, they help in the identification of discrimination, which can be very difficult for an individual worker, as already pointed out. They can do this all the more effectively in that they have special competence in the field of discrimination in general, and wage discrimination in particular. Finally, not having the power to make a binding decision that the tribunal has, but intervening as a formal or informal conciliator, they can reduce the tensions that inevitably occur between employee and employer in cases of litigation. This undoubtedly represents an improvement on the traditional tribunal procedure, although, as we have seen, it does not replace the need for recourse to a tribunal in cases of serious conflict.

In these circumstances, it is obvious that the best procedure will be one that anticipates discrimination by encouraging a systematic evaluation of discriminatory pay practices. In this respect, the Canadian provinces referred to earlier (cf. 2.3 and 3.1) provide an excellent example. But there are other less radical methods, such as affirmative action, which should be a matter for collective agreements, as in France and Sweden. These, however, depend on the will of the social partners to tackle the problem, as we shall see in the next paragraph. Finally, a particular wage-fixing system, associated with a particular system of labour relations, can also further the movement against wage discrimination. This is the case in Australia and New Zealand. We shall now examine all these types of procedure.

4.3 Systematic procedures to combat discrimination

4.3.1 Radical procedures

It is usual to quote the case of certain Canadian provinces as examples of active legislation against pay discrimination. However, this legislation concerns only a relatively limited number of individuals, since it does not cover the entire country and is very often limited to the public sector. This is true of the Manitoba Pay Equity Act, for example. In Ontario, on the other hand, the law also applies in the private sector. In these two cases (and also in Prince Edward Island and Nova Scotia), employers are required, with a few variations, to conduct, in cooperation with the unions and over a certain number of years, a non-discriminatory job evaluation exercise with a view to correcting any discriminatory job classification that might exist. In Ontario, employers are required to set up a fund equivalent to 1 per cent of the annual wage bill to correct inequalities.

Special mention should be made here of the situation in which the nature of the labour relations system is such that it constitutes an effective weapon against wage discrimination. Indeed, though the methods are basically different, the very unusual form of wage-fixing to be found in Australia and New Zealand can produce similar end results. It should, however, be noted that the situation is undergoing rapid change towards a decentralised system, the nature of which is as yet difficult to evaluate.

We have seen that centralised wage-fixing by means of "awards" provides an effective means of preventing wage discrimination. New Zealand's 1972 Equal Pay Act explicitly insists on the application of the principle of equal pay by means of the "award" system of wage-fixing. However, this system will not work unless the wages fixed by the centralised method are close to the actual wages paid by employers. In any case, the present trend in these countries, especially New Zealand, towards decentralised bargaining at enterprise level, may well call in question the effectiveness of this machinery in combating wage discrimination.

This is not the case with the measures introduced in the Canadian provinces. Whatever criticism may be made of the details of these measures, they are clearly, in principle, an ideal weapon in the war against discrimination. Measures of this type have the enormous advantage of avoiding direct individual confrontation between employee and employer, and they also make it possible to reveal discriminatory practices considered "natural" by force of habit. Whether such laws will become more widespread is another question. One can easily imagine the opposition they would give rise to in a number of countries, if only from the point of view of the enormity of the task and the cost of enforcement. For this reason, it would scarcely be realistic to advocate such measures as an immediate objective, as this could meet with outright rejection in certain countries. It would probably be more effective to work out intermediate solutions, while keeping such measures as a long-term objective.

4.3.2 Incentive procedures

From this point of view, the example of countries such as Finland, France and, above all, Sweden can be used as a reference point. As already noted, the Swedish legislation concerning the equality of men and women at the workplace contains an obligation on employers and employees to implement positive measures. These must be written into the collective agreement where trade unions are established. Where workers are not covered by such agreements, the Ombudsman must see to it that the measures are implemented, if necessary by requesting the intervention of the Equal Opportunities Commission. While these measures appear to focus particularly on indirect discrimination, such as in matters of promotion, the procedure could be extended more systematically to wage discrimination in the strict sense of the term. Negotiation between the social partners certainly has the potential to play a major role in this field.

5. The role of the social partners: Future potential

Collective bargaining has always played a pioneering role in labour issues. More flexible than legislation because it is less cumbersome and less general, it can take innovative social practices into consideration. In a number of countries advantages thus obtained may be extended through subsequent legislation. In the social field, it is more often collective bargaining than law that breaks new ground. In the matter of equal pay, on the other hand, the reverse is very often the case: it is the law that introduces the changes. However, we need to qualify this statement.

A review of the British situation shows, in fact, that despite the existence of very elaborate legal procedures, the unions tend increasingly to be considered as the main forum for action on equal pay issues. This takes place both through collective bargaining and by means of assistance to individual claimants. This illustrates the potential role of the social partners in developments in this field. This potential is, in fact, no more than an extension of their present activities, which are conducted in two areas: the individual or collective defence of employees' rights, and collective bargaining to obtain further advantages.

5.1 Recourse within the enterprise: The need for specialisation

In the previous section we noted that the union may provide assistance to employees who are bringing a complaint before a tribunal. Another type of intervention takes place at this level when the union or staff delegate takes up individual cases with management. It is obviously very difficult to estimate the extent of this type of action, but it is probably not inconsiderable. In fact, a number of countries provide appropriate structures for dealing with discrimination issues in this way, though the structures provided may not necessarily be specialised in this matter. Thus, for example, in a number of countries works councils or committees are supposed to be supplied with the information necessary to take action in this field. In Germany and the Netherlands they can also supervise the implementation of the equality principle in job classifications at enterprise level. This type of intervention will obviously depend both on the workers' representatives' capacity for action and on their degree of commitment to discrimination issues. Unions in the United States, for example, potentially have considerable expertise in this field, as a result of their experience in traditional bargaining on wage rates and job classifications, the backbone of enterprise collective agreements. However, declining unionisation levels in the United States, especially in the private sector, may well limit their scope for action. Where, as is the case in a number of European countries, job classifications are established at national or sectoral level, the workers' representatives at enterprise level will probably lack experience in such a complex field.

As can be seen, effective instruments for dealing with discrimination issues do exist. The problem is that they are general tools suitable for use in a variety of areas. However, as is often the case, the discrimination issue can only be dealt with systematically and effectively if the actors involved are sufficiently expert in the subject. It would therefore seem that workers' representatives must be trained in the area of wage discrimination if they are to exploit the machinery that does exist.

5.2 Collective bargaining: A measure to be exploited

Collective bargaining, the purpose of which is to obtain both increased protection and added benefits, seems to be largely underexploited. Admittedly, as we saw in section 1, the earliest measures to combat wage discrimination, especially in respect of the implementation of Convention No. 100, were more successfully promoted when collective bargaining accompanied legislation. This was the case, in particular, with the abolition of differential pay rates for women. We have also seen that, in such countries as Australia and Sweden, collective bargaining has been the main forum for the campaign against wage discrimination. However, this forum appears to be less effective once it is a question of more thoroughgoing measures designed to deal with indirect forms of discrimination. This is true, for example, in the case of comparing work of equal value rather than equal work, and of affirmative action. Sweden provides one example: the legal requirement to negotiate affirmative measures in favour of women has so far produced little effect in terms of collective agreements. It is also true of France, where there is the possibility of negotiating schemes for equality in employment and occupation. The paucity of such agreements bears witness to the long road that has yet to be travelled.

In other words, up to the present, collective bargaining has been an effective way of combating the more flagrant forms of discrimination, with legislation taking over in the fight against the more subtle forms. While we should not underestimate the importance of trade union action in a number of countries in dealing with exemplary discrimination cases, such forms of action are not systematic or regular.

Vigilance is also likely to be necessary in countries like Australia or New Zealand where the wage bargaining structure is such that the unions can relatively easily take action against discrimination. There the trend towards decentralised wage bargaining, referred to earlier, will make it necessary for them to develop new policies if they are to maintain this orientation.

And yet, encouraging signs are beginning to emerge. In Italy, for example, some collective agreements now contain provision for the establishment, at enterprise level, of joint committees responsible for organising affirmative action. Since the spring of 1991, the largest British union, the Transport and General Workers' Union (TGWU), has been conducting a campaign for equal pay in the car industry. In general, the evolution of a concern for the situation of women on the part of the unions, which we can observe in Japan, the United Kingdom and the United States, for example, suggests the emergence of a new stage in the campaign against discrimination against women in employment, especially wage discrimination.

6. Conclusions

National laws and regulations can certainly be improved. There are two areas, in particular, where various types of progress could be made in one country or another. In the first place, where this has not already been done, the comparison of jobs should be extended to work of equal value rather than limited to equal work. Secondly, there should be a more widespread development of intermediary agencies specialising in wage discrimination issues, the importance of which we have emphasised in the course of this chapter. This extension of legal protection is, however, likely to come up against increasingly rigid barriers, as the campaign against discrimination advances, barriers associated with freedom of management in a market economy. We have seen examples of this. Some remuneration systems are based on criteria that in practice discriminate against women. Seniority is the most obvious example. A similar problem arises in the matter of promotion: the dividing line between a discriminatory choice and one based on merit is not very clear-cut. Appropriate action against discrimination would thus presuppose fairly tight control over employers' management policy, which might prove difficult to establish in practice.

For this reason, it would appear essential that collective bargaining, and more generally the involvement of the social partners, should at a certain point take over from legislative action. The law would then play a prescriptive role. This presupposes, however, that the social partners have both the means and the will to combat discrimination. This means, as we have seen, training workers' representatives in discrimination issues, especially in the matter of pay. As for the will, this implies awareness of the problems. It is true that, for a long time, the unions, dominated as they were by men, did not give issues of discrimination the necessary attention. Marked improvements are, however, becoming apparent today. From this point of view, the fact that such improvements are partly associated with the unions' desire to attract new members at a time when unionisation levels are generally declining is of little importance.[5] This is little more than a reflection of changing employment structures in which women are becoming more and more numerous, and thus could make a significant contribution to increased union membership.

Bibliography

Andiappan, P. et al. "Public policy and equal pay: A comparative study of equal pay laws in Canada, USA and UK", in *International Review of Administrative Sciences,* 1985, No. 1, pp. 24-32.

Department of Employment, Women's Bureau. *Pay equity: A survey of seven OECD countries,* Information Paper No. 5, Canberra, Australian Government Publishing Service, 1987.

EEC. *National reports on equal treatment for men and women.* Commission of the European Communities (VA 4), 1983.

Gunderson, M. "Male-female wage differentials and policy responses", in *Journal of Economic Literature,* Mar. 1989, pp. 46-72.

IIRA (International Industrial Relations Association). *Equity and equality of treatment in employment,* Eighth World Congress, 4-7 Sept. 1989.

ILO. *Equal remuneration: General Survey by the Committee of Experts on the Application of Conventions and Recommendations,* Report III (Part 4B), International Labour Conference, 72nd Session, Geneva, 1986.

Meehan, E.M. *Women's rights at work: Campaigns and policy in Britain and the United States.* Basingstoke, Macmillan, 1985.

Nielsen, Ruth. *Equality legislation in a comparative perspective – Towards state feminism?* Copenhagen, Women's Research Centre in Social Science, Feb. 1983.

OECD. *Equal pay for work of comparable worth: The experience of industrialised countries,* Document prepared for the OECD, 1988.

—. "Women's activity, employment and earnings: A review of recent developments", in *Employment Outlook,* Sep. 1988, pp. 129-172.

Osborne, R.J. *Equal pay for equal work: A study of legislation in the United States, Canada, the United Kingdom and New Zealand.* London, University Microfilm International, 1976.

Petman, Fyfe J. *Equal pay for women: Progress and problems in seven countries.* Bradford, MCB Books, 1975.

Treu, Tiziano. "Equal pay and comparable worth: A view from Europe", in *Comparative Law Journal,* Fall 1980, No. 1, pp. 1-33.

Tzannatos, Z. "Equal pay in Greece and Britain", in *Industrial Relations Journal,* (Oxford), Winter 1987, 99, pp. 275-283.

Notes

[1] The growing complexity of economies and societies makes the concept of "social benefit" more ambiguous than it used to be. In this same field of equality in employment and occupation, a controversy is developing today in France on the subject of a union-management agreement designed to promote equality between men and women at the workplace. One of its clauses specifies that nothing sbould impede the access of women to any employment for which they choose to train. This may appear to call in question the ban on night work for women. This is indeed a development, but there is no general agreement between the social partners as to whether it is a beneficial one.

[2] ILO: *Equal remuneration: General Survey by the Committee on the Application of Conventions and Recommendations,* Report III (Part 4B), International Labour Conference, 72nd Session, 1986.

[3] Radio Dalarna Case, *IDS European Report 355,* July 1991, p. 5.

[4] This is the case when no expert opinion is necessary or when the employee does not call in a lawyer of his choice. Furthermore, costs can be paid by the union if the employee is a union member, or to a large extent covered by legal aid.

[5] Undoubtedly, this is not the only reason. Canadian trade unions which seem to have escaped what is referred to as the union crisis, are no less unremitting defenders of equality for women.

2

Equal pay in Australia

*Margaret Thornton**

1. Introduction

Although the Australian workforce displays a marked degree of sex segregation,[1] Australian women in full-time employment are somewhat better off than their English and North American counterparts. In Australia, adult women earn 83.4 per cent of the average weekly ordinary-time earnings of men.[2] The comparable figure for the United Kingdom is 74 per cent, for the United States 70 per cent and for Canada 65 per cent.[3] There are two main reasons for this phenomenon:

- Australia has a centralised wage-fixing system;
- there is a higher rate of female unionisation in Australia (see section 5).

In Australia, as O'Donnell and Golder have pointed out, "general wage fixing principles are probably more important than the existence of mechanisms for pursuing equal pay in explaining the wages of men and women workers".[4] Accordingly, it is proposed to outline these general principles before considering specific measures designed to effect equal pay.

1.1 A centralised wage-fixing system

In Australia, wage-setting is controlled through industrial tribunals at both federal and state levels by means of conciliation and compulsory arbitration. The tribunals set minimum wages, although it is possible for unions to bargain with employers for increased weightings. Generally speaking, however, the comparatively weaker industrial muscle of female-dominated unions has not enabled them to negotiate significant margins. Not surprisingly, it is the powerful male-dominated unions, perceived to be the most productive, which have been able to command the highest wages. Nevertheless, a high award has then to be used as a benchmark by other unions to enforce comparative wage justice at the national or state level. The notion of relativity has constituted the traditional heart of the wage-setting system, although the greater focus on efficiency and productivity, the hallmarks of the late 1980s, must inevitably affect traditional relativities.

* Senior Lecturer in Law, Macquarie University. The author would like to thank Dr. Meredith Burgmann and Dr. Clare Burton for reading and commenting on a draft of this paper.

The specification of minimum wages and conditions is normally incorporated into awards which are formal, legally binding instruments ratified by an industrial tribunal. Likely to be more comprehensive than employment contracts in other countries and to operate at the industry-wide level, they specify minimum rates, together with special rates, such as overtime rates and rates for extreme and hazardous conditions. They also specify the hours of work and whether the employment is weekly, daily, casual or part-time, in addition to stipulating conditions regarding termination of employment.[5] In 1986, 83.4 per cent of male and 87.4 per cent of female employees were covered by award rates of pay.[6] Home-based and peripheral workers are likely to be outside the award structure.[7] While more employees are covered by state than by federal awards, leading wage decisions are made through the federal tribunal, the Australian Industrial Relations Commission (formerly the Australian Conciliation and Arbitration Commission), and, in practice, the state tribunals accept the principles laid down by the Commission, although they are not legally bound to do so.[8] At the federal level, claims with national ramifications are lodged with the Commission by the Australian Council of Trade Unions (ACTU), the central union body, to which most unions are affiliated. Unions must be formally registered in order to have access to the Commission in the event of a dispute, although the Commission may act of its own accord.[9] The Confederation of Australian Industry, the leading management group, is also represented before the Commission. The Government is the third primary social partner. This principle of tripartism, constituted by unions, employer organisations and government, forms the basis of the Australian industrial relations system. Individuals have no standing before the Commission, although interested parties, including women's groups, such as the Council of Action for Equal Pay,[10] may be given permission to intervene in hearings. Structural negotiation between labour and management was instituted at the beginning of the century as an efficient method of fixing wages and conditions of work, primarily to forestall the possibility of strike action.

The fact that wages have been fixed at national or state industry-wide level has been beneficial to those who are industrially weak, that is, those located in small workplaces and women, particularly migrant women. In addition, the status of the formal bodies is such that there has been a spillover of benefits from award-based wage decisions to award-free areas of employment. A high degree of regulation and centralisation would therefore appear to result in a more equitable and egalitarian system of wage distribution.

1.2 The industrial framework: The equal pay decisions

In the light of Australia's historic reliance on an industrial framework for innovations in wage-setting, the industrial rather than either the legislative or the judicial arena has been the primary *locus* of social change. In 1970, the sex of a worker was generally still a formal criterion in wage-setting, but by 1976 it was no longer relevant. The effect of the key decisions was that the minimum hourly (award) rate of women rose from 74 per cent of the male rate in 1970 to 94 per cent in 1976. Actual hourly earnings rose from 68 per cent to 81 per cent. This is a dramatic manifestation of the result of an interventionist stance, given that other variables such as occupational structures are unlikely to have changed in a few short years.

Although Australia did not ratify the Equal Remuneration Convention, 1951 (No. 100), until 1974, the Convention acted as an impetus towards the effecting of equal pay measures prior to that date.[11] The early state measures, however, adopted a narrow formulation of equal pay, for "performing work of the same or a like nature".[12] This was also true of the Australian Conciliation and Arbitration Commission's Equal Pay Cases decision of 1969,[13] which guaranteed equal pay provided that the work performed by men and women was "of the same or a like nature".

This decision resulted from an application from a number of unions before the Commission to consider equal pay for female employees. The unions asked for a flat-rate increase of AuD8.20 for all female workers, which they claimed would effect equal pay, and maintained that the historic needs-based concept of wage fixing was no longer relevant.

It was the Harvester decision[14] of 1907 that formalised the view, which was to prevail for the next 60 years, that the average male worker is a married man with a dependent wife and three children, while the average female worker is a single woman without dependants. This concept of the family wage led to the setting of the rate for work carried out in predominantly female occupations at 54 per cent of the male basic wage.[15] Although it was necessary to raise the pay for women's jobs during the Second World War, the female rate was set at 75 per cent of the male basic rate after the war, again on the basis of assumed needs.[16] This averred needs-based construction conveniently sidestepped the question of equity. Indeed, it has been suggested that the family concept constituted another form of protection for male workers.[17]

The union submission was supported by a number of women's organisations, which were given permission to intervene in the case. Employers' groups opposed the introduction of equal pay, mainly on the ground of cost, while the Commonwealth Government accorded the principle qualified support.

Although the Commission rejected the flat-rate increase, it found that the concept of "equal pay for equal work" was a "socially proper one", while the concept of the family wage no longer carried with it the significance of past days. Acknowledging the considerable costs to employers of the decision, the Commission prescribed graduated implementation over a three-year period.

One major limitation of the decision was that work "essentially or usually performed by females" constituted a specific exception to the equal pay principle. Consequently, the decision helped only about 18 per cent of women in the female labour force, such as teachers and public servants. The decision was a disappointment both to women and to the unions that had been supporting the case, who had sought "equal pay" rather than recognition of "equal work".[18]

Indeed, only three years later, following a further application by the ACTU, the Australian Conciliation and Arbitration Commission formally acknowledged that the concept of "equal pay for equal work" was too narrow in today's world. As a result, the "equal pay for work of equal value" formulation was introduced in the National Wage and Equal Pay Cases decision of 1972,[19] which stipulated "consideration of the work performed irrespective of the sex of the worker". The Commission held that female rates would be determined by work value comparisons, using techniques well established within the Australian industrial culture.

Once again, the decision provided for graduated implementation, so that it would be fully in force by 1975. The decision was subsequently followed by the state tribunals.[20] The principle of equal pay for work of equal value could be formally incorporated into awards either by means of agreement or through arbitration, if agreement could not be reached. The period of implementation was remarkably uncontentious, particularly as the equal pay decisions were persuasive rather than mandatory so far as the unions were concerned.[21] However, once a union had supported an application for equal pay and secured its inclusion in an award, employers were bound by it. Prosecutions could be instituted for underpayment of wages, although there is no evidence of a prosecution arising specifically from the violation of an equal pay ruling.

The economic growth of the 1970s, which attracted married women into the workforce, coupled with the expansion in service industries where women predominate, may have contributed to the peaceful transitional period. The favourable economic climate is significant in view of the fact that the total wages bill for female work increased overall from 18 per cent to 28 per cent between 1964 and 1976, compared with a 2 per cent increase over the previous 14 years.[22]

A limiting factor, so far as giving full effect to the 1972 decision was concerned, was that the minimum wage, which came into being in 1966, applied only to male workers, in recognition of the historic family wage concept. In 1974, this anomaly was corrected when the Australian Conciliation and Arbitration Commission handed down a decision as part of the National Wage Case which secured an adult minimum wage for all workers.[23] This base, below which no worker can be paid, has been particularly beneficial to low-paid women workers, and has also constituted an important step in endeavouring to secure substantive compliance with the principles of the 1972 decision. However, the coincidence of the introduction of equal pay measures and the minimum wage for female workers renders it impossible to isolate their respective impact on pay ratios.[24]

1.3 The definition of "equal work"

In reaching its National Wage and Equal Pay Cases decision in 1972, the Australian Conciliation and Arbitration Commission defined "equal pay for work of equal value" as the fixation of award wage rates by a consideration of the work performed irrespective of the sex of the worker" but no attempt has been made subsequently to develop a more precise formulation of the concept of value. In the United States, the value of jobs is assessed in terms of relative value to an employer. The Australian 1972 decision makes it quite clear that value does not mean value to the employer: "the value of the work refers to worth in terms of award wage or salary fixation, not worth to the employer". The rationale for the difference arises out of a centralised – as opposed to an enterprise-based system, although "worth in terms of award wage or salary fixation" does nothing to illuminate the elusive concept of equal value.

1.4 Scope of the equal pay decisions

As already noted, a major defect of the 1969 decision was that it expressly excluded work performed "exclusively by females". In 1972 this situation was reversed, and the Commission envisaged comparison between female and male classifications:

Work value comparisons should, where possible, be made between female and male classifications within the award under consideration. But where such comparisons are unavailable or inconclusive, as may be the case where the work is performed exclusively by females, it may be necessary to take into account comparisons of work value between female classifications within the award and/or comparisons of work value between female classifications in different awards. In some cases comparisons with male classifications in other awards may be necessary.

Thus consideration was not to be restricted to the situation in one establishment but should extend to the general situation under the determination or award, or if necessary to different awards.

2. Further attempts to narrow the wage gap between men and women

The recession of the early 1980s focused attention on the disadvantaged position of women in the workforce vis-à-vis men, highlighted by the relative poverty of divorced and older women. Furthermore, there was frustration with the fact that there had been no discernible improvement in the male/female wages ratio over a decade, and concern that women in traditionally female occupations had not benefited from the 1972 decision. The view of Gregory and Duncan that equal pay had been "fully implemented"[25] was not universally shared. While women's wages had improved significantly in Australia since that time, a gap of approximately 20 per cent still remained in respect of women in full-time work. Short, for example, argues that this gap may be attributable to a failure to implement fully the 1972 principles, rather than to the different educational and work experiences of women.[26] Indeed, her study reveals that only 35 awards were changed expressly to allow for equal pay for work of equal value.[27] The Australian Conciliation and Arbitration Commission had been reluctant to rule specifically on "work of equal value" in 1972, and the cases which sought to implement the principle made no attempt to invest the concept with any more precise meaning: "Employers and unions merely agreed on integration of male and female classifications without specific studies to see if the work was of equal value."[28] It was therefore felt that the implementation of a formalised job evaluation scheme would cure the omission by forcing attention to be focused on the meaning of equal value. While the 1972 equal pay decision made provision for male/female comparisons, the improvements that occurred were based on conventional "rule-of-thumb" views about the value of different sorts of work rather than on any systematic or analytical method of comparing female occupations with male occupations.

2.1 The rejection of "comparable worth"

As a result of pressure from feminists within the union movement who had been impressed by North American "comparable worth" initiatives, the ACTU accepted the idea of supporting a comparable worth test case. There was, however, considerable hesitancy on the part of the conservative wing of the trade union movement because of the prevailing labour government accord to the effect that, in the interests of the economy, no bids for wage increases would be made except to cure anomalies. However, the ACTU had adopted a Working Women's Charter in 1977, one plank of which was equal pay for women workers, and in 1984 the ACTU adopted an Action Program for Women Workers, designed to implement the principles contained in the Charter. A separate *Equal Pay Manual* was also developed by the ACTU Working Women's Centre and distributed to ACTU affiliates.

A "comparable worth" test case was conducted in 1985 to consider the applicability of the concept in Australia in the light of the principles articulated in the 1972 equal pay decision. It is, however, misleading to refer to this case as a comparable worth case because there was no attempt to compare predominantly female with predominantly male jobs. The case, run by the ACTU, sought to vary the Private Hospitals' and Doctors' Nurses (ACT) Award 1972. The nurses claimed that, as members of a predominantly female occupational group, they were not beneficiaries of the 1972 equal pay decision. Restricted to threshold issues alone, the case sought to establish whether a reaffirmation of the 1972 equal pay decision was appropriate and whether the 1983 National Wage Fixing Principles[29] applied to the applicants.

The Australian Conciliation and Arbitration Commission rejected the term "comparable worth" and reaffirmed its commitment to the "equal pay for work of equal value" principles of the 1972 decision, which were still available for implementation:

> In our view the use of the term comparable worth in the Australian context would lead to confusion, and in particular, we believe that it would be inappropriate and confusing to equate the doctrine with the 1972 principle of equal pay for work of equal value. For all of these reasons we specifically reject the notion.

It was held that applications were to be processed through the Anomalies and Inequalities Principle of the 1983 National Wage Fixing Principles. The Commission felt that adoption of the comparable worth concept in Australia would "strike at the heart of long accepted methods of wage fixation in this country". It believed that comparable worth would involve a new methodology which would be likely to corrode Australia's centralised wage-fixing system. There may also have been a fear that established wage relativities would be upset by a new methodology. The decision was perceived by many as a significant setback to the securing of equal pay for work of equal value.[30]

Although both "comparable worth" and "equal pay for work of equal value" are indeterminite generic terms encompassing various initiatives to effect pay equity for women, the Australian Conciliation and Arbitration Commission could discern no good reason to introduce the new term "comparable worth", a term which had originated in the United States, a country with a quite different system of wage-fixing. The more familiar term, "Equal pay for work of equal value", threatened neither Australia's centralised wage-fixing system nor the informal norms associated with the ascertainment of work value.

2.2 The reaffirmation of equal pay for work of equal value

All was not lost, however, because the 1972 decision had expressly adverted to the possibility of comparing predominantly male and female occupations of the 1983 National Wage Fixing Principles. The Anomalies Principle permitted wage increases to be negotiated if it could be demonstrated that there had been a failure to implement established principles, including the equal pay principle. As a result, anomalies conferences were convened in respect of several nurses' cases in 1986 and 1987.[31] In the first such case, the ACTU presented an exhaustive history of Australian Capital Territory (Canberra and its environs) public sector nurses' wage movements, and compared them with those of a traditionally male occupation, metal tradesmen, in the same area over a five-year period. The idea was to demonstrate that nurses had not received an equal pay for work of equal value wage adjustment. The President of the Australian Conciliation and Arbitration Commission accepted the validity of the case, and as a result equal pay principles formed an integral plank of several nurses' pay cases during 1986 and 1987. In the Victorian Registered Nurses' Pay Case, 1986, it was argued that nurses were paid a lower margin for skill than their male counterparts. Furthermore, comparisons showed that nurses were paid low wages relative to other occupations in the health industry. The Victorian Industrial Relations Commission found the existence of an anomaly in the non-application of the 1972 equal pay principle and granted pay increases accordingly. Registered nurses in South Australia were similarly successful. A federal nurses' case was also run in 1987, as a result of which all nurses who had been involved in the 1985 "comparable worth" claim received increased rates of pay. The nurses were compared to other workers in the health industry, namely, therapists, hospital scientists, medical laboratory technicians, technical officers and pharmacists. Again, however, the comparison was directed towards changes in male pay rates, rather than towards specific work value studies.[32]

In the manual the ACTU sent out to unions as part of its Action Program for Women Workers, it endorsed the running of equal pay claims for women in traditional female occupations and advised as to the criteria necessary to support a claim. The formal support of the male-dominated union council is essential for the running of a successful case. One of the critical concerns about the comparable worth test case was that the ACTU was lukewarm about it, no doubt due to the recognition that it could conceivably reduce hard-won margins in male-dominated awards. The wage-fixing system has been constructed on an edifice of relativities between awards, and the union movement does not want this threatened.

There is, however, a proviso concerning the nurses' cases. While nursing is an example of a paradigmatically female occupation in that the focus is on caring for people rather than on capital accumulation, it is also atypical of the segregated female labour force. First of all, registered nurses are well-qualified professionals with formal credentials. The existence of such credentials means that it is much more possible to quantify the nurses' jobs, either within a formal job evaluation scheme or within the less formal Australian concept of work value, than is the case with the preponderance of jobs performed by women. Such jobs tend to be characterised by an informal rather than a formal skill component. Secondly, nurses provide an essential service within the community and they have been in short supply. Thirdly, nurses in Australia are generally well organised industrially; their status is less contingent on the existence of a personal relationship with their employers than is the case with, say, secretaries. Indeed, industrial action in Victoria during this period was a powerful factor in securing pay increases, and Hunter suggests that it overshadowed the pursuit of theoretical concessions before the Australian Conciliation and Arbitration Commission.[33]

The problem of undervaluation now confronts those focusing on the more elusive question of women's worth in areas such as textiles and clerical work.[34] The work of women who exercise keyboard skills has been significantly undervalued because the industrial culture has perceived it to be monotonous, routine and unskilled – because women do it. These women have not fared well, even when supported by relatively strong public sector unions.[35]

2.3 *Ancillary strategies*

There is a developing awareness on the part of women activitists that the problem of undervaluation has contributed to the intractability of the 20 per cent differential between men's and women's wages, and ancillary strategies are being developed to endeavour to remedy this gap. Many of these strategies transcend the traditional concerns of both wage-setting and the resolution of disputes between employers and employees.

Contemporary pay increases tend to be linked to productivity, while taking into account the new principles of industrial democracy and restructuring. Productivity has always been a problematic variable when applied to women's work. The caring and servicing nature of much of women's traditional work simply does not lend itself to measurement in productivity terms. However, a number of new strategies have been devised by the ACTU which seek to minimise the harm to low-paid workers arising from the focus on contemporary economic imperatives. Such strategies include flat-rate increases and the adaptation of the restructuring and efficiency principle to assist women workers by means of broad-banding, multi-skilling, the development of career paths, training, retraining, and adult apprenticeships. The devising of structural measures is a recognition of the multi-faceted reasons for sex-based wage inequalities, which are resistant to simple quantitative remedies. The ACTU has acknowledged that the following factors should be taken into account when considering the reasons for women's lower earnings:

- Young people who earn less than adults comprise a higher proportion of employed women than employed men.
- Part-time work is more prevalent amongst women than amongst men.
- Women work less overtime than men.
- Women are concentrated in a small range of occupations and industries, and earnings in these occupations and industries are relatively low.

- Women are usually concentrated around the lower grades of any occupation.
- Over-award, bonus, etc., payments made to women are generally less than those made to men.[36]

It is significant that strategies to secure wage increases for women were developed at a time of severe economic downturn in Australia in 1987-88.[37] A two-tier wage system was introduced to replace regular full wage indexation.[38] The first tier included a flat-rate wage increase for all workers rather than the customary percentage. This flat-rate form is advantageous for women, as so many have low incomes. The increase of AuD16, for example, represented a 6.6 per cent increase for a worker earning AuD240 per week, but only 3 per cent for a worker earning AuD520 per week.[39] The second tier included provision for supplementary payments, another special measure designed to assist low-paid workers. However, it was not purely women's predominance in this category that singled them out for assistance: account was also taken on the sex-based differential in respect of over-award payments. While minimum wage rates are set by an industrial tribunal, over-award rates are commonly negotiated with employers; industrial tribunals do not have jurisdiction over these payments. Reflecting male unionists' superior bargaining strength, men earn an average of AuD10.90 per week in over-award payments compared with women's AuD5.50.[40] In the clothing industry, the discrepancy is considerable, with cutters (men) receiving an average over-award payment of AuD49.39 and machinists (women) receiving an average AuD9.14. Many women in this industry in fact receive the base rate. Accordingly, the Australian Conciliation and Arbitration Commission, in granting supplementary payments to low-paid workers, stressed the need for those receiving over-award payments not to receive the increase. The aim was to "reduce wage inequalities by reducing differentials between the highest and lowest paid workers in a *[sic]* award without reference to the historical reasons for those differentials".[41] Low-paid workers in the retail and textile industries and those covered by various clerical awards also benefited from supplementary payments.

The restructuring and efficiency principle was adopted by the Commission in order to promote "improved efficiency in industry".[42] The restructuring of awards entails the detailed review of classifications to remove obsolete ones and to streamline and reduce the number of awards. Restructuring has sometimes resulted in the broad-banding of classifications, for example clerical and administrative ones, which has opened up careers for women in some public sector areas.[43] Jobs have also been re-designed to abolish repetitive single-task functions in process and light assembly work. Attention has, however, been drawn to the ease with which jobs can be redesigned along sex-based lines, in line with stereotypical assumptions about skill with light, repetitive work requiring dexterity being preferred for women and heavy, complicated, demanding work for men.[44]

In the restructuring process, the ACTU has noted the desirability of individual unions taking account of women's particular needs. These arise from factors such as the concentration of women in both a small number of industries and a small number of jobs, as well as from the earnings differentials, the large numbers of part-time women workers, the fact that women tend to possess less formal qualifications than men, and women's primary role with respect to family responsibilities.[45] Family responsibilities are a key factor in respect of opportunities for training, mobility and seniority, all of which contribute to the wages gap. So far as training is concerned, the ACTU has drawn attention to women's low participation in both "in-house" and formal training as areas requiring remedial attention.[46] The attention of unions has also been alerted to the special training needs of non-English speaking migrant women.[47]

2.4 An integrated approach to wage-setting

However, this is not just a matter of special measures for women which may be withdrawn or not implemented in times of recession. Pay equity principles must be considered in conjunction with broader structural strategies.[48] To consider one approach in isolation from the other is inadequate:

None of the wage fixing principles devised over the past 15 or so years has facilitated the implementation of the 1972 equal pay principle and ... in every national wage case the principle of equal pay should be taken into account in setting the principles for the national wage, because ... the national wage principles cannot effectively or properly be set without regard to that principle of equal pay.[49]

In this passage, the National Pay Equity Coalition exhorts the development of an integrated approach towards wage-setting. Such an approach is clearly desirable as a means of countering contemporary trends which militate against women's interests. The trend in favour of deregulation has, for example, operated to increase part-time, contract and casual work, categories which attract disproportionate numbers of women but which erode the conditions and pay secured in full-time, regulated markets. Furthermore, opportunities for promotion and increasing skills are likely to be extremely limited or non-existent in such positions. The contemporary trend away from full-time employment thus runs counter to the pay equity movement. The adoption of across-the-board strategies, such as minimum rates of pay and flat-rate increases, does, however, go some way towards accommodating fringe workers.

In addition, affirmative action strategies need to be devised at the enterprise level to take account of the special needs of women workers. The Affirmative Action (Equal Opportunity for Women) Act 1986 (Cth) makes it mandatory for enterprises with over 100 employees to prepare equal opportunity programmes. The Act requires consultation both with women and with the unions, although the content of the programmes is not specified. Any programme designed to have anything other than a minor cosmetic effect must involve significant input from employees: employers cannot be relied upon to develop a radical proposal for sexual desegregation, for example.

3. Procedures for determining "equality"

3.1 The criteria for comparing work

There has never been any specific focus on the value of the jobs women perform vis-à-vis that of comparable male jobs. As Burton and Innes observe, the primary concern has been with "similarity in job *content*, not in job *value*".[50] It was on this basis that women's jobs were slotted into existing classifications without any real attempt to assess their value. Typing, for example, was simply placed at the bottom of the clerical range since it was assumed to be inferior to other male-defined clerical tasks.[51] This ad hoc methodology has meant that traditional women's jobs, particularly those covered by predominantly female awards, have never received the critical attention that the equal value concept promised. In addition, the deference to historical relativities, in which is embedded the idea that the financial needs of female workers are less than those of male workers, has necessarily militated against the possibility of approaching the concept of equal value free of its ideological trappings. Thus, women's work which had been undervalued at the inception of an award would not escape the straitjacket of historic undervaluation unless the elusive question of value was specifically addresed *de novo.*

During the early 1980s, a close focus on the value of women's work may have been deliberately eschewed because of the likely destabilising effect on the economy of a substantial increase in wages. Several women's orgnisations intervened in the 1983 National Wage Case demanding proper work value studies in the light of the 1972 equal pay decision. However, the Australian Conciliation and Arbitration Commission rejected the idea on the basis that it would provide an opportunity for wage increases which would be "inappropriate in the current state of unemployment especially among women".[52] The inference is that the goal of equal pay may be pursued only at times that suit a male-defined perception of the national good.[53]

As mentioned, consideration was given to equal pay cases for nurses and other professional categories following the so-called "comparable worth" test case. In the Therapists Case, for example, the Australian Conciliation and Arbitration Commission "placed heavy emphasis on educational qualifications rather than on work level descriptions".[54] The suggestion is that formal qualifications may receive disproportionate weighting. This is an example where the component of skill was dealt with in accordance with pre-existing male norms and "value" was not analysed in relation to the more nebulous quality of caring, for example. Also likely to be contested is the evaluation of women's work demanding constant interruption, manual dexterity and close attention to detail. As commentators have observed, if women's work is to be properly valued, the prejudice must be overcome against comparing *dissimilar* work.[55]

3.2 The role of job evaluation

If comparisons of dissimilar jobs were to take place, a methodology with some degree of formality would be required; an informal rule-of-thumb approach would necessarily be inadequate. While work value cases do focus on the traditional components of skill, effort, responsibility and working conditions, there has been a resistance to systematic methods of job evaluation, as the 1985 "comparable worth" case suggests. This resistance may have been partly due to concerns regarding the time and cost involved in formal schemes,[56] in addition to fears as to its destabilising effect on relativities. Indeed, Short's research revealed that a more scientific evaluative method was attempted on only one occasion. This was in the Metal Trades Award (re Work Value Inquiry) of 1966:

The Commonwealth attempted a detailed methodical approach to wage fixation by filling in of check sheets for each job inspected as the case proceeded and in the end producing a table of relative values for each job.[57]

As was subsequently argued in the "comparable worth" case, job evaluation has been depicted by employers and unions as a foreign concept which belongs in collective bargaining countries rather than in a centralised system.

Despite the resistance to developing a formal methodology at the centralised level, employers may voluntarily develop their own schemes, or use well-known schemes such as the Hay system, provided that they meet minimum award wage requirements. For example, the banking industry has introduced the Hay system to replace wage rates determined by years of service.[58] Clare Burton has shown, however, how formal job evaluation schemes, such as the Hay Guide Chart-Profile Method, may insidiously entrench gender bias in the valuation of jobs by mirroring prevailing social values.[59] Burton's study shows how bias may infect every stage of the process, from the design of the scheme to the analysis, description, evaluation and classification of jobs, which is then translated into discriminatory wage rates. Burton proceeds to argue, however, that bias is not the necessary corollary of a formal scheme.

3.3 The scope of comparison

An assessment of the value of an occupational classification necessarily involves crossing occupational barriers. The history of work value cases in Australia reveals a marked disinclination to compare discrete occupational classifications. A search of wage-fixing cases throughout the century by Short revealed no more than a couple of instances and they have not become accepted precedents.[60] Both cases involved male-dominated professional occupations. The first sought to compare the work and training of engineers with those of doctors, lawyers and dentists.[61] The Australian Conciliation and Arbitration Commission rejected the comparisons, which were not of a formalised kind, because it feared that they would set a dangerous precedent. Despite the rejection, engineers received a substantial pay rise and work value cases were lodged by other professional occupations. This case, suggesting a preference for an informal comparison of job classifications rather than a formal comparison of job factors, is illustrative of the ad hoc approach designed to maintain relativity in wages. A somewhat more formal comparison was made in the Journalists' Case,[62] in which journalists were compared with Commonwealth public servants and teachers, and found to be comparable in terms of educational qualifications and work qualities. Although these cases were decided in the 1960s in the pre-equal pay era, and the 1972 equal pay decision expressly adverts to the possibility of comparisons between male and female classifications, the suggestion has never been adopted in equal pay cases. Nor has there been any attempt to specify the proportion of one sex that is necessary for a classification to be regarded as either male-dominated or female-dominated.

4. Enforcement arrangements

4.1 The role of the anti-discrimination agencies

In Australia, the industrial arena has been somewhat proprietorial concerning equal pay issues. Hence, there are no reported decisions arising from allegations of wage discrimination lodged with human rights or anti-discrimination agencies. Indeed, there has been some tension between the two arenas, particularly in New South Wales, where it is Labor Council of New South Wales (the state central union body) policy to remove all discrimination complaints pertaining to employment from the jurisdiction of the Anti-Discrimination Board to that of the State Industrial Commission.[63] This is despite the fact that the awards and decisions of wage-fixing tribunals are expressly excluded from the New South Wales anti-discrimination legislation and even over-award payments are excepted from scrutiny.[64] The decisions of wage-fixing tribunals are also excepted from the federal Sex Discrimination Act 1984.[65] Although the Victorian Equal Opportunity Act 1984 does not expressly except the decisions of wage-fixing tribunals, section 39*(e)*(iii) does except "an instrument made or approved by or under any other Act", which inferentially includes such decisions.

Other states have chosen not to adopt a deferential attitude towards arbitration bodies in their anti-discrimination legislation. South Australia has not concerned itself with awards at all,[66] while the Western Australian Act contains a sunset clause which excepts awards for a period of two years only.[67] It would therefore be possible to lodge a complaint concerning wage discrimination in these states.

At the federal level and in states containing an exception in their legislative schemes, a complaint could be lodged concerning wages only in respect of award-free areas of employment. As increasing numbers of women are employed in part-time, casual and contract work, there is, at least theoretically, some scope for either an individual or a representative complaint in all jurisdictions. The federal Sex Discrimination Act 1984 also permits a union to lodge a complaint on behalf of an aggrieved member or members,[68] although the exception would seem to accord this provision little practical effect vis-à-vis wage discrimination. The fundamental commitment of unions to the classwide resolution of wages disputes through industrial forums conflicts with the philosophy underpinning the individual, complaint-based orientation of anti-discrimination forums, although this is not to deny the important supportive role played by some unions in general complaints arising from discrimination in employment.[69] In view of the New South Wales Labor Council's policy, the lodging of a sex discrimination complaint concerning wages in that state could be viewed as a provocative act by the conservative wing of the union movement.

4.2 The burden of proof

In any case, an equal value case would be difficult to run under the Sex Discrimination Act 1984 (Cth). If not resolved at the informal conciliation level, a direct discrimination complaint would require the claimant to show that she had been treated less favourably than a real or hypothetical man in the same or similar circumstances. This doctrine lends itself most readily to an equal work case, not an equal value case.

As far as indirect discrimination is concerned,[70] the relevant section of the Sex Discrimination Act is worded in such a way that it places an onerous burden upon a claimant at the formal inquiry level. The claimant would first need to establish that a higher proportion of men than women were able to comply with a particular requirement or condition; secondly, that the requirement or condition was not reasonable in the circumstances and, thirdly, that the claimant herself did not or was not able to comply with that requirement or condition. The embeddedness of sex discrimination in wages renders this three-pronged requirement difficult to meet, unless a material benefit, such as, say, eligibility for superannuation or training, were contingent upon having reached a particular wage level not generally attained by women. Furthermore, the individualised focus of anti-discrimination legislation means that the respondent, as well as the claimant, must be clearly identifiable. Hence, the jurisdiction favours complaints in which linear causality can be established. It is much more difficult to establish a causal nexus in an indirect discrimination complaint than it is in a direct, or overt, discrimination complaint.

4.3 Remedies

Seeking to render a sole employer liable in an equal value case, in respect of which it is impossible to separate the mutifarious causal strands, highlights the uncertainty of securing a remedy in an anti-discrimination forum. Even if an individual complaint were successful, the decision would be unlikely to have the significant classwide effect that could be expected from a national pay decision within the industrial arena. While anti-discrimination legislation does permit the hearing of a representative complaint (a form of class action), the fragmented nature of a great deal of women's employment militates against concerted action. For women who lack access to a union, however, there may be no other formal avenue available.

An anti-discrimination complaint dealing with work practices might pose a less onerous burden of proof and might be viewed with less suspicion than one dealing with wages *per se*. Generally speaking, however, the conclusion is that pursuing a wages claim through the normal industrial channels is less fraught with uncertainties than the anti-discrimination route. The Human Rights and Equal Opportunity Commission (which administers the federal Sex Discrimination Act), or a state anti-discrimination agency, could intervene in a national wage case. Intervention by the Human Rights and Equal Opportunity Commission before the Australian Industrial Relations Commission on behalf of women generally could constitute a constructive strategy in bridging the gap between the industrial and the human rights arenas.

4.4 Legal costs

With regard to cost, the industrial route involves no cost to individuals as a case is conducted by a union, a number of unions or a central union body on behalf of members. Nor is there any cost involved in lodging a complaint with a human rights or anti-discrimination agency, which then has a duty to investigate and to endeavour to conciliate. If the agency is unable to conciliate, the complaint is referred on to a tribunal. Any legal representation is then the responsibility of the individual claimant or claimants. Unions have undertaken to pay claimants' costs in some anti-discrimination inquiries but, as suggested, union support would be unlikely to be forthcoming in a pay case. Some anti-discrimination legislation provides for the parties to pay their own costs at the tribunal level, whether unsuccessful or not, an alteration of the customary court rule that the loser pays.[71] This is a powerful disincentive to pursuing a pay equity complaint through an anti-discrimination jurisdiction. Expert testimony, including a possible job evaluation consultancy, would also have to be paid for by the claimant unless an agency, such as the Human Rights and Equal Opportunity Commission, were prepared to intervene formally. In addition, legal aid for civil cases is generally limited, and the complexity of an equal value case suggests that it would be unlikely to be supported, particularly in the light of the perceived availability of an alternative industrial avenue.

5. The role of the unions

The overall rate of unionisation in Australia is 53 per cent: 60 per cent for men and 43 per cent for women.[72] Public sector unionisation is approximately 71 per cent, compared with approximately 34 per cent in the private sector.[73] Unions tend to be organised around a particular trade or craft, although they may be based on an industry or occupation. Despite an increase in female unionisation in Australia over the past decade, the female rate still falls considerably below that for men. It is clear that there is a correlation between an increase in female membership and improved pay and conditions for female workers. Indeed, unionisation is the keystone to the formal implementation of the "equal pay for work of equal value" principle in Australia. If a union cannot be persuaded to pursue the issue on behalf of its women members, a case cannot be run. The union movement has been criticised for its past failure to respond to the dramatic changes in the workforce participation of women. One commentator has claimed that unions still persist in treating women in the same way as they did 50 years ago.[74] However, issues such as equal pay, affirmative action, maternity leave and child care have been pursued in more recent years. Currently, the ACTU is seeking ratification by the Australian Government of the Workers with Family Responsibilities Convention, 1981 (No. 156), in addition to running a test case on paternity leave.

Although male workers have not been anxious to support wage increases for women in female-dominated occupations, they have been assiduous in ensuring that women who do the same work should be paid the same wage in order to prevent any possibility of employers hiring cheaper female labour at their expense. This principle has a long history in Australian arbitration and is clearly articulated in early cases such as the Fruitpickers Case.[75] The somewhat vexed element of male self-interest apart, women have been stigmatised by the stereotype that women's commitment to the workforce is less *because* their financial needs are less, women workers not being likely to have family responsibilities.

Despite the ambivalence evinced by male unionists towards women as workers, women have benefited from union activity in securing superior pay and conditions for all workers at both federal and state level. For example, sick leave, long-service leave and three to four weeks' annual holiday, including a holiday weighting, are regarded as basic remuneration entitlements within the employment contract. It is through the union movement, primarily through the federal and state central bodies, that such initiatives have originated. These bodies also carry out research, conduct training courses and prepare promotional material for distribution to members. In addition, they exert an influence on government policies, although this is likely to be more apparent when a Labor Government is in power.

The tradition of centralised wage-fixing, together with a relatively high rate of unionisation, thus enabled a dramatic change to take place in women's wages in Australia over a relatively short span of time once equal pay initiatives had been instituted.

6. Conclusions

While specific equal pay measures have assisted women workers in Australia in their search for pay equity, the values of a centralised wage-fixing system and a high level of unionisation among women cannot be denied; specific equal pay measures have not been solely responsible for reducing the male-female wage gap. A centralised system of awards specifying wages and conditions has had the effect both of suppressing untrammelled wages growth at the upper levels and of ensuring wage justice at the lower levels. Since women predominate in the latter categories, they have benefited from the establishment of minimum wages and wage decisions with across-the-board effect.[76] If Australian women had had to depend on collective bargaining at the enterprise level, the male-female wages differential would undoubtedly be significantly greater.

A recent Green Paper on industrial relations in New South Wales recommends a stronger enterprise focus, decentralisation, collective agreements and enterprise bargaining units in line with the contemporary reviews of industrial relations conducted in other parts of Australia and at the federal level.[77] While this trend towards partial deregulation will arguably contribute towards greater productivity, efficiency, flexibility, competitiveness and industrial harmony in the interests of the greater good, it does not bode well for women. The Australian experience over the 20-year period 1969-89 underlines the advantages for women of a high degree of centralisation and regulation. The new trends do not envisage the abandonment of centralisation altogether, but its restriction to determining matters of principle. But even this limited deregulation is likely to leave women subject to the vagaries of their respective unions and employers. The reality is that the records of unions have been patchy in pursuing equal pay on behalf of women members. The disadvantage for women of enterprise-centred bargaining is compounded by the fact that it is largely invisible to the public eye. These factors, which at present militate against the interests of women workers in the negotiation of over-award payments, would be likely to disadvantage women further if enterprise-based wage rates were to become the norm. The wages gap would then widen rather than narrow, despite the innovative measures designed to effect structural changes presently being devised at the national level.

Nevertheless, formal measures alone are unlikely to ameliorate the conditions of women's working lives, as women have always been peripheral to the informal, as well as to the formal, decision-making processes within industrial relations. And the devising of appropriate strategies to counteract the subtlety of informal discrimination is likely to be even more difficult and elusive than is the case with formal discrimination. The point may be illustrated by reference to the industrial context which forms the backdrop to the stage on which the equal pay issues are played out. Henderson coined the phrase "the industrial relations club" to describe the clannish relationship which exists between "members of employer and employee organisations, public servants, academics, journalists and industrial lawyers – all of whom have a vested interest in the perpetuation of the system".[78] The overriding characteristic of this club is that it is a largely male preserve. Indeed, of the 46 members of the Australian Industrial Relations Commission appointed to hold office from 1 March 1989, only four are women. Although it would not necessarily follow that the appointment of more women would effect an instantaneous change in the Commission's value system, the composition of the Commission is illustrative of the overwhelmingly male ethos which has been resistant to squarely confronting the meaning of the "equal pay for work of equal value" prescript.

Thus, while the equal pay movement has recognised that the wages gap cannot be reduced without remedying structural inequalities in the workforce generally, the gendered nature of traditional industrial relations policies and personnel practices constitutes a significantly less tractable problem. However, it is this contextual animus which has traditionally informed and contributed to the negative evaluation of women's work. More recently, it has permitted the trend towards deregulation to be rationalised in the averred national interests of efficiency and productivity, despite the likely deleterious impact of deregulation on women workers.

Notes

1 According to an OECD study a decade ago, Australia had the highest degree of sex segregation of any advanced OECD country. See Organisation for Economic Cooperation and Development: *Women and employment* (Paris, OECD, 1980).

2 All employed workers are included in the computation of average weekly ordinary-time earnings. When overtime earnings are taken into account, the figure falls to 78.8 per cent of average male weekly earnings; when part-time employment is taken into account, the figure falls to 65 per cent. Australian Bureau of Statistics: *Average Weekly Earnings, Australia, November 1988,* Cat. 6301.0 (Canberra, AGPS, 1989). Other relevant statistics are as follows: 41 per cent of the Australian workforce is female; the female workforce participation rate is 51.3 per cent; 78 per cent of part-time workers are female. Australian Bureau of Statistics: *The Labour Force, Australia, January 1989,* Cat. 6203.0 (Canberra, AGPS, 1989).

3 Women's Bureau, Department of Employment, Education and Training: *Pay equity: A survey of 7 OECD countries,* Information Paper No. 5 (Canberra, AGPS, 1987), p. 67.

4 Carol O'Donnell and Nerolie Golder: "A comparative analysis of equal pay in the United States, Britain and Australia", in *Australian Feminist Studies,* 1986, 3, p. 59.

5 S. Deery and D. Plowman: *Australian industrial relations* (Sydney, McGraw Hill, 2nd ed., 1985), p. 331.

6 Australian Bureau of Statistics; *1988 Year Book* (Canberra, AGPS, 1988), p. 319.

7 However, this is not the case for all awards. The Federal and State Clothing Trades Award, for example, specifies rates of pay and conditions for home-based workers.

8 The Australian Constitution (s. 51 xxxv) limits the powers of the Commonwealth to industrial disputes extending beyond the limits of a state.

9 Industrial Relations Act 1988 (Cth), s. 33.

[10] This organisation, formed in 1937, was responsible for encouraging the ACTU to support the principle of equal pay in 1941.

[11] Mary Gaudron and Michal Bosworth: "Equal pay?", in Judy Mackinolty and Heather Radi (eds.): *In pursuit of justice* (Sydney, Hale and Iremonger, 1979), p. 163.

[12] Industrial Arbitration (Female Rates) Amendment Act 1958 (NSW); see also In Re Clerks (State) Award and Other Awards (1959) AR 470. cf. Public Service (Equal Pay) Act 1966 (Tas.); Industrial Code 1967 (SA); Industrial Arbitration Amendment Act 1968 (WA). Queensland had effected an amendment to its Industrial Conciliation and Arbitration Act as early as 1916, although little progress was made in implementation. See J. Hutson: *Six wage concepts* (Sydney, Amalgamated Engineering Union, 1971), p. 119.

[13] Equal Pay Cases (1969) 127 CAR 1142.

[14] *Ex parte H.V. McKay* (1907) 2 CAR 1.

[15] *Federated Clothing Trades* v. *J.A. Archer* (1919) 13 CAR 647.

[16] (1949-50) 68 CAR 698.

[17] Edna Ryan and Ann Conlon: *Gentle invaders: Australian women at work 1788-1974* (Melbourne, Nelson, 1975), p. 110.

[18] Hutson, op. cit., p. 126.

[19] (1972) 147 CAR 172.

[20] In the case of New South Wales, for example, see the State Equal Pay Case [1973] AR 425.

[21] Christine Short: "Equal pay – What happened?", in *Journal of Industrial Relations,* 1986, 28, pp. 315, 320.

[22] R.G. Gregory and R.C. Duncan: "Segmented labour market theories and the Australian experience of equal pay for women", in *Journal of Post Keynesian Economics,* 1981, 3, pp. 403, 422.

[23] (1974) 157 CAR 293.

[24] cf. Women's Bureau: *Pay equity,* op. cit., p. 71.

[25] op. cit., p. 411. cf. Curthoys, who takes the view that the 1972 "equal pay for work of equal value" decision was a comparable worth decision in priciple, and responsible for the reduced wage differential for women in Australia vis-à-vis the United States. See Ann Curthoys: "Equal pay, a family wage or both: Women workers, feminists and unionists in Australia since 1945", in Barbara Caine, et al. (eds): *Crossing boundaries: Feminisms and the critique of knowledges* (Sydney Allen and Unwin, 1988), p. 140.

[26] Short, op cit, p. 321.

[27] ibid. p. 324.

[28] ibid.

[29] National Wage Case 1983 (1983) 291 CAR 3. The Wage Fixing Principles were designed to restrict wage rises unless rewarding increased productivity. Wage increases which did not conform to the enumerated principles were prohibited. Narrow exceptions were permitted to operate through an "anomalies" provision.

[30] Jane Innes: "The ACTU's comparable worth test case", in *Legal Service Bulletin,* 1986, II, p. 86. cf. David Brereton: "Comparable worth concept rejected", in *Legal Service Bulletin,* 1986 II, p. 87.

[31] Australian Council of Trade Unions: *Equal pay for work of equal value: Criteria for establishing a pay claim* (Melbourne, ACTU, 1987), p. 12.

[32] Short, op. cit., p. 330.

[33] Rosemary Hunter: "Women workers and federal industrial law: From *Harvester* to comparable worth", *in Australian Journal of Labour Law,* 1988, No. 1, pp. 147, 169.

[34] Clerical workers constitute approximately 34 per cent of the female workforce in Australia.

[35] e.g. Universities (Equal Pay) Case, Industrial Commission of NSW (unreported, 1980). See also Margaret Thornton: "(Un)equal pay for work of equal value", in *Journal of Industrial Relations,* 1981, 23, p. 466.

[36] Australian Council of Trade Unions: *Women workers: The effect of the two-tiered wages system* (Melbourne, ACTU, 1988), p. 1.

[37] ACTU: *Women workers,* op. cit., p. 32.

[38] National Wage Case, Mar. 1987, Print G6800.

[39] ibid.

[40] ACTU: *Women workers,* op cit., p. 14.

[41] Women's Bureau: *Pay equity,* op cit., p. 53.

[42] National Wage Case, Mar. 1987.

[43] ACTU: *Women workers,* op. cit., p. 19.

[44] *Restructuring awards issues for women workers* (Melbourne, ACTU, July 1988), p. 4.

[45] ibid., p. 2.

[46] ibid, p. 4.

[47] ibid.

[48] New Zealand was moving in the direction of integrated equal employment opportunities/equal pay legislation. See *Towards employment equity: Report of the Working Group on Equal Employment Opportunities and Equal Pay* (Wellington, GP, 1988). However, the Employment Equity Act, enacted in August 1990, was repealed in December of the same year by the new Government.

[49] Submission from National Pay Equity Coalition: National Wage Case, Aug. 1988, p. 23.

[50] Clare Burton and Jane Innes: *Report to the New Zealand Law Commission on Equal Opportunities and Equal Pay for Work of Equal Value in Australia* (Sydney, May 1988, unpublished) pp. 12-13.

[51] Short, op. cit., p. 325. cf. Thornton: "(Un)equal pay", op. cit.

[52] National Wage Case (1983) 4 IR 429, 453.

[53] Margaret Thornton: "The equality principle and the sexual division of labour", in *Women's Studies International Forum,* 1986, 9, pp. 13, 16.

[54] Burton and Innes, op. cit., p. 22.

[55] Hunter, op. cit., p. 164.

[56] Cf. Brereton, op. cit., p. 88.

[57] 121 CAR 587, 749.

[58] ACTU: *Women workers,* op. cit., p. 21.

[59] Clare Burton et al.: *Women's worth: Pay equity and job evaluation in Australia* (Canberra, AGPS, 1987).

[60] Short, op. cit., p. 323.

[61] The Association of Professional Engineers, Australia (1961) 97 CAR 233.

[62] (1967) 120 CAR 186.

[63] See Margaret Thornton: "Discrimination law industrial law: Are they compatible?" in *Australian Quarterly,* 1987, 59, p. 162.

[64] Anti-Discrimination Act 1977 (NSW), s. 54 (1)*(d)-(e)* and (2).

[65] s. 40(1)*(e).*

[66] Equal Opportunity Act 1984 (SA).

[67] Equal Opportunity Act 1984 (WA), s. 69(1)*(e)* and (2). See also *Confederation of Western Australian Industry* v. *The Trades and Labor Council of Western Australia* (1988) EOC 92-218 (WA Industrial Relations Commission).

[68] s. 50(1)*(d).*

[69] E.g. *O'Callaghan* v. *Loder and Anor* (1984) EOC 92-022 and 92-023 (NSW EOT); *Hill* v. *Water Resources Commission* (1985) EOC 92-127 (NSW EOT).

[70] SDA (Cth), s. 5(2).

[71] Anti-Discrimination Act 1977 (NSW), s. 114; Equal Opportunity Act 1984 (WA), s. 128.

[72] Australian Bureau of Statistics: *Trade Union Statistics, Australia, 30 June 1988,* Cat. 6323.0 (Canberra, AGPS, 1989). As is the case with other parts of the English-speaking world, Australia is experiencing a decline in the rate of unionisation. Over the past four years, for example, there has been a decline of approximately 4 per cent. The lower unionisation rate for women reflects, in part, the sex-segregated nature of the workforce, women's lesser commitment to the workforce, arising from their predominance in part-time, casual and contract work, and the fact that women may work in the home or in small, scattered workplaces. In part, the lower rate for women may also be explained by sociological factors such as the somewhat alienating, male-dominated milieu of traditional unionism, together with its historic antipathy towards the specific issues which have an impact upon women as workers.

[73] Australian Bureau of Statistics: *Trade Union Membership, Australia, 1986,* Cat. 6325.0 (Canberra: AGPS, 1986).

[74] Kate White: "Women and unions in Australia", in Women and Labour Publications Collective: *All her labours,* Vol. I: *Working it out* (Sydney, Hale and Iremonger, 1984), p. 119.

[75] (1922) 6 CAR 21.

[76] At the time of writing (May 1989), the ACTU was developing a strategy designed to increase the minimum wage for Australian workers quite substantially. Sex-neutral measures of this kind also have the advantage of not carrying with them the seeds of invidiousness which attach to sex-specific measures.

[77] *Transforming industrial relations in New South Wales,* Green Paper prepared by John Niland, Vol. I (Sydney, NSW GP, 1989). cf. Committee of Review: *Australian industrial relations law and systems* (Hancock Report), 3 Vols. (Canberra, AGPS, 1985); *Inquiry into the delivery of services by the Industrial Relations Commission of Victoria* (Marshall Report) (mimeograph, 1986).

[78] Gerard Henderson: "The industrial relations club", in John Hyde and John Nurick (eds.): *Wages wasteland: A radical examination of the Australian wage fixing system* (Sydney, Hale and Iremonger, 1985), p. 42.

3

Equal pay in Canada

*Dr. Patricia C. McDermott**

1. Introduction

Canada is a federal State with 14 different jurisdictions that have some form of wage discrimination legislation: one federal, ten provincial and three territorial districts.[1] Given this multiplicity of jurisdictions, it is a somewhat complex task to summarise the nature and scope of Canadian equal pay legislation. The best way to describe the history of legislation directed at reducing the persistent gender-based wage gap is to discuss the three trends in legislative reform, namely: the initial "equal pay for equal work" approach, which is also referred to as "equal work" legislation; the subsequent "equal pay for work of equal value" initiative or "equal value" legislation; and the current wave of "pay equity" legislation, recently introduced into four Canadian jurisdictions. Because this pay equity legislation has such a significant potential for reducing the gender-based wage gap, this chapter will focus primarily on this initiative.

1.1 Equal pay for equal work

By the end of the 1950s most Canadian jurisdictions had "equal pay for equal work" provisions in their basic employment standards statutes. These provisions were complaint-based and required employees to initiate actions against their employers, a fact which has clearly reduced their effectiveness. Since its introduction to Canada in 1951, equal pay legislation has involved a form of job evaluation based on the four standard internationally accepted factors: skill, effort, responsibility and working conditions. Until the mid-1970s equal pay complaints could only be made if the jobs being compared were identical. In 1970 a court decision in the province of Ontario found that female nurses' aides and male orderlies, although not doing exactly the same jobs, were performing "equal work" within the meaning of the statute. This decision resulted in Ontario's Employment Standards Act being amended to change the "same work" to "*substantially* the same kind of work".[2] This reform was subsequently introduced into the equal pay legislation throughout Canada.

Although this reform did broaden the scope of the equal pay remedy, the method of determining what was "substantially the same kind of work" remained quite

* York University, Toronto.

restrictive. Basically the jobs done by women and men had to involve substantially the same skill, effort, responsibility and working conditions. This meant that a job done by a woman which involved more skill but less responsibility than a similar job done by a male worker would not qualify for remedial action. Whether a job has "more" or "less" skill, of course, has been determined within the context of traditional job evaluation techniques.

The equal pay provisions throughout Canada have also included exemptions, such as merit systems, which allow an employer to justify a pay differential that would otherwise be found discriminatory under the legislation. The restrictive method of defining "substantially the same", the complaint-based structure of the legislation, and these exemptions have all operated to make Canadian equal pay laws relatively ineffective, even in the limited areas where men and women do the same type of work. The major reason why equal pay laws have not been able to reduce the wage gap significantly is, however, the high degree of gender segregation of the labour market. The increasing realisation that, on the whole, men and women do different types of work, has generated a push for equal value legislation that would redress systematic wage discrimination by ensuring that "women's work" is paid what it is worth, both to the employer and to society.

1.2 Equal pay for work of equal value

Only three Canadian jurisdictions, the federal Government (1978),[3] the province of Quebec (1976)[4] and the Yukon Territory, have introduced "equal pay for work of equal value" legislation. In all three cases the equal value provisions are contained in human rights legislation. Again the method of comparing jobs has involved a job evaluation process which uses the four standard factors: skill, effort, responsibility and working conditions. However, the *total evaluation score, not the score for each factor,* is compared. Since it is not necessary for each factor to be equivalent as they have to be under "equal work" systems, completely different jobs can be compared. This ability to compare so-called "apples and oranges" represents the most significant feature of the move from equal work to equal value legislation.

The federal Government's equal value scheme introduced the closely related concepts of "occupational groups" and "gender predominance" into its provisions. Rooted in the notion of systemic discrimination, both the requirements that a complaint be remedied for a homogeneous occupational group (within the establishment) and that the group have a majority of female incumbents[5] set the stage for future "proactive" pay equity legislation. In essence the gender predominance concept acknowledges the reality that a highly segregated labour force is at the heart of wage discrimination.

It should also be noted that the equal value legislation is still complaint-based and contains a list of exemptions, similar to those found in the equal work provisions, that can be used to justify an otherwise discriminatory wage practice. In over a decade equal value provisions have not proved effective in significantly narrowing the wage gap. The Canadian Human Rights Commission has handled only a dozen equal value cases since the provisions came into force in 1978. Although these cases have resulted in significant wage increases for those involved,[6] the activity under this initiative is unlikely to bring about a significant reduction in the wage gap for federally regulated employees. The recent trend among equal pay advocates and some policy-makers is to move to a "proactive" pay equity system that places the onus of eliminating discriminatory pay practices on the employer, rather than placing the burden solely on employees, who are often reluctant to bring a complaint.

1.3 Pay equity

The first Canadian jurisdiction to pass a proactive Pay Equity Act was was Manitoba (1984), followed by Ontario (1987), Prince Edward Island (1988) and Nova Scotia (1988). Rather than introducing pay equity provisions into other employment statutes, all four Canadian jurisdictions have passed separate Acts dealing solely with pay equity; they have also set up new administrative agencies to deal specifically with pay equity matters.

Basically, Canadian proactive pay equity schemes operate by evaluating all female and male job classes in an establishment and comparing the female jobs with the male ones to ensure that the female jobs are being paid using the same measure of value. In other words, if, after an evaluation process, a female job is found to have the same value as a comparable male job although the pay is lower, pay equity would require that the wages for the female job be raised to those for the the male. Thus, proactive pay equity differs in a fundamental way from "equal work" and "equal value" legislation, both of which are complaint based. Under pay equity legislation employees do not have to make complaints if their problems are to be remedied. It is the responsibility of employers to demonstrate that they are not engaged in discriminatory pay practices in any of their establishments. If it is found that they are, the legislation requires that the situation be remedied within a set period of time.

Although there are some in male-dominated jobs who experience wage discrimination, typically because of race, ethnicity or age, pay equity legislation is only directed at redressing the arguably more pressing and widespread gender-based wage gap. Not considering the discrimination against low-paid males presents a serious problem in both Ontario and Nova Scotia, where the legislation operates in such a manner that underpaid male jobs can function, as we will discuss, to lower significantly the adjustments female-dominated jobs will receive in the pay equity process. Furthermore, not addressing the impact of race, ethnicity and age on wage structures within the female labour force itself will compound, for those doing women's work, the problem of being compared to low-paid males whose wages are depressed by such factors.

1.4 The definition of pay

The four Canadian pay equity statutes all include definitions of "wages",[7] "pay"[8] or "compensation"[9] that go beyond basic salaries. In Manitoba, Ontario and Prince Edward Island the definition includes pay *and benefits* provided. But Nova Scotia's Act is the only one that actually provides guidance on what should be included when calculating the total wage to be used for the purposes of a pay equity exercise.

The provision explicitly excludes gratuities, payments in lieu of overtime, and living, car and clothing allowances.[10] The exclusion of these items seems to be an attempt to introduce some logic and equity into the calculation of wages that are to be compared and adjusted. For example, it would seem unfair to give those in a female job class a wage increase because those in the male job class receive a payment that must go towards a work-related expenditure, such as a uniform or a car. One could also argue that it is unfair to give a group of non-unionised employees a benefit that has been won, via collective bargaining, by another group. This would be particularly true if the unorganised group had had the option of joining a union and negotiating similar benefits but, for whatever reasons, had declined to do so.

Since three of the statutes are, at present, unclear about what should be included when calculating wages, there will undoubtedly be debates and confusion about how this critical component of a pay equity exercise should be established. This uncertainty could have been avoided if clear guidance had been given in either the legislation or the regulations.

1.5 Scope of the pay equity provisions

Of the four pay equity statutes in Canada, only Ontario's Pay Equity Act covers *both* the private and the public sectors. The other three Acts restrict their coverage to the public sector, which includes both the so-called "narrow" public sector, defined primarily as the provincial government as employer of civil service workers, and some "broader" public sector employers. Although the definition of "broader" public sector could include all the publicly run and/or funded hospitals, educational institutions, crown corporations and agencies, as well as municipal employers, only Ontario's legislation contains this inclusive list in its definition of "broader" public sector. Unlike the other three statutes, Ontario's Act includes all municipalities, all school boards and any employer who receives significant provincial funding. The Ontario Act is also the first proactive statute in the world to require all private sector employers with 100 or more employees to introduce a pay equity plan.[11]

It should also be mentioned that in 1988 the province of Newfoundland announced that it would be implementing a proactive pay equity programme for its public service employees. The decision was made, however, not to introduce legislation but simply for the provincial government, as employer, to take the initiative. Given that the programme will only cover the narrow public service, this represents the most limited coverage of all current proactive schemes.

In terms of coverage generally, all of the four pay equity statutes in Canada include both full-time and part-time positions of a permanent nature. In Nova Scotia, for instance, this includes "term" employees who are employed for more than one year.[12] Although Ontario's Act specifically excludes students who are employed during vacations,[13] it does have a very generous definition of "casual" employees that includes seasonal work, work performed for at least one-third of a normal working week, and even work performed on a regular and continuing basis for less than one-third of the normal working week.[14] It appears that when a group of employees is excluded from this type of legislation they are excluded for the purposes of calculating occupational classes as well as receiving wage adjustments.

Another important point that must be made when discussing the coverage of Canadian pay equity legislation is that there must be at least one "comparable" male job class in the employer's establishment in order to establish a discriminatory pay practice. In other words, those in all-female workplaces, such as child-care centres or nursing homes, cannot use the current Canadian pay equity legislation. Even where female employees tend to be located at the bottom of the wage hierarchy, as in the retail sector, those employees would not be able to use the legislation to seek equal pay in at least two Canadian jurisdictions because of the need for a male job class for comparison.[15]

2. Procedures for determining "Equality"

2.1 Permitted justifications for differences in pay

Only Manitoba's Pay Equity Act does not include the exemptions present in both the equal work and equal value provisions discussed earlier; Ontario's Prince Edward Island's and Nova Scotia's Acts each list the all too familiar exemptions that can so seriously undermine pay equity. The exemptions listed in these statutes include seniority systems, training programmes, merit systems, skills shortages and "red circling" (a procedure by which an employee is downgraded as a result of a re-evaluation of his position, but his wages are temporarily fixed until the wages appropriate to the downgraded position are equivalent to his current wages). All three statutes do, however, provide that exclusions must operate without gender discrimination. In other words, such schemes as merit pay or training programmes must be, where feasible, equally open to both male and female workers in the establishment.[16]

2.2 The role of job evaluation

All pay equity jurisdictions in Canada have maintained the four standard factors that have traditionally been used in both the "equal work" and the "equal value" provisions: skill, effort, responsibility and working conditions. It should also be noted that these factors are set out in the text of each statute; consideration of them is thus mandatory when conducting a pay equity exercise. Three of the four statutes clearly state that a "job evaluation" procedure is to be used in the pay equity process. Although Ontario's Act uses the term "job comparison" instead of "job evaluation", given the structure of Ontario's pay equity process and its use of the four standard factors typically employed in job evaluation, it appears that a job evaluation methodology is assumed.

2.3 Sex bias in job evaluation

All four jurisdictions also require that the job evaluation methodology employed in a pay equity exercise be either "gender-neutral"[17] or one that "does not discriminate on the basis of sex".[18] None of the statutes, however, defines precisely what gender-neutral means. Two jurisdictions, Manitoba and Ontario, have produced educational literature about how gender bias can be introduced into job evaluation methodology, but these efforts have only been at an introductory level. For example, the relative weighting of the four factors, and the possible impact on evaluation results that different weightings can produce, have not been discussed in any detail.

Another critical issue, the introduction of gender bias and errors into the collection of "job content data" by simply using current, often gender-biased and inaccurate job descriptions, has not been examined. Most significantly, the class bias and gender stereotyping that can enter a job evaluation process by the common practice of using so-called "evaluation teams" has also not been explored in this literature.

It is an understatement to say that a pay equity exercise based on job evaluation, with its gender predominance calculations, factor weightings, job information data and so on, is a somewhat complicated process. Thus an attempt to remove gender bias from the process can, in itself, become a complex task. It is, however, absolutely essential to do so if equitable pay practices are to be achieved. Legislation that requires a "gender-neutral" job evaluation procedure, but does not provide detailed guidelines or regulations describing how this should be achieved, raises serious questions about its ability to reduce significantly the gender-based wage gap.

Clearly the reticence about evaluating the job evaluation methodology itself occurs partly because to do so would be to question the way job evaluation has been carried out historically – in such a way as to create, in most instances, a justification for the undervaluation of women's work. But such a critique would also question the way much job evaluation is currently being done by consulting firms implementing pay equity throughout Canada.

Two leading researchers in the area of pay equity have noted that "most" pay equity exercises in the United States have employed "the very management consulting firms that have been using biased job evaluation systems for decades".[19] Unfortunately this same pattern is beginning to emerge in Canada. Some public sector pay equity processes have opted to use consulting firms that have been judged by some authors to be gender-biased. In Ontario, a province where literally thousands of private sector employers must comply with pay equity legislation, the lack of guidance on this critical issue presents a serious weakness.

2.4 Gender-dominated occupational categories and jobs

All four Pay Equity Acts require that each establishment's workforce be divided into "job classes"[20] at the beginning of a pay equity exercise. A "job class" is defined as a group of positions that have similar qualifications, duties, responsibilities and pay schedules. Ontario's Act allows a job class to consist of one position,[21] but in Manitoba and Nova Scotia an occupational class must have ten or more incumbents to qualify as a job class,[22] a restriction that clearly reduces the number who can seek equitable pay under the legislation.

As already mentioned, all four Canadian Pay Equity Acts include a gender predominance requirement for job classes that are used in the job evaluation process. Manitoba's Act, the first to be passed, requires that both male and female job classes be at least 70 per cent male or female to qualify as either a "female-dominated class" and seeking pay adjustments, or a "male-dominated class" for purposes of comparison in the pay equity scheme.

Ontario's Pay Equity Act, the next to come into force, also requires a 70 per cent or more standard for male job classes, but lowers the female job class requirement to 60 per cent. This means that more female job classes will be eligible for wage adjustments. The two other jurisdictions that subsequently enacted pay equity statutes adopted the figure of 60 per cent for both male and female job classes.

Clearly the lowering of the female gender predominance requirement to 60 per cent, as has occurred in three jurisdictions, has given more people in female job classes access to the remedial legislation. The lowering of the requirement to 60 per cent for male predominance in both Nova Scotia and Prince Edward Island has also meant that more male job classes are available for comparison purposes. Although this could help provide a much-needed male comparator in establishments where there are few male job classes, a lower male gender predominance requirement does not necessarily mean that more favourable male comparators can be found. It is possible that introducing more male job classes that are less clearly "men's work" will result in a lower-paid male job class being made available to serve as the comparator for a female job class. One study for the Ontario Public Service Employees' Union, which analysed wage data for unionised public service workers, found that for each 1 per cent increase in the number of women in a job class, there was a decrease of Can$1.15 in weekly wages, thus creating an annual differential of Can$5,980 for a job class that was 100 per cent female.[23]

Even if legislation allows female job classes to receive an average of the wages of possible male comparators, as in Manitoba and Prince Edward Island, the lowering of the male predominance requirement may mean that lower-paid male job classes decrease the average wage adjustments for the female-dominated classes. Of course, if the statutes require that an exact match for each female job class must be found, as is the case in both Ontario and Nova Scotia, the introduction of lower-paid male comparators is very problematic indeed.

Gender predominance is a concept that deserves further theoretical and quantitative study. Given that both Ontario's and Nova Scotia's statutes only require employers to raise the wages of the female job class to the *lowest* wage of all possible "comparable" male job classes (those which have similar job evaluation results), lowering the male predominance requirement could seriously undermine the pay equity process. As noted, however, where there is a limited number of male jobs for comparison purposes, the lower requirement could serve to make available a much-needed male comparator, without which current pay equity legislation in Ontario and Nova Scotia is ineffective. When more is known about the effects of gender premominance requirements, it will be easier to assess how they should be adjusted to further the goal of equitable pay.

2.5 The scope of comparison

All four Canadian pay equity jurisdictions limit liability for discriminatory pay practices to the employer's "establishment". Thus a separate pay equity exercise must be carried out in each establishment or establishments, as defined by the specific Act. Since in Manitoba, Nova Scotia and Prince Edward Island the pay equity statutes limit their coverage to the public sector, it is relatively easy to identify the employer. In Ontario, however, where pay equity legislation covers the entire private sector as well, it can be difficult, especially in non-unionised settings, to establish who is liable for discriminatory pay practices. For example, if an employer runs a franchised outlet, or a division of a large multinational, it may be necessary to "pierce the corporate veil" to obtain access to the information, the authority and, most importantly, the funds necessary to implement pay equity.

Not only can identifying the employer be difficult under Ontario's statute, but the definition of "establishment", which appears to have been developed to accommodate regional differences, is also somewhat complicated. It is basically a geographical definition that follows the county, district and regional boundaries of the province. If, for instance, an employer has an office in city A and another in city B, these would constitute two "establishments" and require two separate pay equity plans. It is, however, possible for the employer, for the purposes of non-union pay equity plans, to join geographical units in any combination and create a variety of "establishments". Unfortunately, this gives employers the opportunity to construct their province-wide pay equity scheme in such a way as to avoid costly comparisons and thus clearly represents a weakness in the legislation.[24]

Ontario's pay equity scheme differs in another significant way from those in the other three jurisdictions. In Manitoba, Nova Scotia and Prince Edward Island, the statutes explicitly state that a "*single*" gender-neutral job evaluation scheme must be used in the employer's establishment[25] to cover both organised and non-unionised employees. This is not the case under Ontario's Act, which stipulates a separate pay equity plan for each bargaining unit and another for non-unionised employees. This can prove to be a rather complex undertaking. A typical Ontario hospital, for example, has employees in at least ten different bargaining units, each represented by a different union, and would therefore require 11 separate pay equity plans, one for each of the ten units and one for the non-unionised employees. The problem is that since each bargaining unit has the right to negotiate its own pay equity plan,[26] the hospital could conceivably end up with 11 *different* job evaluation schemes.

Each female job class must first seek an appropriate male comparator within their own plan, and only if none is available can they search in other plans. Given the incompatibility of job evaluation schemes, the task of searching for a comparable male job class "throughout the establishment" is rendered extremely difficult, if not impossible. It is very likely that, given the highly segregated nature of the labour market, many female job classes will need to look outside their own pay equity plans. Just how this can be done, given incompatible job evaluation schemes, is, at this point, unclear.

3. The process of wage adjustment

3.1 *The different methods of making adjustments*

The calculation of wages is a significant element in any pay equity exercise. Since women's wages are to be raised to the level of comparable men's wages, how the wage adjustments are to be decided upon will also be crucial. Manitoba's and Prince Edward Island's pay equity schemes include a significantly different model of wage adjustment from those in Ontario and Nova Scotia.

In both Manitoba and Prince Edward Island, the Acts contain no explicit provision as to how pay equity adjustments should be made, but leave decisions about "the quantum, allocation and orderly implementation" of wage adjustments to negotiations between the employer and the agents bargaining on the employees' behalf.[27] Both Acts also permit comparisons which involve the "average or projected average schedule or grade of pay".[28] This means that an "average pay line approach"[29] can be used to establish wage adjustments. In other words, each female job class need not be matched with a precise male comparator.

As we will see when we discuss the wage adjustment process in Ontario and Nova Scotia, this explicit ability to use an average of possible comparators, or even an "average pay line" approach for an entire establishment, not only avoids the problem of throwing a compensation system into disarray, but also avoids conflict with collective bargaining relationships. Another advantage of an average pay line approach is its focus on the gender-based wage gap that exists within each establishment. Since this is precisely the problem pay equity is attempting to remedy, the extent to which an individual organisation's pay gap is closed will indicate, to some extent, the success of a particular pay equity exercise.

Nova Scotia's and Ontario's manner of handling wage adjustments differs from that in the other two jurisdictions in that they outline very explicit procedures, rather than leaving it to the parties to decide.

In both Nova Scotia and Ontario the "pay" or "compensation" for a job class that is used in a pay equity exercise is the maximum wage for that job class. In Ontario the maximum is called the "job rate"[30] while in Nova Scotia it is simply referred to as the "top rate of pay".[31] In essence, it is these maximum rates that are compared. If a female job class has the same value as a male job class (as established by the job evaluation), and if the male job class has a higher "job rate" or "top rate of pay", the female job class is entitled to that rate. When this occurs, the job/top rate (the maximum) of the female job class becomes the same as that for the male job class[32] and all those in the female job class receive the differential between the female and male job/top rates.[33] This is the heart of how pay equity operates in both Nova Scotia and Ontario.

This is what happens when a female job class has the same or comparable value as only *one* male job class. If, however, there is *more than one* possible male job class with the same or comparable value, the female job class is entitled only to the *lowest* job/top rate of the possible male comparators. As noted earlier, this means that in establishments where male job classes are experiencing discriminatory pay because of ethnicity or race, pay equity operates to bring those in female job classes only up to this low discriminatory standard. There is no doubt that this provision seriously lowers the level of wage adjustments for thousands of employees seeking pay equity, and also removes the possibility of receiving any wage adjustment at all for thousands of others.

We should note that it is possible to use an average pay line approach in Nova Scotia or Ontario and this would clearly offer a higher standard of pay equity. However, both the employer and the bargaining agent would have to agree on this. Since it is likely that such an approach would cost the employer more than the adjustment procedure contained in the legislation, it is doubtful that many would opt for this route. Similarly it is probable that Ontario employers, who are allowed to implement pay equity plans without the involvement of non-unionised employees, would comply with only the statutory minimum when implementing wage adjustments.

To make matters more complicated, in both Ontario and Nova Scotia, if there are *no* appropriate male job classes to serve as comparators but only those of lower value, the female job class is entitled to the highest job/top rate of the lower valued male job class. Not only is this confusing, but it could result in lower valued female job classes receiving higher wage adjustments than other higher valued female job classes. This would happen if the lower valued female job class was fortunate enough to find a higher paid male comparator. This is, of course, more probable in Ontario where, unlike in all three other jurisdictions, comparisons are made across a multitude of pay equity plans for different bargaining units and a single male job match must be found rather than moving to an average wage line as allowed in other jurisdictions. In other words, if the average wage line methodology is employed, female job classes end up with an average of the wages for comparable male jobs rather than the wage of an exact match, as in Ontario. Thus in Ontario the rare female job class could "get lucky" and be matched to a lower valued but much higher paid comparator – perhaps a job in the shipping department organised by a union with a more than usually aggressive bargaining style such as the Teamsters.

3.2 *The relationship between pay equity and existing wage relationships*

It seems that the drafters of Nova Scotia's legislation anticipated the problem of wage adjustments altering existing wage relationships, and introduced a clause allowing employers to make further wage adjustments in order to avoid this situation. This clause states that an employer shall consider "the pay of every person to whom the employee is responsible or subordinate" to determine whether additional adjustments should be made in the light of the duties and responsibilities of that person "in relation to" the duties and responsibilities of other employees.[34]

Such a clause is obviously highly problematic in terms of pay equity. If the current pay structure in place in an establishment is inequitable, it allows that inequity to continue. It also raises serious questions about the validity of a job evaluation exercise. On the whole, such a clause is clearly antithetical to pay equity. It demonstrates a compromise between a statute that is willing to insist on the total revamping of a compensation system and one that will allow equity to be set aside in favour of maintaining internally consistent, if inequitable, compensation relativities.

It should be pointed out that all pay equity legislation in Canada is characterised by a similar tension between the goal of what could be termed "full" pay equity and maintaining so-called "internal relativities" in compensation. Some of this tension appears to be focused on the role job evaluation is allowed to play in the legislated scheme. In Manitoba, for example, a "job evaluation is a science" approach is tempered by permitting collective bargaining, guided by the job evaluation results, to establish the final wage adjustments. In a description of how the Manitoba public service pay equity exercise proceeded, one observer stated:

> We had agreed that we were not involved in a mechanical "pay for points" exercise. There is no magic formula which can be fed into a computer to spit out solutions. Rather, we viewed the rating exercise as a means to give us the information on our gender-dominated classifications. That data *then served as guidelines* to the negotiations teams who bargained the adjustments [emphasis added].[35]

Allowing the final adjustments to be collectively bargained, rather than incorporating specific job comparison procedures in the legislation, can be seen as reflecting both an apparent lack of faith in the precision of job evaluation and a concern about disrupting existing compensation relationships. Similarly, as noted, the Nova Scotia Act permits employers to determine whether a wage adjustment should also be given to other employees when a comparison of the "duties and responsibilities" is made between those not receiving pay equity adjustments and those entitled to an increase.[36] This is clearly designed to readjust the wage relationships disrupted by the pay equity process.

3.3 Stipulations as to time-limits and the total sum required for wage adjustments

Before we leave the topic of wage adjustments, it must be noted that all four pay equity jurisdictions in Canada have some provisions regarding the money an employer must make available for pay adjustments on an annual basis, and in some cases provisions that limit the length of time within which pay equity must be achieved. Manitoba, for example, not only requires that employers put 1 per cent of their total payroll towards pay equity adjustments annually, but limits what they are required to pay to this amount. The Manitoba Act also limits the length of time over which employers must make pay equity adjustments to four years.[37]

Although Nova Scotia's legislation similarly requires that public sector employers should complete the pay equity process in four years, it does not limit the amount an employer is required to pay out annually in wage adjustments, and it makes employees "entitled" to the adjustment 24 months after the start of the pay equity process.[38] Ontario's and Prince Edward Island's Acts also both require that at least 1 per cent of an employer's total payroll be available annually for wage adjustments.[39] Prince Edward Island's legislation actually forbids a public sector employer from making pay adjustments "in an amount in excess of 1 per cent of the total payroll" unless the employer is paying retrospective payments or is combining the final payout, which is less than 1 per cent, with the payment for the preceding year.[40] Rather than restricting the amount of any payout to 1 per cent of the payroll, Ontario's Act, like Manitoba's protects employers from having to pay more than 1 per cent annually, but allows them to pay out more if they so desire.[41]

Prince Edward Island's legislation does not stipulate the number of years in which public sector employers must achieve pay equity. While Ontario's Act does not limit the length of time in which private sector employers must complete pay equity adjustments, it does set a seven-year limit on the completion of public sector payments and does not limit the final payment to 1 per cent of an employer's province-wide payroll.[42] This is an interesting contrast to the Manitoba Act, which anticipates only a four-year payout period at a rate of 1 per cent of the total payroll.[43]

4. Enforcement arrangements for implementing pay equity policies

4.1 The different methods of enforcement and the government bodies involved

The Manitoba Act gives the power to settle disputes arising from the pay equity process to the arbitration procedures available in the provincial labour legislation for solving disagreements arising during normal collective bargaining.[44] This is an option that builds on the legitimacy of a system of dispute settlement already in place. There is, nevertheless, a concern that current arbitrators lack the expertise needed to handle often complex pay equity matters, especially those involving gender neutrality.

The Manitoba Act requires that the parties negotiating the civil service pay equity plan identify the job classes and select a gender-neutral job evaluation scheme within a ten-month period.[45] At this point the first of two "agreements" must be filed with the Executive Director of the Pay Equity Bureau. Sixteen months later, a second agreement regarding the quantum, allocation and implementation of wage adjustments must also be filed with the Bureau.[46] If, at any point, there is a breakdown in the negotiations, either party may refer the matter to arbitration.[47] The Director of the Bureau may also, after consultation with the parties, refer the matter to arbitration if agreements are not filed in a timely manner.[48] The civil service began their pay equity exercise in October 1985 and the broader public sector began one year later.

Under the Prince Edward Island Act, if a disagreement arises during the pay equity process, either party may file a complaint with the Pay Equity Commissioner. At this point the Commissioner investigates the complaint, and if no settlement is reached, the matter is referred to arbitration under the procedures set out in the provincial Labour Relations Act.[49]

The Prince Edward Island Act assumes that pay equity is a continuing process in that pay equity must be maintained. After pay equity has been achieved, "any employee or bargaining agent" may file a complaint with the Pay Equity Commissioner to the effect that a public sector employer has either engaged in a "discriminatory practice" or "failed to maintain pay equity".[50] At this point the commissioner settles the matter without reference to arbitration.[51] One wonders, however, precisely what "maintaining" pay equity means. It is unclear whether job classes that have been found comparable are to receive the same compensation indefinitely. Surely beginning to pay the male job class more would not be "maintaining" pay equity. It will certainly be interesting to see how ongoing pay equity is defined, particularly within the context of collective bargaining. If pay equity wage relationships are indeed a permanent feature of the compensation scheme of employers, once pay equity has been achieved and the 1 per cent is no longer explicitly required to be put into adjustments, theoretically the employer will be left with an increased wage bill, unless cuts can be made in the wages of some other groups. The concern for some male-dominated unionists is that closing the gender-based wage gap will be done at the expense of male wages.

As noted earlier, the Prince Edward Island legislation does not contain a time limit for the completion of wage adjustments; however, like the Manitoba Act, it does require that wage adjustments should begin after a two-year implementation period and that the civil service should start the process a year before the broader public sector.[52] Again, as in Manitoba, parties must file copies of their agreements with the Commissioner of the Pay Equity Bureau.[53]

The Nova Scotia Act, like those in Prince Edward Island and Ontario, sets up a separate commission to deal with pay equity. This commission settles matters when there is a failure to agree over such issues as job evaluation and the "quantum of allocation" of wage adjustments.[54] It does not, however, make use of regular dispute settlement procedures available under provincial labour legislation; rather the commission itself settles these issues.

Like the legislation in both Manitoba and Prince Edward Island, the Nova Scotia Act has a two-year implementation schedule whereby the civil service began the process in 1988, followed a year later by the broader public sector.[55] Again, as in the other two jurisdictions, agreements are to be filed with the Pay Equity Commission and, as in Manitoba, wage adjustments must be completed within four years.[56]

Ontario has also opted to set up a separate body, the Pay Equity Commission, to handle a broad range of pay equity disputes. Complaints go first to the Review Services provided by the Commission. If they fail to settle the matter or a request is made for an appeal from this initial decision, the case then moves to the Commission's Hearings Tribunal for a full hearing.[57] As noted, the Ontario Act contains a unique feature that allows claimants before the Hearings Tribunal to remain anonymous. It should also be pointed out that although the Review Services' initial investigation and attempt to reach a settlement is free, the much-needed representation by experienced counsel before the Hearings Tribunal can become quite costly even for relatively minor matters.

The Ontario Act also contains the clearly important but somewhat nebulous provision that employers must "maintain compensation practices that provide for pay equity".[58] This clause is accompanied by another, allowing employers, "once pay equity has been achieved", to argue that "bargaining strength" makes it necessary to pay comparable male and female job classes differently. This appears to be the only reason available for altering the job rates of two job classes once they have been matched in a pay equity exercise. As discussed with reference to the Prince Edward Island Act, the

Ontario Act also fails to give any guidance as to whether these wages are to remain the same indefinitely.

Unlike the legislation in all three other jurisdictions, the Ontario Act does not require that pay equity plans be filed with the Commission; they must simply be "posted" in the workplace and made available, upon request, to those covered by the plan.[59] The reason for this probably has to do with the volume of plans that would be generated by the large number of private sector employers in Ontario. Nevertheless, the fact that plans do not have to be filed presents a serious weakness in the Ontario Act, as it will be extremely difficult to monitor the extent to which the Act is complied with. In addition, the complexity of Ontario's pay equity legislation clearly makes it difficulty for employees covered by the Act to understand the process sufficiently to be able to formulate a complaint about a plan once it is posted.

The Ontario Act contains a two-year implementation period for all public sector employers. At this point plans are to be posted and wage adjustments are to begin, and they must be completed within five years.[60] Although private sector employers with 500 employees or over must also post their plans within two years, they do not have to begin wage adjustments for a further year, and again there is no deadline by which wage adjustments must be complete.

Private sector employers in Ontario with between 100 and 499 employees must post their pay equity plans within three years of the Act coming into force and begin wage adjustments a year later. There are similar schedules for small employers with at between 50 and 99 employees and between ten and 49 employees.[61] They can opt to post their plans in the fourth and fifth years after the implementation of the Act and begin wage adjustments a year later; however, these are not mandatory time-limits for these two groups of employers. It simply means that they can wait for five or six years after the passage of the Act before becoming seriously concerned about pay equity. It appears that they then become vulnerable to complaints that they are engaged in discriminatory pay practices.[62]

The rather lengthy implementation period, the lack of mandatory compliance for employers with 10-99 employees, and the complete exclusion of employers with less than ten employees, represent serious weaknesses in Ontario's legislation. These shortcomings, combined with the absence of a filing requirements discussed earlier, will make it difficult to assess the level of compliance throughout the province.

4.2 Protection against victimisation

Ontario's Act is the only one that contains an explicit "protection from reprisals" clause which prohibits anyone from intimidating or coercing a person for exercising their rights under the Act.[63] The Act also includes a truly unique and potentially powerful feature which allows an employee to complain *anonymously* to the Pay Equity Commission.[64]

4.3 Progress reports on the pay equity process

The filing requirements and the complaints procedures, together with the power of the Pay Equity Commissions to initiate their own complaints, are all forms of enforcement. Some of the legislation has further provisions to encourage, monitor and enforce compliance. All four Acts stipulate that the Commission or Bureau should educate and provide information and advice about the pay equity process.[65] Three jurisdictions, Ontario being the exception, also require that the Commission "prepare and maintain statistics" relating to the implementation of pay equity.[66] In Manitoba the Pay Equity Bureau is also required to file a "detailed report" every 12 months "setting out the progress in the implementation of pay equity".[67] This report is subsequently tabled before the provincial Assembly.[68]

Both the Nova Scotia and the Prince Edward Island Acts also require the Commission or Bureau to submit a report on the implementation process every six months to the Minister of Labour, who will table it in the provincial Assembly.[69] There is an additional requirement in the Nova Scotia Act that each public sector employer should file a monthly report with the Commission "setting out the progress in implementing pay equity".[70]

The Ontario Act contains a provision that the Commission shall make an "annual report" on its "activities and affairs" to the Minister of Labour, who will table the report before the provincial Assembly.[71] This is not, of course, a report on the implementation of pay equity as is provided for in the other three statutes, but will probably contain a summary of the cases settled by Review Services and the decisions of the Hearings Tribunal.

5. The role of collective bargaining

Manitoba, Nova Scotia and Prince Edward Island have adopted a similar approach to the role of collective bargaining in the pay equity process. Each Act has the bargaining agents (the unions) represent the members as they would in normal collective bargaining. All three statutes also require that "employee representatives" be elected[72] or selected[73] by employees who are not unionised. These representatives will bargain on their behalf in matters relating to pay equity. Both the union negotiators and the employee representatives come together to bargain over pay equity with the employer. It is somewhat unusual to have employees who are not unionised negotiate with the employer alongside certified bargaining agents. Each statute requires that the parties bargain in "good faith" to reach an agreement on the implementation of pay equity, and that employers disclose to the employee agents information in their "possession and control relevant to the implementation of pay equity".[74]

The major item to be bargained in these three jurisdictions is the "single" gender-neutral job evaluation scheme.[75] As already discussed, all the employees of each employer, whether unionised or not, are evaluated under the same job evaluation scheme, and those in female job classes are entitled to wage adjustments established by comparisons with male job classes within this single scheme.

Ontario, as outlined earlier, takes a quite different approach. Instead of requiring a single job evaluation scheme, each bargaining unit negotiates a separate one; this makes comparisons across the establishment, although permitted under the Act, quite difficult. Ontario also differs in that there is no provision for "employee representatives" for those not in unions. These unorganised workers are not entitled to a role in the pay equity process, but have their pay equity plan developed and implemented for them by the employer. Thus only unions and employers can engage in "good faith" bargaining, while non-unionised employees have to wait until the employer has a plan in place before they can complain.[76]

The Prince Edward Island and Nova Scotia Acts both stipulate that pay equity negotiations take place "separate and apart" from normal collective bargaining,[77] while the legislation in both Manitoba and Ontario is silent on this point. In Manitoba, since union and non-union employee agents bargain together for a single job evaluation scheme, it would be difficult to combine pay equity negotiations with normal bargaining. In Ontario, however, pay equity negotiations and bargaining for a new collective agreement could take place together, although it is likely that numerous potential jurisdictional conflicts would emerge between these two somewhat contradictory undertakings.

For example, if pay equity negotiations and ordinary negotiations were merged and allegations of "bad faith" bargaining arose, where would the complainants take their problem – to the Labour Board or the Pay Equity Commission? If the matter involved disclosure of information needed for both pay equity and normal collective bargaining, it would again be unclear which body had jurisdiction. These are only a few of the numerous conflicts that could emerge in combined bargaining. Indeed, the very nature of a pay equity process that only delivers wage increases to those in female-dominated jobs, and potentially in a somewhat random fashion, runs counter to the goals of normal bargaining. It is likely that most unions, when possible, will engage in the pay equity process first and then try to bargain increases for those who did not receive adjustments, and also, no doubt, attempt to restore traditional compensation relationships. It appears, at least in Ontario, that this will be difficult, since such attempts could be found to contravene the Act.[78]

The relationship between collective bargaining and the pay equity process is unclear. Both the Prince Edward Island and the Ontario Acts contain provisions stating that a pay equity plan "prevails over" the provisions of all relevant collective agreements and that wage adjustments shall be "deemed to be incorporated into and form part of the relevant collective agreements".[79] Nova Scotia's Act contains a similar clause, which also maintains that the pay equity agreement "prevails over the provisions of other agreements with respect to pay".[80] This is clearly an attempt to ensure that the wage relationships established in the pay equity process are not undermined by collective bargaining; precisely what this means for collective bargaining is not clear.

Are these new wage relationships to be maintained indefinitely? One would assume so since the adjustments are, as we have noted, "incorporated into and form part of the relevant collective agreements". This is, of course, particularly problematic in Ontario, where non-unionised female job classes can be matched with male job classes within other bargaining units. It is, as discussed earlier, open to employers in Ontario to argue, once pay equity has been achieved, that wage relationships established under the pay equity process may be altered if the difference in compensation that will be created as a result of a higher increase to a male job class is the result of greater "bargaining strength" on the part of the male bargaining unit.[81] This same problem is, of course, true for other pay equity jurisdictions; however, only Ontario's Act gives the employer an explicit right to alter the wage relationships established by the pay equity exercise.

6. Conclusions

The most important area to watch in Canadian pay equity implementation exercises will be the commitment to, and development of, the concept of "gender neutrality". This notion has the potential to challenge the way job evaluation has been carried out for decades. Since the Canadian legislation, like so many other pay equity exercises in the world, is based on job evaluation, it is quite clear that unless a serious attempt is made to evaluate and correct the gender-biased methodologies and assumptions built into traditional job evaluation schemes, the wage gap will persist.

It may also, of course, become essential to develop alternative ways of closing the wage gap without systems based on job evaluation. The most fruitful avenue to explore here is surely the one of statistical analysis to examine the impact of labour market segregation on wages. Even if no such option is developed or accepted, it is likely that sound statistical tools can be used to reveal the biased performance of some job evaluation schemes.

The major obstacle to the implementation of pay equity in Canada has, to date, been the reluctance of jurisdictions to move towards any form of positive action. Without the legislation in place, the theoretical debates about how best to close the wage gap cannot be tested. So far, only four out of 14 provinces have introduced proactive pay equity statutes. Of these, only one, Ontario, has opted to cover the private sector. Until legislation has been introduced in every Canadian jurisdiction covering both the public and the private sector, and comprehensive measures are taken to monitor compliance, the gender-based wage gap will continue to be a feature of the labour market in Canada, as it has been in all other industrialised nations for so long.

Notes

[1] Approximately 10 per cent of the Canadian workforce is covered by federal employment legislation. This includes employees who work directly for the federal Government as well as those employed in a "federal undertaking", whether in the public or private sector.

[2] The current s. 33(1) of this Act includes the equal pay provisions.

[3] Canadian Human Rights Act, s. 11.

[4] Quebec's Charter of Human Rights and Freedoms provision covers "equivalent work", which includes substantially similar work and the equal value standard.

[5] The federal legislation uses a "sliding scale" to establish gender predominance. If a female occupational group has under 100 incumbents it must be at least 70 per cent female to qualify for an equal value complaint. If it has 100 to 500 it has to have 60 per cent or more and if it has over 500 the group has to be 55 per cent or more female.

[6] For an overview of these cases see *Equal pay: Collective bargaining and the law,* prepared by Mary Cornish for the Ministry of Labour, Minister of Supply and Services, 1986.

[7] Manitoba, s. 1, Prince Edward Island, s. 1.

[8] Nova Scotia, s. 1*(o)*.

[9] Ontario, s. 1.

[10] Nova Scotia, s. 3*(o)*.

[11] Although it could be argued that Ontario's Pay Equity Act requires small employers (ten to 99 employees) to implement a pay equity plan, this appears only to occur if a complaint is launched against the employer in the sixth or seventh year (depending on the employer's size) after the Act came into force (s. 21).

[12] Nova Scotia's *Pay Equity Act,* SNS 1988, c. 16, s. 1*(f)*.

[13] Ontario's *Pay Equity Act,* SO c.34, 1987, s. 1.

[14] ibid., s. 8(3) and (4).

[15] As we will discuss shortly, both Ontario and Nova Scotia require a comparison with a specific male job class to be established for each female job class. Without that comparison, and without the explicit right to compare "indirectly" as can be done in Manitoba, those in female job classes appear to be out of luck in these two jurisdictions.

[16] Exemption provisions are found in s. 8 of Ontario's Act, s. 13(4) of Nova Scotia's and s. 8 of Prince Edward Island's. Note that Nova Scotia's provision does not include red circling, while Prince Edward Island's does not include red circling or temporary training programmes.

[17] Manitoba, s. 9(1); Prince Edward Island, s. 14(1)*(a);* Ontario, s. 12.

[18] Nova Scotia, s. 12.

[19] See "Equitable compensation: Methodological criteria for comparable worth", in Christine Bose and Glenna Spitze (eds.): *Ingredients for women's employment policy* (New York, SUNY Press, 1987).

[20] Ontario's Act uses the term "job class", while Nova Scotia refers to "classifications", and both Manitoba and Prince Edward Island simply refer to a "class".

[21] Ontario, s. 1(6).

[22] Both Manitoba's Pay Equity Act and Nova Scotia's Act outline some flexibility on this issue. See ss. 1 of the Manitoba Act and 1*(j)* and *(m)* of the Nova Scotia Act.

[23] This study was done by Sonja Greckol. See Debra Lewis: *Just give us the money* (Vancouver, British Columbia, Women's Research Centre, 1988), p. 120.

[24] See P. McDermott: "Pay equity in Ontario: A critical legal analysis", in *Osgoode Hall Law Journal,* spring, 1990, for a more detailed discussion of this and other weaknesses in Ontario's Act.

[25] It should be noted that these three statutes use a "functional" definition of establishment that basically coincides with the definition of employer.

[26] Ontario, s. 14(2)*(a)*.

[27] See Manitoba, ss. 9(1)*(c)* and 14(1), and Prince Edward Island, s. 14.

[28] Manitoba, s. 6(2); Prince Edward Island, s. 7(2).

[29] An average pay line approach has been used in most implementations of pay equity in the United States and has also been used in the federal jurisdiction in Canada for implementing equal value legislation.

[30] Ontario, s. 1.

[31] Nova Scotia, s. 14(2)*(a)*.

[32] Ontario, s. 6; Nova Scotia, s. 17.

[33] Ontario, s. 9(3); Nova Scotia, s. 14(2)(6).

[34] Nova Scotia, s. 16.

[35] Roberta Ellis-Grunfeld: "Pay equity in Manitoba", in *Manitoba Law Journal* (Winnipeg, Manitoba), Vol. 16, No. 3, p. 231.

[36] Nova Scotia, s. 16.

[37] Manitoba, s. 7(3)*(a)*.

[38] Nova Scotia, s. 14(1) and 15(1).

[39] Ontario, s. 13(4) and (5); Prince Edward Island, s. 10*(a)* and *(b)*.

[40] Prince Edward Island, s. 11(1).

[41] Ontario, s. 13(6).

42 S. 13(7) of Ontario's Act stipulates that public sector employers should fully implement adjustments in compensation by the seventh anniversary of the effective date and thus creates, via this section, an exemption to the 1 per cent limit.

43 This section of Manitoba's Act has been the subject of a successful legal challenge using the equity clauses (s. 15) of Canada's Charter of Rights and Freedoms. In this case the court found the annual 1 per cent of payroll limit, together with the four-year limit, to violate the equity provisions.

44 Manitoba, s. 10(1), (4) and (6).

45 Manitoba, s. 8(1).

46 Manitoba, ss. 9(2) and 14(2).

47 Manitoba, ss. 10(1) and 15(1).

48 Manitoba, ss. 10(2) and 15(2).

49 Prince Edward Island, s. 15(1).

50 Prince Edward Island, s. 6(2).

51 Prince Edward Island, s. 5(2) and (3).

52 Prince Edward Island, s. 17(1) and (2).

53 Prince Edward Island, s. 14(4).

54 Nova Scotia, s. 12.

55 Nova Scotia, s. 11.

56 Nova Scotia, ss. 20 and 14(1).

57 Ontario, s. 23.

58 Ontario, s. 7(1).

59 Ontario, s. 1(2) and (3).

60 Ontario, 13(7).

61 Ontario, s. 10*(c)* and *(d)*.

62 Particularly the s. 7 requirement to "establish and maintain compensation practices that provide for pay equity".

63 Ontario, s. 9(2).

64 Ontario, s. 32(4).

65 Manitoba, s. 5; Nova Scotia, s. 7; Ontario, s. 33; Prince Edward Island, s. 5.

66 Manitoba, s. 5; Nova Scotia, s. 7; Prince Edward Island, s. 5.

67 Manitoba, s. 5(2)*(c)*.

68 Manitoba, s. 5(4).

69 Nova Scotia, s. 9; Prince Edward Island, s. 5.

70 Nova Scotia, s. 9(1).

71 Ontario, s. 33(5).

72 Manitoba, s. 1; Prince Edward Island, s. 1*(f)*.

73 Nova Scotia, s. 1*(g)*.

74 Manitoba, ss. 8 and 13; Nova Scotia, s. 18; Prince Edward Island, s. 13.

75 Manitoba, ss. 9(1)*(a)(i)* and 14(1)*(a)(i)*; Nova Scotia, s. 12; Prince Edward Island, s. 14(1)*(a)(i)*.

76 Ontario, ss. 15(4), (5), (6) and (7).

77 Nova Scotia, s. 18(3); Prince Edward Island, s. 13(3).

78 Specifically s. 7(1) and (2).

79 Ontario, s. 13(10); Prince Edward Island, s. 14(5).

80 Nova Scotia, s. 19.

81 Ontario, s. 8(2).

4

Equal pay in Finland

Jukka Heikkerö, Pirkko K. Koskinen** and Paavo Nikula****

1. Introduction

1.1 The legal basis for equality of pay

Paying different wages to female and male employees on the basis of sex is expressly forbidden only in the Act on equality between women and men, which came into force in 1987. The Employment Contracts Act of 1970 includes only a general provision to the effect that employers shall treat their employees equitably, while the Finnish Constitution includes a provision according to which all citizens are equal before the law. But this rather general provision only seems to place an obligation on all public authorities in relation to citizens, and to prohibit the enactment of laws that will place them in unequal positions without justification.

In the private sector separate wage brackets for women were abolished from collective agreements by the middle of the 1960s. The Equal Remuneration Convention, 1951 (No. 100) may be considered the main factor contributing to this development. On the other hand, the collective agreements do not include provisions positively obligating the promotion of equal pay.

Before the abolition of separate wage brackets in the public sector, statutorily different wages were paid for certain posts, depending on the sex of the office-holder; the best-known example is provided by primary schoolteachers. The wages of male teachers were higher, and the houses provided for them were larger than those for female teachers. Such differences were abolished from employment relationships in the public sector by the end of the 1960s. Nowadays the wages of civil servants are mainly determined by collective agreements, in certain cases as so-called contractual salaries, and office-holders are paid mainly on the basis of the post they hold, regardless of sex. The length of the employment relationship and the locality of the office also affect the pay.

* Trade union lawyer.

** Deputy Parliamentary Ombudsman, former Professor of Labour Law.

*** Member of Parliament, former Equality Ombudsman.

Discrimination based on sex in employment relationships in the private sector was not prohibited until 1970 by the Employment Contracts Act; the original form of section 17, paragraph 3, being the following: "The employer shall treat his workers impartially without making any unwarranted discrimination on the basis of origin, religion, sex, age, political or trade union activity or any other comparable circumstance."

The Employment Contracts Act applies to employment relationships in general. It includes provisions relating to the making and duration of employment contracts, the basis for the payment of wages and the termination and annulment of employment contracts. More specific provisions on terms of employment are contained in laws such as the Working Hours Act, the Annual Holidays Act and the Labour Protection Act. The Equality Act also includes provisions relating to employment. According to the Employment Contracts Act, discrimination in an employment relationship is a punishable offence. This has not, however, had the effect of making the provision effective, at least not in practice: during a period of about ten years, only some ten cases in which this provision of the Act has been appealed to have been brought to the Supreme Court, and none of these has been concerned with discrimination based on sex.

In 1987 the prohibition of discrimination based on sex was transferred from the Employment Contracts Act to the Equality Act. The Finnish Equality Act includes provisions of two types: target-oriented ones, obligating, for example, both public authorities and private employers to promote equality, and concrete ones, prohibiting discrimination on the basis of sex. According to which:

> Discrimination on the basis of sex is prohibited. For the purposes of this Act discrimination means the placing of women and men in different positions on the basis of sex. Discrimination also includes any procedure whereby women and men are *de facto* placed in clearly different positions in relation to each other.

Section 8, paragraph 2(1), applies particularly to wage discrimination. According to this provision, an employer's procedure is to be considered discriminatory if the employer applies to an employee conditions of payment or employment less favourable than would be applied to an employee of the opposite sex employed in the same work or work of equal value. However, the employer shall not be deemed to have practised wage discrimination if he can prove that his procedure is based on an acceptable reason other than the employee's sex. The burden of proof here lies with the employer, who has to show that there is some acceptable legal reason for the wage differentials between employees of different sex performing the same kind of work or work of equal value. In simpler terms: the employer has to prove that his procedures are not discriminatory.

Finally, section 14 on discriminatory advertising makes it illegal for an advertisement for a job or training vacancy to invite women or men only to apply, unless there is a weighty and acceptable reason related to the nature of the job or duties, or unless this is based on an equality plan that makes positive special treatment possible (see 4.1 below).

1.2 The definition of pay

The wages referred to in section 8 of the Equality Act include all the elements of pay, both basic wages and various kinds of bonuses. The basic wages may be monthly, weekly, daily, hourly or piece-work, or different combinations of these. Bonuses, on the other hand, can be statutory, such as overtime or Sunday work compensation, stand-by or holiday compensation, or they may be based on the employment contract or collective agreement, such as language proficiency and dirty work bonuses or end-of-holiday pay. Emoluments in kind, such as lunch, health care, company car, etc., are included in the concept of pay.

Employees are entitled to wages determined on the same grounds and of the same amount regardless of their sex and regardless of the kind of pay, whether it is basic wages, bonus or emoluments in kind. It is contrary to the Equality Act to pay piece-work wages to female employees while a man receives time wages for the same work or work of equal value. Thus the total amount of the wages is not the only decisive factor in the comparison; rather, each item constituting wages is taken into consideration separately.

It has been presumed by the equality authorities (the Equality Ombudsman and his assistants) that any extra benefits derived from employment should also be granted to female and male employees equally. In general, if it is possible for the employer to use discretion under a collective agreement, it should be applied to women and men on the same grounds. In the public sector, for example, the placing of employees in salary brackets within the same official job title should take place on the same grounds for female and male employees. Thus it may be considered as discrimination if men have mostly been placed in the upper wage brackets, whereas women doing work of equal value are more evenly distributed in the different wage brackets. The equality authorities have also taken the view that the practice of giving the wives of male employees free health care (although they are not in the service of the employer) but not allowing it to the husbands of female employees is a discriminatory one.

In Finland welfare benefits for employees are mainly statutory, and welfare benefits related to the employment relationship, whether in the private or the public sector, to a large extent depend on the employees' income level during their period of employment. The earnings-related pension is also affected by the length of time the person concerned has been an active participant in the labour market in general or has been in the service of a particular employer.

Certain Finnish companies have pension regulations according to which female employees may retire on a pension at an earlier age than male employees in similar jobs. After the Equality Act came into force, there was discussion as to whether such arrangements complied with the Act. Since the cancellation of these would have involved difficulties and consequences not aimed at by the Equality Act, a special provision was added to the Act (section 25, paragraph 4) to the effect that such schemes could be applied after 1 January 1987 if they were in force prior to that date. New pension schemes including such a provision would be contrary to the Equality Act, however. No other welfare benefits can be tied to the sex of the employee in this way – with the exception of the special treatment of women during pregnancy and childbirth which is allowed by the Act. Older agreements of this kind became illegal after the

Equality Act came into force, as indicated by the example concerning workplace health care mentioned above.

In Finland, minimum levels of wages are specified in collective agreements, which does not prevent wages being paid which are higher than the minimum level; in practice this is quite common in certain fields, though not in the public sector where the wages specified are the wages actually paid.

1.3 The definition of "equal work"

The Equality Act does not contain definitions of "the same work", "comparable" or "equal value". This has not yet come up as an issue in labour market practice in respect of equality issues, but rather when the admissibility of changing the terms of employment is being discussed.

In 1990 a working group was established by the central organisations of employers and employees to define the criteria for comparable and equal work. The group will continue its work until the end of 1992.

The Finnish Equality Act equates the same work and work of equal value In practice, the difference lies in the significant fact that the contents of jobs of equal value may be different, whereas the same work conceptually requires similarity of content. Insignificant differences are not taken into consideration: in one company, for example, a female engineer in the planning division was, in addition to her planning tasks, in charge of dealing with incoming mail, but it was not considered possible to draw the conclusion that her work was different from that of the male engineers doing only planning jobs.

1.4 Scope of the equal pay provisions

The Finnish Equality Act applies to all employment relationships, whether in the private or public sector, irrespective of whether the work is full time or part time, temporary or permanent, done at home or whatever. In practice, the comparison of jobs does entail difficulties. As a matter of fact, certain groups, such as part-time employees and those working at home, are mainly composed of women, and the actual emoluments of these groups of employees may be inferior to those of others. The question as to whether a special law would be needed to ensure that these employees are properly protected against wage discrimination has not yet become topical.

One significant weakness in both the Employment Contracts Act and the Equality Act is that they are both employer-oriented: the prohibition on paying different wages to female and male employees performing the same work or work of equal value applies only to the employees of the same employer.

2. Procedures for determining "equality"

2.1 *Permitted justifications for differences in pay*

Section 8 of the Equality Act simply prohibits the paying of different wages to employees of different sex for the same work or work of equal value. It does not list the grounds by virtue of which different wages can be paid. In fact the question of whether different wages can be paid according to the working hours, training, skill, work results or responsibility of the employee has not even been raised. Likewise it seems to be accepted that the content of the work and the working conditions (dirtiness, noise) will affect wages. Within the public administration, wages also vary according to the duration of the employment relationship and the locality where the work is done (cost-of-living bonus and the bonus for living in a border area).

The legality of wage differentials must also be examined taking into account the prohibition of discrimination in the Employment Contracts Act, which forbids the placing of employees in different positions due to, for example, age or trade union affiliation. It has not been considered that this provision would prevent employees' wages varying according to how long their employment relationship has lasted.

Depending on the collective agreement, the factors affecting wage differentials may either be listed more or less exhaustively or left completely unlisted. Whatever the situation, such arrangements can hardly be considered as favouring particular employees or as discriminatory in a way that violates the Employment Contracts Act. Such factors should rather be understood as criteria offering benefits to all employees belonging to a certain group, to which all employees can belong, at least in theory, during their employment history.

Some of the criteria permitting wage differentials do, however, seem to be in need of reassessment. The issue of responsibility as a wage-raising factor has been a frequent subject of discussion. It is to be suspected that the work done by men is more easily considered as responsible, responsibility being assessed mainly on the basis of economic factors, such as the prevention of damage to materials or tools, and so on. The responsibility involved in typical women's jobs, such as nursing, is not perceived or recognised as easily, since human rather than economic values are involved. The same seems to apply even more generally when the characteristic features of women's and men's jobs are being evaluated (for example, the monotony of work, so-called static stress or strain, in contrast to the occasional need for physical strength).

2.2 *The criteria for comparing jobs*

Grounds for deciding whether jobs are of equal value have not been laid down in the Equality Act. According to its preamble, attention should be paid to the quality and content of the jobs, on the one hand, and to the working conditions, on the other. It is also necessary to decide what kind and frequency of differences will result in jobs not being considered of equal value. In this context the question of what kinds of differences are emphasised when determining wages is decisive. When making comparisons to determine whether employees of different sex are doing work of equal value, this would, according to the preamble, mainly have to be based on the practice and norms that are observed in the particular field, for example, in connection with job evaluation. The Act does not make it compulsory for job evaluation to be used to determine whether different jobs are of equal value. The legislation neither prohibits nor requires it.

In so far as the assessment of work is based on the wage groups specified in the collective agreements of various sectors, there are many different systems for classifying wage groups. In the field of tyre retreading, for example, the wage group is mainly determined according to the number of years of employment in the field.

The wage group may be based on a classification list including hundreds of items, in addition to which a certain amount of occupational experience measured in years may be required. In Finland this is true of both the clothing industry and the shoe and leather industry. The classification has developed as the result of years of practice, and is not based on analytical job evaluation.

Where job evaluation is used, it is largely based on the "difficulty" of the jobs concerned, according to a classification of difficulties, and working conditions are also taken into consideration. This is what happens in the chemical industry.

In practice, the equality authorities have stressed four factors in the comparison of jobs: education and training, occupational experience, working conditions and responsibility. Similar concepts, possibly under different names, are used in the relatively few job evaluation schemes that have been used in Finland. The most recent is the one introduced in the metal industry in the late 1980s.

In their statements, the equality authorities have recommended that training and experience should be assessed in relation to the training and occupational experience needed for the job. As far as working conditions are concerned, it has been stressed that attention should be paid not only to noise and dirt problems, but also to the strain caused by monotony or by doing several jobs at the same time. The definition of responsibility is problematic, since it is only really possible to compare the economic responsibility involved in different jobs. It is difficult to compare responsibility involving people and economic responsibility. According to the Equality Ombudsman, human responsibility has tended to be underestimated with relatively too much emphasis being place on economic responsibility.

The basic data used in job evaluation schemes, in accordance with the collective agreements, have been uncovered only to a limited extent when equal pay issues have been examined in accordance with the Equality Act. The internal groupings of the difficulty classes appear in the documents, but the grounds for awarding points are not clarified.

In practice it has not yet, since the implementation of the Equality Act, been necessary for the courts to reach a decision on the question of how jobs are to be compared when an employer does not use any job evaluation scheme. From the point of view of the Equality Act, it is evident that they will at some point have to do so. Their conclusions will then have to be based on the four job evaluation concepts referred to above, and on the job descriptions of the different employees.

2.3 Sex bias in job evaluation

The possibly discriminatory nature of job evaluation has not yet been examined in Finland. The equality authorities have stressed the importance of not over-emphasising the difficulty factors characteristic of male-dominated fields and correspondingly underestimating those characteristic of female-dominated fields when comparing jobs. Relevant research into the extent to which the job evaluation schemes being used do *de facto* discriminate against women was initiated by four female-dominated unions of the Central Organisation of Finnish Trade Unions (SAK) in spring 1989. In the "general job evaluation system within industry", published by the employers' organisation, it can be observed that physical strain earns the maximum of ten points, whereas the maximum number of points earned by mental strain is five. The difficulty factors used in the system seem to be weighted in favour of "heavy" work rather than work requiring dexterity. It is for these reasons, among others, that the workers' organisations have not accepted this evaluation system for the labour-intensive consumer goods industry, which is on the whole female-dominated.

Different collective agreements include quite a variety of evaluation systems, and even the same collective agreement may result in a different outcome in different cases. In the shoe industry, for example, men and women are placed in the different wage brackets contained in the collective agreement in a relatively equal way, but the men receive somewhat higher wages in practice. The same collective agreement, but with a different job classification, applies to the leather industry. Here the men are placed in the highest wage brackets, again outstripping the women in their wages. In this case, however, women and men are not placed in different wage brackets as such. Rather they are place unequally in the different wage groups contained in the collective agreement. When looking at the leather industry, it is possible to compare the "heaviness" of the different jobs. Heaviness and dirtiness, both characteristic of men's work, are traditionally highly valued in job evaluation. The implementation of equal pay in such cases requires a reassessment of the job evaluation scheme, which may require cooperation between employer and employee. The implementation of the Equality Act has in fact resulted in quite an active interest in the reform of job evaluation. These examples of the impact of the job classifications and evaluation criteria contained in collective agreements on the wages of women and men cannot be considered exceptional.

2.4 Gender-dominated occupational categories and jobs

Neither the labour legislation nor the collective agreements contain criteria by which jobs can be judged to be mainly women's or mainly men's jobs. In practice the Finnish labour market is trongly segregated by sex: more than half of the workforce are in female- or male-dominated fields, in which the share of either sex exceeds 90 per cent. Only about 6 per cent of employees work in balanced fields, in which the share of either sex is not less than 40 per cent.

2.5 The scope of comparison

The provision on equal pay in the Equality Act can only be applied to workers in the employ of the same employer. In this respect it is significant that the municipality, the State, or a group of companies can be considered as single employers. The different occupational groups employed by these major employers can thus be compared under the equal pay provisions.

In practice, the comparison of jobs usually involves only wages of those performing the same work, as determined by the collective agreement binding on the employer. The comparison of different jobs is considered problematic, so often this comparison has not been made. Nor does the Equality Act place any obligation on the labour market organisations to specify whether jobs are placed in different wage groups as traditional "women's jobs" or "men's jobs". It is basically at the discretion of the labour market organisations whether or not jobs are re-evaluated in order to establish their equality. Relevant initiatives can be taken both by the equality authorities and by individual employees, but ultimately the parties to the collective agreements (i.e. the organisations and unions of employers and employees) decide on the measures to be taken. At the most concrete level, the labour market parties must be unanimous if corrective measures are to be taken.

Collective agreements do not apply to the top management of enterprises, whose members are paid according to separate agreements, which are hardly known to outsiders. This is of little significance, however, when considering the wage differentials between women and men, since there are so few women in top management.

3. Enforcement arrangements for implementing equal pay policies

3.1 The different methods of enforcement

In general the Equality Act is supervised by the Equality Ombudsman and his Office and the Equality Board, on which there are more detailed provisions in a separate Act. This supervision is administrative rather than judicial in nature.

As already mentioned, the Equality Act contains both target-oriented provisions and concrete prohibitions of discrimination on the basis of sex. No special consequences of non-compliance with the target-oriented provisions of the Act have been prescribed by law; it is not, for example, possible to demand that employers should meet their obligation to promote equality by taking them to court. But the Equality Ombudsman does have an obligation, whenever he observes that the obligations prescribed by the Equality Act are not being met, or that the provisions of the Act are being violated, to make efforts, by means of counselling and advice, to prevent the continuation or recurrence of the illegal procedure. For the performance of these tasks the Ombudsman receives the information he considers necessary from both public authorities and private employers; he may even impose a fine for the withholding of such information. The Ombudsman is also entitled to carry out inspections at workplaces and to receive assistance for this purpose.

The counselling and advice provided by the Equality Ombudsman are not binding and so cannot be legally enforced. On the other hand, it is in practice possible to implement the target-oriented provisions by agreement between the labour market parties; the matters mentioned in these provisions (for example, equal placement of women and men in the different jobs and career stages) are thus negotiable issues (see 4.1 below).

Where a violation of the prohibitions on discrimination is concerned, the Equality Ombudsman may bring the matter to the consideration of the Equality Board. The Board may then, under penalty of a fine if necessary, prohibit the continuation or recurrence of the discriminatory procedure. An appeal against the decision may be made to the Supreme Administrative Court, but the prohibition must be observed in spite of the appeal, unless otherwise prescribed by the Equality Board or the Supreme Administrative Court.

Alternatively, violations of the equal pay provisions can be dealt with in general courts, when wages are not fixed by collective agreement (as would be the case with, for example, top managers or, at the other end of the scale, domestic staff), or in the labour court, when wages are based on such an agreement. If it is considered that a provision of a collective agreement is contrary to the Equality Act, the matter is again within the competence of the labour court.

In addition to the means available to the equality authorities, it is thus also possible for individuals to take measures when they consider that they have been discriminated against on the basis of sex.

If the general prohibition on discrimination contained in section 7 of the Equality Act has been violated, an action, which is carried out in the names of the parties concerned, is instituted in the general court of first instance. It is a normal case of action for damages in which the claimant has to prove not only the damage for which compensation is claimed, but also deliberate or negligent discrimination on the part of the employer. The Equality Ombudsman may assist the person who has been discriminated against.

The injured person may also claim compensation for a violation of the prohibition on discrimination in working life; the action concerned is then carried on in his/her own name in the general court of first instance in the area in which the employer is resident. Compensation in this case is not dependent on damage being proved, and must be paid regardless of the intent or negligence of the offender. A period of limitation of one year has been prescribed for the taking of action.

The Equality Ombudsman's opinion can also be requested on issues concerning equal pay. The Equality Ombudsman has clarified the different alternatives offered by the Equality Act and the guidelines for determining whether jobs are of equal value. In cases where wages are not based on a collective agreement, the Equality Ombudsman has been able to give an opinion on the level of wages paid for different jobs. In some, an adjustment of wage levels has been recommended by the Ombudsman; in others, it has been concluded that the jobs concerned are not the same or of equal value.

When wages are based on a collective agreement, whether in the private or the public sector, the Equality Ombudsman has recommended that the precise value of the different jobs should be clarified by the parties and that a possible adjustment of wage levels should then be considered. The Equality Ombudsman has indicated that the equality authorities are willing to take part in the continued consideration of the matter, but collective agreements basically provide that individual wage disputes should be settled by local negotiations between the employer and the employees' representatives, or, at the final stage, by negotiations between the respective labour market organisations.

3.2 Government bodies involved in implementing equal pay

The Office of the Equality Ombudsman is responsible for supervising the implementation of the entire Equality Act. Specialisation in wage issues has not as yet been possible, given the limited resources of the Office. The need for such expertise is obvious. The equality authorities have made efforts to increase the expertise available concerning the handling of wage issues in accordance with the Equality Act, particularly within the labour market organisations.

The Equality Ombudsman can issue statements, advice and instructions in individual cases concerning the application of the Equality Act, for example, on the raising of the wages of a female employee (or employees) to the same amount as that of a man (or men) performing the same work or work of equal value and employed by the same employer. These statements, advice or instructions are not binding on the employer or the court. Nor is it necessary that the Equality Ombudsman should deal with a matter for it to be brought to court.

The Equality Board works part time, having no office of its own. The Board includes a chair and four other members, as well as a part-time secretary. The Board does not take up matters on its own initiative, only at the request of the Equality Ombudsman or the courts. It can be characterised as an expert body which makes decisions on the application of the Equality Act after the Equality Ombudsman has dealt with the matter. The Equality Board can give its opinion on matters under consideration in court, however, even when the Equality Ombudsman has not dealt with the matter at all, and this has in fact happened in practice. The Board need not be asked for its opinion, however, nor is it binding on the court. The courts will no longer hear the Equality Ombudsman.

In individual disputes, the equality authorities can act only on the initiative of the interested party, but more general equal pay issues can also be taken up on the authorities' own initiative.

3.3 Legal costs

Legal expenses often constitute a real obstacle to court proceedings. Unionised employees may receive legal aid from their trade unions in matters concerning discrimination based on sex. In most legal proceedings under the Equality Act, well over ten of which had been initiated by spring 1989, employees have received legal aid from their trade union. In such proceedings the main principle of compensation is that the loser is obliged to pay the other party's legal expenses. Where the union has granted legal aid, it is liable for these legal expenses as well if the employee loses her case.

3.4 Remedies

An employee may request that a discriminatory wage term in a contract of employment be declared null and void. Section 50 of the Employment Contracts Act prescribes: "If any term in the contract of employment is null and void because it is contrary to statutory provisions for the employee's protection, this shall not affect the validity of the remainder of the contract."

Thus a discriminatory term is null and void in principle, and the employee is entitled to receive "proper" wages backdated to the beginning of the employment relationship. In practice, the application of this principle is not easy, however. First, it is usually impossible for individual employees to obtain information on the wages of their fellow employees in order to find out whether or not they are being discriminated against. Where wages are covered by a collective agreement, the trade unions also supervise the payment of wages, for example, receiving the wage statistics, but top managers, whose wages are also affected by sex, are not covered by collective agreements. Nor are the wages of individual employees easily extracted from the statistics. The wages are agreed upon individually, and often there is no person of the opposite sex to compare with in the enterprise.

If the general prohibition on discrimination contained in section 7 has been violated, the party concerned may claim compensation for the damage caused by the discrimination. For the action to be successful, the discrimination must have caused damage or suffering to the injured person.

The injured person may also claim compensation for a violation of the prohibition on discrimination in working life. Depending on the nature of the offence, compensation might be between FIM11,100 and FIM35,100. The amount of compensation is not bound to the damage, for which the offended person may claim compensation separately.

3.5 Protection against victimisation

There are no special provisions for the protection of employees against possible reprisals by the employer, in the Equality Act or anywhere else. In practice, the general regulations concerning protection against arbitrary dismissal seem to provide the only means of protection: an employer may not dismiss an employee without a particularly weighty reason, the existence of which has to be proved by the employer in case of dispute. But this form of protection has its flaws: an employer may give the employee notice all the same, and the employment relationship will be terminated after the period of notice has expired. An employee who has been illegally dismissed may be paid wages for a minimum of three months and a maximum of 20 months in compensation. The compensation is not compensation for damage, and it is therefore possible for the employee to get it even when no damage has been caused by the dismissal. The job is lost, however, and although the court may find the dismissal illegal, it cannot order that the employee should be taken back.

According to information received by the equality authorities, dismissal is not the only conceivable form of reprisal. Employees who have requested equality may find their working conditions are made worse, their career development hindered, their training prevented. Alternatively, they may be pressured into giving notice themselves, in which case they will receive no compensation. There are no special provisions to prevent such reprisals, although a sufficiently persistent employee could make a new report to the Equality Ombudsman and bring a new action on the grounds that she is still being discriminated against on the basis of sex.

When adopting the equality legislation, the Finnish Parliament assumed that the Government would follow closely possible reprisals due to reference to the Equality Act. A relevant report will be submitted to Parliament when the Act has been in force for five years (1991), and the Government will then consider possible special provisions for protecting employees against reprisals. The necessity of such provisions is not really at issue – of course they are necessary – but rather their effectiveness. The difficulties of producing evidence constitute one practical problem.

3.6 The burden of proof

There is a specific provision on the burden of proof in section 8, paragraph 3, of the Equality Act: "An employer shall not be deemed to have violated the prohibition on discrimination stipulated in subparagraphs (1) or (2) of paragraph 2 of this section if he can prove that his procedure was based on an acceptable reason other than the employee's sex."

The employee must first prove that her wages are lower than those of a male comparator employed by the same employer, and that the work she does, her training and education, etc., are the same or of equal value as those of the comparator. In other words, the employee has to prove the inequality of the wages and the equal value of the work. Thereafter, as already mentioned, the burden of proof is transferred to the employer, who has to prove that there is some acceptable legal reason for the differences in wages.

3.7 Access to information on wages

By virtue of the shop steward agreement of the labour market parties, shop stewards receive certain wage statistics from the employer. The original purpose of this was not, however, the promotion of equality of pay between men and women but to enable them to supervise compliance with the collective agreement.

The Equality Ombudsman may request the information needed for the settlement of an equal pay matter from the employer, and may obtain confidential information which the employer is not obliged or even entitled to give even to the employee who considers herself to be discriminated against. The Equality Ombudsman is obliged to maintain secrecy concerning such information.

3.8 Experience with equal pay claims

As far as is known, only a few equal pay issues have been brought to court, and there are no final judgements from the High Court of Justice. The Equality Ombudsman has received dozens of requests for an opinion on such issues, usually concerning the application of the equal pay provisions and the criteria for assessing whether work is of equal value. Equal pay may of course come up as an issue between the labour market parties. During the past couple of years issues of equal pay between men and women have been increasingly prominent in collective bargaining. Individual issues concerning equal pay may also be dealt with within the negotiating procedure of the labour market system, and shop stewards deal with such issues at the workplace. Finally, there have been signs that the equal pay issue might become a cause of industrial action in female-dominated sectors. There is no uniform system for collecting data concerning the number of issues raised under the equal pay legislation.

4. The role of the social partners

4.1 Union-management involvement in implementing equal pay

The joint procedures of the labour market parties for the implementation of equal pay policies are based on voluntariness. According to the Act, a plan designed to promote equality between women and men can be drawn up, but there is no compulsion to introduce such a measure. Such a plan might include, for example, measures aimed especially at bringing more women into managerial positions. Ways of reforming the criteria for the classification of jobs might also be included, and special measures to improve women's career development. Since the purpose of the Finnish Equality Act is to improve the status of women, particularly in working life, such plans should be expressly concerned with improving the status of women. One possible approach might be to decide on special job quotas for women, but these have not yet been introduced in Finland. Up to now, only a few such plans have been prepared. On the other hand, collective agreements usually include the principle that issues relating to wage differentials based on sex should be settled at the workplace.

The immediate impact of the programmatic provisions of the Equality Act has thus been extremely limited, but in the long run they may affect attitudes in a favourable way. The trade unions themselves are generally committed to promoting equality, particularly as far as wages are concerned. Programmatic measures have been prepared for this purpose, and a few bodies have been set up for the further development of the work. So far, only one trade union has decided that a certain number of women and a certain number of men should always be elected to the bodies of employees' representatives (minimum quotas). Several unions have decided to promote equality in their internal administration and personnel policy, but have not yet confirmed special quotas. Four trade unions have set up a joint working group on equality, the recommendations of which will be discussed by the labour market central organisations.

A special equality item was included in the stabilisation settlement of autumn 1988. Employers agreed to pay a bonus, calculated by multiplying the number of women working in each sector covered by the agreement by FIM0.10 per hour. Each sector then decided for itself how it would make use of the fairly modest resulting sum of money. The practice varied: in some sectors the bonus, contrary to its original purpose, was distributed equally to all employee groups, while in others it was directed to the lower income groups, mainly including female workers. The distribution of the equality bonus was very important in principle, as it was an acknowledgement that gender is a factor that determines pay. This was the first time that a special effort had been made to improve the wages of women in the wage settlement. The stabilisation settlement was nationwide, although certain unions broke away from it.

A settlement of the same type was reached in 1990, with a slightly higher level of bonus, and implementation to take place by means of collective agreements for each union. In the education sector, the equality item in the 1990 settlement was about 0.4 per cent of the sum total for the sector, and it was used for raising the wages of certain female-dominated groups of teachers (grades 1-2 in comprehensive schools), the few men working in the same job also receiving the wage increase.

4.2 Union-management involvement in determining job evaluation criteria

There is cooperation between the central labour market organisations (the Central Organisation of Finnish Trade Unions (SAK) and the Finnish Employers' Confederation (STK)) in the Advisory Board on Rationalisation, which has put forward quite a few recommendations on such issues as job evaluation. In practice the wage groupings and job evaluation factors are agreed upon by the central organisations of employers and employees. The aim of the organisations on both sides is to achieve an outcome that is generally the best possible from their point of view. Aspects related to equality between the sexes may thus easily be overlooked, given that job evaluation is regulated on other grounds than those concerning such equality.

The job evaluation scheme which came into force at the beginning of 1989 in the metal industry aims to determine wages solely on the basis of the jobs done. Working groups have been set up at workplaces with the purpose of specifying the difficulty of the different jobs. Employees' representatives are entitled to participate. The difficulty of the jobs is determined by people who have a training agreed upon jointly by employers and employees and who are well informed about job evaluation.

4.3 Monitoring collective agreements

If a regulation concerning wages in a collective agreement is considered to be discriminatory against either sex, the labour court can declare the regulation null and void, following a suit brought by the employees' (or employers') organisation. Such cases have not occurred in practice. In fact, it is assumed that an employer who observes the collective agreement will not be guilty of discrimination and that, if the agreement is found to be discriminatory on the basis of sex, the parties to it will negotiate a revision of the discriminatory provisions.

Employers are obliged to send copies of collective agreements to the Ministry of Social Affairs and Health, but this obligation is not connected with the supervision of the equal pay legislation. No approval by the authorities is required in order for collective agreements to be valid. In Finland, the labour market central organisations cooperate over the compilation of statistics, even to the extent that the Finnish Employers' Confederation compiles the statistics for the Central Statistical Office. Statistics including, for example, data on the average wages of employees of opposite sex in different fields are compiled for every quarter of the year. The statistical system has, however, been developed mainly for reasons other than equality.

5. Conclusions

The provisions and regulations concerning equal pay do not seem to have prevented wage differentials based on sex, nor even to have reduced them, according to the latest reports. Women's wages are on average approximately 75 per cent of men's.[1] The situation is different in different fields, and there are of course women receiving so-called top wages and men with quite low pay.

Part of the wage differential between women and men can be explained on grounds other than sex: on average, women's working hours (the time used for paid work) are shorter than men's as they tend to look for jobs in fields with shorter than average working hours, they more seldom work overtime, and they are left behind as regards career development because of maternity and parental leave. There are also differences in training: women tend to receive an all-round, general, liberal education, which is not highly valued on the labour market, or they seek vocational training that leads to a field dominated by women. Men, on the other hand, mostly look for "hard" vocational training. But even when all these factors are taken into account, there still remain differentials which cannot be explained by anything other than sex.

However, the Finnish Equality Act has only been in force since 1987. There have not been many cases of its application in the courts, and consideration of these cases is still not complete. It is therefore difficult to estimate the practical effects of the Act, and particularly of its equal pay provision. The increase in the general consciousness concerning problems of equality, especially the position of women on the labour market, may perhaps be considered its most significant effect. A change in attitudes, and consequent improvements in wage practices, may well come about as a result of this increased consciousness.

Note

[1] See e.g. *Women and men in the Nordic countries: Facts on equal opportunities* (Copenhagen, Nordic Council of Ministers, 1988), p. 94.

5

Equal pay in France

*Christophe Pettiti**

1. Introduction

The principle of equal pay for men and women is derived in French law from the general principle postulated by the Preamble to the French Constitution of 1946, the third paragraph of which states: "The law guarantees to women equal rights to those of men in all areas." The Preamble to the 1946 Constitution is an integral part of the French Constitution in force since 4 October 1958.

In order to give effect to this principle, French legislation has incorporated various provisions that place an emphasis on monitoring compliance with the principle and promoting its implementation. This chapter is a study of these provisions.

Promoting the principle of equality between men and women in the context of basic rights is perfectly in keeping with French legal and political tradition, though its assertion has been somewhat belated in the field of social legislation, especially in respect of remuneration. The principle of equal rights was in fact asserted for the first time in legislation concerning the family and inheritance, under pressure from public opinion.

1.1 The legal basis for equality of pay

The Equal Remuneration Convention, 1951 (No. 100), was incorporated into French law through the combined effect of the Act of 10 December 1952 authorising its ratification[1] and the Decree of 16 April 1953 concerning its publication.[2]

The existence of a general principle of non-discrimination in the Constitution, the ratification of Convention No. 100, and Article 119 of the Treaty of Rome would not, however, suffice in themselves to ensure compliance with the principle of equal pay, in the absence of national laws and regulations.

* Barrister at the Paris Appeals Court; Member of the Commission of the European Communities Team of Experts on the Implementation of Equality Directives. This study is based on the research jointly conducted by Marie-Thérèse Lanquetin, Clair Sutter and the author on behalf of the Commission of the European Communities. It expresses the opinions of the author and not those of the Commission.

The Act of 1950 concerning collective bargaining did refer to the principle of equality but it had little legal or practical effect in the field of gender equality.[3] It was by the Act of 22 December 1972 concerning equal remuneration for men and women[4] that a statutory provision was explicitly introduced into French law. The 1972 Act reiterates the principles set forth by the ILO in Convention No. 100 in respect of the concept of "work of equal value". The 1972 Act, codified in article L 140-2 of the Labour Code, specifies in its first paragraph that "every employer shall ensure equal remuneration for men and women for the same work or for work of equal value".

No immediate changes in French law followed the adoption in February 1975 of the European Community Directive 75/117/EEC concerning the implementation of the principle of equal remuneration for male and female workers.[5] However, in view of the difficulties encountered in giving effect to the 1972 Act, the law enlarged on article L 140-2 of the Labour Code by establishing criteria for the concrete assessment of the value of work. This amendment was adopted in the Act of 13 July 1983[6] concerning equality in employment, which should be regarded as the key text on the question of equal treatment and opportunity for men and women in French law.

1.2 The definition of pay

The 1972 Act defined the concept of pay in the same terms as those adopted by the International Labour Conference in Convention No. 100. Paragraph 2 of article L 140-2 of the Labour Code specifies:

> for the purposes of this Chapter, the term "remuneration" means the ordinary basic or minimum wage or salary and all other benefits and supplements paid directly or indirectly in cash or in kind, by the employer to the worker on account of the latter's employment.

This concept of pay can and should be extended and given the widest possible interpretation. Thus, the Council of State considered that housing benefits consisting of free accommodation or a monthly accommodation allowance constituted an element of remuneration and must therefore be granted according to criteria consistent with the principle of equal remuneration for men and women.[7] Similarly, the Court of Appeal ruled that a "regular attendance" bonus *(prime d'assiduité)* constituted an element of remuneration.[8]

It is not clear whether the principle of equal remuneration also applies to social security benefits. The laws and regulations governing such benefits contain no express provision in respect of equal treatment for men and women, but it is to be assumed that the principle of equal remuneration propounded by the ILO and the European Community will be respected.[9]

As regards welfare benefits, in particular retirement pensions, which are directly regulated by law without any element of participation at company or sectoral level, the European Court of Justice pointed out, in its ruling of 25 May 1971,[10] that a retirement pension founded on this principle does not constitute a benefit paid directly by the employer to the worker and arising out of the worker's employment within the meaning of Article 119, paragraph 2, of the Treaty of Rome. Bearing in mind the vagueness of article L 140-2 of the Labour Code, it is to be feared that a similar solution would be adopted by the French courts if the question were referred to them.

On the other hand, the European Court of Justice did consider as discrimination, in violation of Article 119, a compulsory contribution to a pension scheme imposed by the employer on male employees only, to whom it was refunded in part if they left that employment, and which was used to establish the level of certain allowances and social benefits.[11] A French court confronted with the same question might therefore be obliged to follow this interpretation.

Article L 140-2 of the Labour Code does not specify whether the principle of equal remuneration should apply in the case of each individual element of remuneration or of total remuneration. French courts have not had occasion to make an express ruling on this point, but it may be considered, in the light of jurisprudence, that, where a man and a women perform the same work or work of equal value, they are entitled to the same elements of remuneration, unless these elements of remuneration can be considered as equivalent alternatives.

1.3 The definition of "equal work"

We have seen that the 1972 Act adopted the concept of "same work or work of equal value", as used in Convention No. 100. This differs from that used in EC Directive 75-117, "identical work or work considered as being of equal value", in that the French wording allows for a comparison at the time of the dispute, whereas that of the Directive presupposes a preliminary objective assessment.

The Act of 13 July 1983 specifies further that:

> Work shall be deemed to be of equal value if it requires on the whole a comparable level of knowledge in the occupation in the form of a degree, a certificate or practice in the occupation, of ability acquired through experience, of responsibility and of physical or nervous stress.

These factors had been the cause of difficulties in legal disputes prior to the Act of 13 July 1983. Moreover, the Act takes up the demands that workers' and employers' organisations had been putting forward. The departmental circular on the interpretation of the law specifies that:

> Equal value should be recognised in cases where, notwithstanding differences that might possibly be identified between two occupations under comparison, these occupations, evaluated as a whole, entail comparable knowledge in the occupation in the form of a degree, a certificate or practice in the occupation.[12]

The courts and tribunals have also contributed to the formulation of a definition (see 2.2 below).

If this broader concept of equal work, not necessarily implying identical work, had not been established, the principle of equal pay would have been largely devoid of meaning. In France, as in other EC countries, there is a tendency towards occupational segregation, which results in women being confined to certain types of employment. As we shall see later, the Act of 13 July 1983 stressed the importance of all jobs being open to both men and women, which could lead to genuine equality of pay.

1.4 Scope of the equal pay provisions

The equal pay principle is given the widest possible scope. Article L 140 of the Labour Code, in common with all provisions of the Labour Code, applies to all employees bound by a (written or oral) contract of employment, including apprentices and trainee employees under employment training contracts.[11]

This therefore covers employees in the public sector, referred to in article 6 of the Act of 13 July 1983[13] and in article L 140-5 of the Labour Code (which also stipulates that the principle applies in particular to employees bound by contract made under public law), and to employees of private companies and public corporations such as SNCF and Air France.

Exceptions include the armed forces, which are not covered by the public service statute, a Decree of 23 March 1973 having defined the special status of the women's army corps. Since there is such a special corps, there cannot be "mixed" male/female occupations; consequently, the principle of equal pay obviously does not apply. As for the private sector, exceptions include workers employed without contracts in family businesses (small workshops, retail outlets, farms).

As regards working arrangements, especially working hours, the equal pay principle applies whatever form the employment may take (part time, temporary, casual, home-based). Part-time workers and outworkers (homeworkers) are protected by a legal principle of equal rights (articles L 212-4-2 and L 721-6 of the Labour Code).

2. Procedures for determining "equality"

2.1 Permitted justifications for differences in pay

French law concerning equal pay is based on a positive obligation imposed on employers to ensure equal pay for men and women workers for the same work or work of equal value. Although, as we have seen definitions have been established to clarify the terms "pay" and "equal value", the law contains no express provision as to what justifications will be admitted for differences in pay. In cases of dispute, therefore, it is for the judge to decide what factors might justify a difference in pay for men and women, but the differential can only be justified in terms of the work performed not having the same value.

It must, however, be admitted that employers are allowed considerable latitude in the matter of proving that work is not of the same value. Thus, the work is not of equal value if one employee is more experienced than another and hence contributes more to the business.[14] The courts also consider the fact that one job is more arduous than another as a justification for differences in pay. For example, a female assembly worker who performs her work sitting down may have a less ardous job than a male labourer who is required to handle heavy loads, though the labourer and the assembly worker may belong to the same occupational category.[15]

Criteria unrelated to the nature and quality of the work may not be used to justify non-compliance with the equal pay principle. Thus the concept of "market forces" cannot be invoked to justify differences in pay, since the principle of equality is independent of economic constraints. In practice, however, the powers of company managers in the matter of personnel do enable them to differentiate when it comes to recruiting, and this can have serious consequences for the principle of equal pay.

Not many employers invoke particular conditions of employment to introduce a differentiated system of hourly wage rates, for example, the ban on night work for women, if such an hourly wage differential is a pretext for indirect discrimination.[16]

2.2 *The role of job evaluation*

While Article 3 of Convention No. 100 provides for the possibility of States taking measures to promote objective appraisal of jobs on the basis of the work to be performed, the French legislation does not make job classification and evaluation central to the application of the principle of equal pay for men and women.

The sectoral collective agreements contain job classification and evaluation schemes involving a wage or salary grid or scale. Job evaluation in France is based on schemes adopted at various different times. In the 1950s, minimum wages at sectoral level were determined in accordance with classifications established on the basis of the length of apprenticeship required for a particular trade or occupation. Jobs were classified by category without a description of their content. Since 1970, sectoral agreements have based classifications on job content. This new type of classification is carried out according to a grid comprising qualification levels defined by general criteria: independence, responsibility, type of activity, skill or training required. Divided into grades, these levels also enable the complexity and difficulty of the work to be taken into account.

Job classifications and evaluations make no distinction between men and women. The elements defined in the collective agreements apply to both sexes. Article L 140-3, paragraph 2, of the Labour Code specifies that "The categories and criteria for job classification and upgrading schemes and all other bases for calculating remuneration, such as job evaluation systems, shall be the same for workers of both sexes".

However, these job evaluation schemes cannot constitute an effective instrument of protection, inasmuch as they allow employers the possibility of establishing different job levels within the one occupational category. Employers have a certain latitude in the matter of placing a newly created job on this or that level in the classification grid. It is they who analyse the work required, the necessary qualifications and the responsibilities involved, in order to determine the grid level and coefficient corresponding to these characteristics. Once employers, consciously or otherwise, undervalue the work of women, discrimination will occur.[17] Discrimination tends to appear especially where there is segregated employment.

The Supreme Court of Appeal *(Cour de Cassation),* in its ruling of 24 November 1976,[18] dismissed the argument based on the employers' obligation to give equal pay to all workers belonging to an occupational category defined in the collective agreement. In this particular case, the court pointed out that it was a matter for the judge to "ascertain whether, within each of the occupational categories established by the collective agreement, and especially Category VIII, certain jobs did not involve particular characteristics or difficulties, which might, regardless of all considerations of the employee's sex", entail a difference in pay.

Once the judge has established that the woman does work of equal value to that of the man, the employer is obliged to pay them equally. In one instance, the employer paid men employed as knitters a "regular attendance" bonus *(prime d'assiduité)* which was not paid to women employed as "folders" or "ironers", on the pretext that the men's work affected the work of all other employees in positions further down the production line and was therefore more important than the women's in the manufacturing process. The Supreme Court of Appeal considered that, while it was true that the jobs performed by the men and the women were different, it was certain that in this case "the women were performing work of equal value to that of the men".[19]

To ascertain whether workers are performing the same work of work of equal value, the judge may have recourse to an expert who must examine whether the occupations are similar.[20] The courts may also consider more subjective factors, such as the employees' personal qualities and aptitudes as reflected in results.[21]

It is easier to prove non-compliance with the equal pay principle where jobs are "mixed" (that is, hold by men and women without distiction). In such cases the judge has the means of examining whether the elements invoked to justify different pay for men and women engaged in the same occupation are genuine or whether there is a hidden intention to discriminate. Thus, where it is established that the alleged difference in knowledge of the occupation or value of the work claimed by the employer is based neither on certificates nor on experience acquired in previous jobs, discrimination has clearly been practised.[22]

The Supreme Court of Appeal does, however, impose on the judge an obligation to investigate all elements that might justify a difference in pay. In a decision of 31 May 1988, it ruled that different rates of pay for men and women in the same occupational category at the same level of seniority could be justified in terms of the versatility and length of training of male workers, even when the male and female workers were performing equally arduous work.[23]

The supervision exercised by the courts may sometimes be considered excessive. However, the ruling of 31 May 1988 demonstrates that the job classification schemes used in France are not, in general, in themselves adequate to be used as models for the purpose of investigating whether the principle of equal pay is being applied. On the other hand, the establishment of a job classification system that would be adequate for this task appears to be out of the question.

Given that the job classifications adopted in collective agreements are no more than the result of negotiations between the parties to the agreements, it would, perhaps, be advisable to provide the social partners with technical assistance to help them determine the classification criteria on a more egalitarian basis. A greater effort needs to be made to apply the principle of equal pay and equal treatment in job evaluation and classification systems.

The job classifications adopted in collective agreements could in theory be subject to legal dispute in cases of non-compliance with the equal pay principle. In fact, such complaints have not been brought before the courts – which does not in itself mean that discriminatory practices do not occur. Besides, negotiations between the social partners alone can bring about concrete progress in this field.

2.3 Gender-dominated occupational categories and jobs

It has been emphasised that the chief obstacle to the application of the principle of equal pay for men and women arises in situations where employment is segregated. In such situations, discrimination is likely to be indirect and therefore more difficult to prove.[24] Furthermore, even if the jobs are different, the fact of segregation has the effect of confining women to certain types of employment, which are usually the least skilled and bring the fewest advantages or benefits of any kind.

The fact that a particular job is performed by a majority of workers of the same sex is not taken into consideration by the law, and up until now there is no legal precedent admitting the existence of discrimination in such a case.

2.4 The scope of comparison

Before the adoption of the Act of 13 July 1983, the Supreme Court of Appeal had rejected pay comparisons between two establishments within one enterprise.[25] The new article L 140-2, paragraph 4, stipulates that henceforth differences in pay between establishments of a single enterprise may not, for the same work or for work of equal value, be based on the sex of the workers. The term "enterprise" having been interpreted in the broad sense in labour legislation (it is not only a separate individual), one might expect that this law would be given a broader interpretation, but this has not so far been the case.

3. Enforcement arrangements for implementing equal pay policies

3.1 The different methods of enforcement

The implementation of the principle of equal pay was based initially, at the time when the 1972 Act was passed, on the simple obligation on employers to respect this principle, an obligation sanctioned at both civil and criminal levels. Responsibility for ensuring that this principle was applied lay with the labour inspectors, the employees and the trade unions.

In the face of wage discrimination based on sex, employees can apply individually and directly to the employer to bring the alleged discrimination to his notice. Employees can also request the intervention of the staff representative or union delegate to try to reach agreement with the employer. They can apply to the labour inspector, who can insist on being given information about the various elements involved in wage fixing in the enterprise, especially wage norms, occupational cetegories, and the criteria and basis for calculating wages. The labour inspector may or may not conduct a hearing involving both parties.[26]

If all this produces no results, employees can refer their case to a tribunal. Civil proceedings before the labour tribunal can be instituted individually and directly by the employee. The law also allows the representative union organisations at the workplace the possibility of bringing civil or criminal actions on behalf of employees, regardless of whether they are members of the union in question. The employees, in this case, must be informed in writing and not have stated any objection to the action. In any case, employees can always intervene in any proceedings initiated by the union.

Subsequent to the 1972 Act, the powers of the institutions representing employees were increased, especially in order to enable them to obtain information on wage policy in respect of men and women at the workplace. Concurrently with this obligation to supply information, the Act imposed on employers an obligation to negotiate wages on an annual basis, both at enterprise and at sectoral level, and to examine wage trends by sex.[27]

Side by side with these measures designed to supervise the implementation of the equal pay principle, the Act of 13 July 1983 opened up the possibility of introducing measures to remedy persistent discriminatory practices and to bring about the concrete attainment of equal pay and equal treatment.[28] These remedial measures can be introduced at the workplace in particular. Their purpose is to bring pressure to bear in the area of training and qualifications and ultimately to enforce the principle of equal pay. Finally, at national level, the law has set up a special organisation to promote the social debate on questions relating to equality in occupation and employment, the Central Council on Equality in Employment between Men and Women (see 3.2 below).

The implementation of the equal pay principle in France can thus be said to be based on a profusion of measures, which can be classed under various headings: information-giving, negotiation, positive actions, and recourse to civil and criminal courts.

3.2 Government bodies involved in implementing equal pay

Unlike a large number of EC Member States, France has not established a special commission responsible for ensuring compliance with the principle of equal pay at local level. The only administrative authority responsible for ensuring the concrete implementation of the principles of equal pay and equal treatment at local level is the labour inspector. Labour inspectors are responsible, under the authority of the Departmental Directors of Labour and Employment, for ensuring that all regulations of the Labour Code are observed within the area assigned to them.

Labour inspectors are given no particular specialised training in the matter of equal treatment or equal pay. Rather, their general competence and the professional training they receive in labour law, social security, and occupational health and safety enable them to supervise the implementation of the principles of equal pay and equal treatment.

In the face of discriminatory pay practices, labour inspectors have the authority to establish that a contravention of the principle of equal pay has occurred by drawing up an official report. This report enables the Public Prosecutor's Office to bring proceedings against the employer before the Police Tribunal.[29]

While labour inspectors can initiate criminal proceedings, they may not bring an action before the civil courts on their own behalf or on the behalf of the employees.

However, in view of their powers in the matter of criminal action, they have, in practice, a good chance of reaching an agreement with the employer on the observance of the principles of equal pay and equal treatment.

The labour inspectors themselves play no particular role as regards the promotion of the principle of equal pay. However, the Act of 13 July 1983 did confer a specific role on the Departmental Directors of Labour and Employment in relation to the adoption of plans and agreements on equality in employment concluded at the workplace (see 4.1 below). These plans, the object of which is to promote equal opportunities, cannot be put into operation until they have been referred to the Departmental Directors of Labour and Employment for approval as to their legality.

As mentioned earlier, the Act of 13 July 1983 also established a special organisation designed to promote the social debate on questions relating to equality in employment, the Central Council on Equality in Employment between Women and Men, attached to the ministers responsible for women's rights, labour, employment and vocational training. The Council takes part in defining and implementing policy relating to equality in employment between women and men, and draws up an annual report on its activities. It comprises representatives of the various ministries involved, representatives of the workers' and employers' organisations, and other persons appointed by virtue of their competence or experience. The Council has no jurisdiction at local level.

3.3 Legal costs

The regulations concerning the initiation of legal action in matters of equal pay are the same as those applicable to general labour disputes.

Employees are not obliged to be represented by a lawyer in the criminal courts. As a general rule, criminal proceedings are instituted either by the Office of the Public Prosecutor or by a union. In the case of such proceedings, employees can associate in a court action with the Public Prosecutor to obtain compensation for damages, either appearing in court themselves or being represented by a lawyer or a union.

Where criminal proceedings are instituted by a union or an employee, the procedural costs are minimal, unless an expert opinion is required, and do not constitute an obstacle to legal action. Such costs, where applicable, are borne by the employer if he is convicted.

In the civil courts (labour tribunals), employees may either appear themselves or be represented by a member of a union organisation, a family member or a lawyer. In practice, employees are usually represented by a lawyer or a union representative.

Procedural costs are practically non-existent for cases brought before the labour tribunals, unless an expert opinion is required. These costs are borne by the losing party, and again they constitute no obstacle to legal action. The employee will only be required to pay her lawyer's fees, if she employs one, or the payment occasionally demanded by the union, if she is represented by the union.

If the employee wins her case, the tribunal may award compensation for costs incurred. The compensation granted is quite modest (between FF500 and FF3,000).

As a general rule, equal pay issues are extremely complex. Cases of this kind often involve detailed preparation, and sometimes require an expert opinion. The employee is therefore obliged to call upon a lawyer or a union representative. Where the action has been initiated by the union, the union itself usually prefers to call on the services of a lawyer. The complexity of equal pay issues that constitutes an obstacle to legal action, if the employee cannot be represented by a union willing or able to pay her costs.

As far as individual action taken by an employee is concerned, France has a system of legal aid which enables people whose means are below a certain level to obtain the services of a lawyer free of charge. This legal aid may be granted in full or in part.

3.4 Remedies

French law provides for both civil and criminal sanctions to enforce the principle of equal pay.

Article L 140-4 of the Labour Code stipulates that regulations contrary to the principle of equal pay are null and void. In such cases, the higher rate of pay is substituted for the previous rate and the employee may also claim back-pay for a maximum of five years.

Non-compliance with the principle of equal pay is also subject to criminal sanction, according to article R 154-0-1 of the Labour Code. The employer is liable to a fine of between FF2,500 and FF5,000 for each worker paid at the illegal rate. The court may also order that the judgement be posted (article 471 of the Penal Code).

The Act of 13 July 1983 also introduced a system whereby the pronouncing of sentence is adjourned with the obligation on the employer to remedy the situation of non-compliance with the equal pay principle. In this case, the employer is declared guilty, and is ordered by the court to define, after consultation with the workers' representatives, appropriate measures to re-establish equality in pay between men and women, in the enterprise that is party to the proceedings.

To conclude, the sanctions applicable in respect of equal pay do enable claimants who have taken legal action to obtain redress. However, they do not appear to act as a deterrent. It should, furthermore, be noted that very few legal actions have been brought before the civil or the criminal courts.

3.5 Protection against victimisation

The Act of 13 July 1983 introduced a system of sanctions to prevent dismissal of a worker as a result of a lawsuit instituted by the worker or on her behalf for non-compliance with the equal pay principle.[30]

Where it has been established that the dismissal in question lacks real grounds and is in fact a measure adopted by the employer as a consequence of the lawsuit, the dismissal is null and void. By law, the employee must be reinstated, unless she refuses; in this case she must be awarded damages and compensation. In the case of minor sanctions, the employee is also entitled to demand nullification.

3.6 The burden of proof

In equal pay and equal treatment cases, the Act of 13 July 1983 introduced a major exception to the general principle that the burden of proof lies with the person demanding the fulfilment of an obligation.

Under the terms of the Act, the burden of proof lies with neither party of with both. Article L 140-8 of the Labour Code specifies that, where legal action is taken with respect to equal pay:

the employer shall furnish to the judge any elements which may justify the inequality of remuneration at issue. In the light of these elements and of those furnished by the worker in support of his complaint, the judge shall make his decision, having ordered, where necessary, such inquiries as he deems appropriate. The worker shall have the benefit of any doubt which remains.

This new regulation obliges the employer to supply proof that the principle of equal pay has been respected. Bearing in mind that this regulation is of recent date, it is as yet too early to examine how it has been applied in practice. However, in the case of the regulation concerning disciplinary sanctions (other than dismissal), where the same principle applies, the courts appear to have been somewhat reluctant to apply in full the principle of giving the employee the benefit of the doubt. In practice, the employee must take an active part in the legal debate, otherwise she will not be awarded the benefit of the doubt. On equal pay issues, it is always in the interest of the employee to substantiate the alleged discrimination. The adoption of the European Community draft directive concerning the burden of proof in the matter of equal pay and equal treatment will undoubtedly reinforce the regulations adopted by French law and promote concrete implementation of them.[31]

3.7 Access to information on wages

In enterprises employing more than 50 workers, the employer is obliged to submit to the works committee or staff delegates a written report on the comparative situation as regards the general employment and training conditions of men and women in the enterprise. This report must include figures on the actual pay of men and women in each of the occupational categories in the enterprise.[32] The report is also to be placed at the disposal of any worker who requests it.[33] In the event of a legal dispute, the claimant is thus entitled to require the employer to communicate this report.

Within the framework of the annual wage negotiations, the employer must supply the bargaining parties with the necessary information to conduct a comparative analysis of the situation of men and women in respect of jobs and qualifications, wages and actual hours worked.[34]

3.8 Experience of equal pay claims

An analysis of equal pay claims suggests that the courts tend to recognise discrimination only in cases of flagrant and direct discrimination. As far as the Supreme Court of Appeal is concerned, discrimination cases mostly come before the Court of

Criminal Appeal and not before the Court of Civil Appeal. The Court of Civil Appeal very frequently allows the employer to justify non-compliance with the equal pay principle by proving that the work is not equal or not of equal value.

In most cases, the courts have not recognised that there has been a violation of the principle of equal pay. A recent ruling by the Supreme Court of Appeal on 31 May 1988 in the case of *Masson* v. *Bocama SA* provides a good illustration of the difficulties encountered by claimants as regards enforcement of the equal pay principle.

In the case in question, women workers assigned to work on ironing presses claimed that they were being discriminated against in respect of pay in that male workers in the same occupational category and with the same seniority coefficient were receiving higher pay for work which the women considered to be similar. The women also claimed that a male assistant storekeeper was in a higher category with a higher coefficient and being paid a higher wage, although his duties and responsibilities were similar to those of the women workers.

The Court of Appeal had declared the employer guilty of non-compliance with the principle of equal pay. This ruling was quashed by the Supreme Court of Appeal *(Cour de Cassation)* on the following grounds:

> while the Court of Appeal had recognised, on the one hand, the equivalence between the work of the female employee assigned to administrative duties and that of an assistant storekeeper and, on the other hand, the equivalence between the physical and mental stress imposed on the women assigned to work on the presses and their male fellow-workers, it could not, however, in the case of the 13 women workers, take the arduousness of the work as a sole point of comparison, without also investigating, as the defendant and the company responsible under civil law had proposed, whether the difference in remuneration could not be justified by the versatility and training of the male workers.

It must be emphasised, however, that there have been very few such lawsuits, so that the legal debate can be considered to play very little importance in the enforcement of equal pay policies.

4. The role of the social partners

4.1 Labour-management involvement in implementing equal pay

In the absence of specialised bodies responsible for promoting and monitoring compliance with the principle of equal pay for men and women, French legislation tends to encourage the social partners to take this principle into account in all collective bargaining issues.

The 1983 Act in particular was designed to give the social partners a dominant role in the implementation of the principle of equality. Collective bargaining, at both sectoral and enterprise level, provides the forum in which the workers' and employers' organisations can play this role, but it is they who must take the initiative. There is, in fact, no legal obligation on the social partners to take any concrete measures in respect of equal treatment or equal pay.

As already mentioned, employers are obliged to submit a report to the workers' representatives and union organisations within the framework of the annual negotiations at sectoral or enterprise level. This report must state among other things, the situation of men and women in respect of pay. However, they are not obliged to come to any kind of agreement on this subject. Apart from the reports submitted in the context of bargaining, the employer is under no obligation to communicate any type of report to any administrative body.

In order to extend the scope of sectoral agreements concluded at national level, the Act requires the inclusion in such agreements of a clause relating to remedial measures designed to correct or eliminate existing inequalities. These measures concern, above all, recruitment, training, promotion, the organisation of work and working conditions.

At the level of the workplace, the Act has introduced the possibility of adopting plans for equality in employment between men and women, negotiated by the employer and the workers' organisations. Such plans may involve various measures, such as reserving certain types of training or job vacancies for women, or modifying the environment and the constraints of the work organisation in the case of women. The adoption of such plans will inevitably have positive repercussions for the implementation of equal pay.

The Departmental Directorates of Labour and Employment have responsibility for monitoring the content of plans for equality in employment. The National Agency for the Improvement of Working Conditions (*Agence Nationale pour l'Amélioration des conditions de Travail* – ANACT) may also intervene and collaborate in the negotiation of plans for equality in employment. The Act further introduced the possibility of state financial assistance to promote activities carried out in accordance with such plans.

Up to the present, some 20 such plans have been adopted. They have been introduced in several large companies such as Moulinex (household applicances), the Bull group (but only in the Angers establishment), Jacques Vabre (farm produce) and the Crédit industriel de Normandie (banking). The measures adopted include paid technical training courses leading to new qualification, priority for women in recruitment to jobs in which they are underrepresented, and retraining with a view to removing obstacles to promotion.[35]

Small and medium-scale enterprises can also conclude contracts with a view to achieving a more equitable representation of men and women in certain occupations with financial assitance from the State. Unlike the plans referred to earlier, these contracts take the form of individual measures on a case-by-case basis, oriented towards action in the field of training and adaptation of working conditions.[36]

These positive actions reflect the transition from the traditional logic of protecting women to the egalitarian logic arising from earlier legislation.

4.2 Labour-management involvement in determining job evaluation criteria

It is within the framework of collective bargaining at sectoral level that the employers' and workers' organisations are expected to determine and adopt job evaluation criteria. The employers' and workers' organisations, which are bound by sectoral collective agreements or occupational agreements, are obliged to meet at least once every five years to examine the need to revise job classifications. The reports drawn up by the Central Collective Agreements Committee, which is responsible, among other things, for examining the collective agreements for compliance with the principle of equal pay, indicate that these questions are not of great immediate interest. Moreover, as we have seen, although jobs are defined without reference to sex, such definitions do allow employers a certain latitude in the matter of determining the pay attaching to the various jobs in each category.

According to some authors, the revision of job categories would not in any case affect one of the most basic causes of inequality in the pay of men and women, that is the distribution of employment according to sex (segregation). The adoption of occupational equality plans at the workplace, involving measures concerning vocational training and promotion, may lead to a more just distribution of jobs and thus to greater equality in respect of pay.[37]

5. Conclusions

An examination of French legal instruments indicates that the principle of equality in employment and pay between men and women has been recognised and sanctioned by law. However, it is also obvious that genuine equality in the matter of pay has not yet been achieved. Contrary to tradition, as far as equal pay is concerned, the law is not ratifying a situation that is already established in fact but acting as a vector of social change.[38]

The delay observed in the implementation of the equal pay principle (the remuneration gap is probably between 20 and 25 per cent) is due above all to sociological causes. Awareness of the importance of the issue was late in developing, not only in the trade unions but also among women themselves. The Act of 13 July 1983 reflects a twofold policy: an assertion of equal rights, designed primarily to prevent discrimination based on sex, and the promotion of equal opportunity for men and women in employment and occupation.[39] The cause of equality of opportunity has been considerably advanced through positive discrimination, such as remedial measures. It is essential now to open all types of employment to both men and women in order to implement the principle of equal pay.

The French approach to the enforcement of equal pay policies is based on a legal system which is satifactory from the point of view of definition, supervision and sanctions. However, the absence of a specialised body responsible for counselling and helping victims of discrimination may possibly discourage the latter from taking legal action. On the other hand, such bodies are not in keeping with French legal traditions.

Job evaluation and classification systems, in their present form, are not sufficient to promote the implementation of the equal pay principle. The 1983 Act made employers' and workers' organisations responsible for renegotiating these classifications. This, reinforced by positive action to promote vocational training and jobs that are open to men and women alike, could create a situation in which the principle of equal pay for men and women became an established fact in the field of employment.

On the whole, French law can be said to place increasing emphasis on equality between men and women, in line with the principles propounded by the ILO and the Commission of the European Communities.

Notes

[1] Act No. 52-1309 of 10.12.52, JO (Law Gazette) 11.12.52.

[2] Decree No. 53.335 of 16.04.53, JO 26.07.53.

[3] Act No. 50-205 of 11.02.50.

[4] Act No. 72-1143 of 22.12.72, JO 24.12.72.

[5] EEC Council Directive 75/117 of 10.02.75.

[6] Act No. 83-635 of 13.07.83, JO 14.07.83.

[7] CE 11.06.82, Dame Diebolt, *Droit Social (Dr. Soc.),* 1983, No. 2, p. 138, Conclusions, B. Genevois.

[8] C. Cass. Crim. 22.06.77, *Dr. Soc.,* 1978, No. 3, p. 132, note, J. Savatier.

[9] Y. Saint-Jours: "L'Egalité de l'homme et de la femme en droit français de la securité sociale", in *Revue Trimestrielle de droit sanitaire et social,* 1985, No. 3, p. 354.

[10] ECJ 25.05.71, Case No. 80-90, *Gabrielle Defrenne* v. *Belgian Government.*

[11] ECJ 11.03.81, Case No. 69-80, *Susan Jane Worringham and M. Humphreys* v. *Lloyds Bank Limited.*

[12] Circ. 02.05.84, JO 07.06.84, NC 4995.

[13] Act No. 83-635 of 13.07.83, JO 14.07.84.

[14] C. Cass. Crim. 01.12.81, *Dame Weill* v. *Hoepff.*

[15] C. Cass. Soc. 18.03.81, quoted under 20 below.

[16] T.I. de Guebwiller, 06.12.79, DO, 1981, p. 391.

[17] See B. Sousi-Roubi: "Réflexions sur les discriminations sexistes dans l'emploi", in *Dr. Soc.,* 1984, p. 339.

[18] C. Cass. Soc. 24.11.76, BVC, No. 619, p. 503; *Dr. Soc.,* 1978, No. 3, p. 132, note, J. Savatier.

[19] C. Cass. Crim. 22.06.77, quoted under 8 above.

[20] C.A. Paris, 22.06.81, DO, 1981, p. 334, Trib. Police Paris, 07.11.80, DO, 1981, p. 392; C. Cass. Soc. 18.03.81, B. Civ. V., No. 229, p. 172.

[21] C.A. Paris, 14.06.82 Bosh, quoted by C. de Marguerye: "Les Juges français et la discrimination sexuelle", in *Dr. Soc.,* 1983, No. 2, p. 122.

[22] C.A. Versailles, 15.04.85, Juri. Soc., 1985, F. 60.

[23] C. Cass. Crim. 31.05.88, Société Anonyme Bocame, unpublished.

[24] See D. Rossi: "Emploi des femmes et mixité: Droits et pratiques", in *Dr. Soc.,* 1987, No. 2, p. 155.

[25] C. Cass. Soc. 09.06.82, B. Civ. V. No. 381, p. 183; Juri. Soc., 1092, F. 65.

[26] Labour Code, art. 140-1.

[27] Labour Code, art. L 132-28 and L 132-12. See C. Sutter: "L'Egalité professionnelle dans les droits nouveaux", in *Dr. Soc.,* 1983, p. 684.

[28] The Constitutional Council, however, opposed the adoption of a law which stipulated that the lists of candidates for local government elections should contain at least 25 per cent of one or the other sex. Cons. Constit. 18.11.82, *Dr. Soc.,* 1983, p. 131, note, D. Loschak. This was not referred to the Constitutional Council at the time of the passing of the 1983 Act.

[29] Labour Code, art. R 154-0-1.

[30] Labour Code, art. R 123-5.

[31] Draft Council Directive relating to the burden of proof in the area of equal treatment and equal pay between men and women, COM (88) 269 Final 24.05.88.

[32] See A. Junter-Loiseau: "La Division sexuelle des emplois à l'épreuve de la loi du 13 juillet 1983 relative à l'égalité professionnelle", in *Dr. Soc.,* 1987, No. 2, p. 143.

[33] Labour Code, art. L 432-3-1.

[34] Labour Code, art. L 132-28.

[35] On these plans see C. Alezra, J. Laufer, M. Maruani and C. Sutter (eds.): "La Mixité du travail: Une strategie pour l'entreprise", in *Cahier Entreprises,* No. 3 (Paris, la Documentation Française, June 1987).

[36] Circular CF4-87 of 17.07.87. For the application of the law on equality of men and women in employment and the new regulations for small and medium-scale enterprises, see "Le contrat pour la mixité des emplois", in *Liaisons sociales,* Leg. Soc. No. 5994 of 21.08.87.

[37] See Sutter, op. cit.

[38] This observation was made during a European Colloquium in Louvain La Neuve, by M. Verwilghen: "L'Egalité juridique entre homes et femmes dans la Communauté Européenne un combat inachevé", in M. Verwilghen (ed.): *Proceedings of the Colloquium Louvain La Neuve,* 1986, Vol. 1, p. 177.

[39] On the principle of equal opportunity, see M.T. Lanquetin: "De l'Egalité professionnelle entre les femmes et les hommes", concerning a draft bill, in *Dr. Soc.,* 1983, No. 4, p. 238.

6

Equal pay in Japan

*Akira Okuyama**

1. Introduction

1.1 The legal basis for equality of pay

In the field of equal pay there are two significant pieces of legislation in Japan – the Labour Standards Law (hereafter the LSL) and the Equal Employment Opportunity Law (hereafter the EEOL). The former was enacted in 1947 and covers all categories of workers except national government employees engaged in general affairs. The latter was passed in 1985 in order to promote equal opportunity and treatment for women workers in all aspects of employment.[1]

Article 4 of the LSL specifies that employers shall not discriminate against female employees in respect of wages simply because they are female.[2] It is generally understood that this provision embodies the equal pay for equal work principle and applies only to discrimination relating to actual wages. But, as explained later, it covers not only discrimination as regards the amount of wages but also wage disparities resulting from the discriminatory application of wage systems or bases for payment between men and women workers. Wage differentials between men and women which result from discrimination as regards hiring, job assignment, promotion, job training, etc. do not, however, constitute direct violation of article 4 of the LSL.

While article 4 of the LSL applies only to sex discrimination as regards wages, the EEOL is wider in its application. Wage differentials between male and female workers derive mainly from sex discrimination in such areas as recruitment, job assignment, promotion and job training. If real equality, including pay equality, between men and women is to be achieved, it is therefore necessary to prohibit all kinds of discrimination against women in employment, and more fundamentally to end job segregation between men and women. The EEOL was enacted to accomplish such objects, its aim being to guarantee equal employment opportunity and treatment between men and women in employment. It lays down the five areas of employment in

* Professor of Law, Seijo University.

which the principle of equal employment and treatment for women should be achieved. These are:

(1) recruitment and hiring;

(2) job assignment and promotion;

(3) education and training;

(4) employees' fringe benefits; and

(5) mandatory retirement age, retirement and dismissal.[3]

The law requires employers to "endeavour" to give equal opportunity and treatment to women in regard to the first two categories, and prohibits them from discriminating against women because of their sex in regard to the last three categories.[4]

The EEOL has no provision that generally prohibits sex discrimination in employment, nor does it directly forbid wage discrimination between men and women. These facts contribute to the widely held view that the EEOL cannot be applied to wage discrimination. It appears, however, that such a view is not totally accurate. One influential view, held by an eminent professor of labour law, is that, in the light of the objects of the EEOL and its nature as a general law relating to equal opportunity and treatment in employment, the principle of equal opportunity and treatment in employment enshrined in it can be applied even to discriminatory practices that are not explicitly referred to in the legislation.[5]

Leaving aside such interpretative controversy over the significance of the legislation and its applicability to wage discrimination, it must be emphasised that the EEOL, together with the public order or good morals clause in article 90 of the Civil Code and the constitutional guarantee of equality contained in article 14 of the Japanese Constitution, does have a good deal of influence on wage discrimination between men and women. It is certainly the case that, since the enactment of the EEOL, women's initial pay is becoming more comparable with men's. It should also be emphasised that the EEOL can be applied to wage differentials between men and women that arise from sex discrimination over job assignment, promotion, fringe benefits, and so on. It thus appears that, alongside article 4 of the LSL, which prohibits wage discrimination as an infringement of the equal pay principle, the EEOL can be seen as a significant and useful legal resource for the elimination of wage discrimination against women.

1.2 The definition of pay

Article 11 of the LSL defines wages to mean all kinds of remuneration, paid by employers to their employees in return for their work no matter what such remuneration is called. The term thus covers not only basic wages but also bonuses, lump-sum allowances, welfare benefits and other allowances (family allowance, spouse allowance, housing allowance, seniority allowance, commuting allowance, etc.). Even retirement pay or gratuities can be regarded as wages if the employer is obliged to pay them under the terms of individual employment contracts or collective agreements.

1.3 The definition of "equal work"

Although article 4 of the LSL does not include the words "equal work", it is generally understood that it establishes the principle of equal pay for equal work. In theory, it must be established that both male and female employees do equal work if wage discrimination against women is to be demonstrated. So how is "equal" work defined legally? In other words, how do women workers know that their work is "equal" to that done by men? The equal pay legislation does not provide any objective measures in this respect. The word "equal" is generally regarded as synonymous with "same". From the legal standpoint, however, this is not quite right. For jobs to be equal it is not required that they should involve exactly the "same" or "identical" tasks, but simply that these tasks should be substantially "similar". In other words, "equal" work should be interpreted as meaning not the "same" work, but work that is on the same level, namely work of "equal value".[6]

1.4 Scope of the equal pay provisions

In principle, the LSL covers all categories of employees, except national government workers (national public servants) engaged in general affairs. It does cover local government workers (local public servants) engaged in general affairs, but they are exempt from some of its provisions (for instance, those concerning joint determination of working conditions by worker and employer).

However, special legislation exists regarding the salaries of public servants. The National Public Employees Law[7] states that the salaries of national government workers shall only be paid in accordance with the Rules and Regulations on Salaries established by law.[8] These Rules and Regulations specify salary scales, the criteria for rises in salary, allowances, etc. Furthermore, article 27 of the National Public Employees Law lays down the principle of equal treatment for all public servants. Very similar legislation exists for the local public servants.[9] It can thus be said that there is no wage discrimination as such between male and female public servants, since all their terms and conditions of employment, including hours of work, job categories, grades and salaries, are prescribed by law and apply to men and women equally.

2. Procedures for determining "equality"

In theory, two requisites must be satisfied in order to establish that article 4 of the LSL, prohibiting wage discrimination against female employees, has been infringed. First, the male and female jobs that are compared must be "equal". Second, the discrimination must have occurred purely for reasons of sex.

2.1 The criteria for comparing jobs

It should in theory be possible to determine whether jobs are equal by comparing jobs done by male and female employees. Under the Equal Pay Act of 1963 in the United States, "equal value" seems to imply that the jobs compared are on the same level in respect of skill, effort, responsibility and working conditions.[10] In Japan, however, it is difficult to determine whether or not two different jobs involve equal skill, effort and responsibility. There are two reasons for this. First, the job categories and job contents at the majority of Japanese companies are extremely vague; they are not necessarily defined or demarcated strictly, nor are precise classifications or evaluations of each job made. Japanese labour law never requires employers to undertake job evaluations of this sort. This obviously makes it quite difficult to compare one job with another. Second, the great majority of Japanese companies have established groups of job categories to which women are never assigned. To take the example of "office workers", the female workers have traditionally continued to work as assistants to male workers who are management trainees. Their work involves routine tasks with low pay, low status and no opportunities for promotion. In other words, although it can be maintained that the female and male jobs both belong to the same category of "office work", they differ greatly in content and nature. Under these circumstances, it becomes difficult to determine whether two different jobs are "equal".

2.2 *Permitted justifications for differences in pay*

According to the juridical interpretation of article 4 of the LSL, even when male and female employees are paid different wages in spite of doing equal work, this will not always and automatically constitute wage discrimination. In order to constitute a violation of that provision, wage discrimination must occur simply because of the employees "being female". In other words, the equal pay for equal work principle enshrined in article 4 is applicable only when discrimination takes place on the basis of sex. Typical meanings of "on account of being female" are as follows: women are generally inferior or inefficient compared to men; their years of service are on average short compared to men's; women have no family dependants, and so on. It is nevertheless difficult to determine whether actual wage disparities between male and female employees amount to discrimination on account of being female. It has to be determined individually and concretely, case by case. In this respect, if the employer cannot prove that such disparities are based on anything other than sex, it can be assumed that they do amount to unlawful discrimination because the employees are female.

This means that wage differentials between men and women on the basis of some reasonable cause other than sex do not constitute unlawful wage discrimination. These reasonable causes include differences in age, qualifications, length of service (seniority), efficiency (results of work), the existence of dependants, and so on. They are not specifically enumerated by the LSL or other related laws or regulations but have emerged entirely as a result of the administrative interpretations of the National Labour Standards Bureau of the Ministry of Labour and the academic views of university professors, lawyers and other specialists.

2.3 *Examples of unlawful wage discrimination against women*

As already noted, it is extremely difficult, as a matter of law, to make a general decision as to what kinds of facts or practices make wage inequality between male and female employees unlawful discrimination on the grounds of "being female". What we can do, however, is to give some examples of unlawful wage discrimination against women.

The Akita Cooperative Bank case

It violates article 4 to pay men and women different starting salaries when the work they perform is equal in content.[11] It is also unlawful to pay male employees on a monthly basis and female employees on a daily basis. Another form of illegal wage discrimination against women is the practice of putting men and women on separate salary scales. A good example is provided by the court decision in the Akita Cooperative Bank case.[12] The facts established by the court were as follows: compensation at the bank consisted of two elements, namely the "personal wage", calculated solely on the basis of age and length of service, and the "functional wage", based on job and ability. In computing the former element, the bank utilised two kinds of schedules, a higher schedule A and a lower schedule B. The bank applied schedule A to men and schedule B to women. Later, the bank changed this pattern of treatment in response to administrative guidance by the Prefectural Labour Standards Inspection Office that this constituted a violation of article 4. Consequently, the bank began to apply schedule A only to men with dependants and to apply schedule B to all women whether married or not. However, men without dependants were paid adjustment premiums in order to bring their compensation up to the level of schedule A. As a result, there was still a wage differential between men and women. In this case, the district court affirmed that a violation of article 4 had taken place and the claimants (seven women) were awarded back pay. The court stated that, by considering all the facts of the case, it was possible to conclude that the bank had treated the claimants adversely as regards wages on the ground of being female, so long as the employer could not prove other special factors that would make such a wage system lawful. The court concluded that the employer's counter-evidence on this point was insufficient, and that the employer had discriminated against the claimants by establishing separate salary scales for men and women and applying the more disadvantageous one only to women without any reasonable cause.

The Iwate Bank case

It also violates the equal pay for equal work principle to pay men and women different amounts of family allowance, housing allowance, living allowance and so on, or to apply different criteria for the payment of such allowances. The Morioka District Court made a decision regarding this type of discrimination in the Iwate Bank case.[13] There, the claimant was a female employee of the respondent bank (her salary was almost double that of her husband) and claimed family allowance. But the bank refused to pay. One of its provisions relating to the payment of family allowance stated that "The bank shall pay family allowance to the employee who is a head of household with dependants. But if his/her spouse also works, only male employees as husbands shall be treated as the head of household". The court held that such provision was illegal because it treated female employees as wives less favourably than male employees as husbands; it also noted that this less favourable treatment of female employees was solely on the grounds of their being female. In short, the court did not question the reasonableness of using the criterion "head of household" but simply declared that it was unlawful to use a criterion that linked with gender alone in order to limit the payment of family allowance beforehand to either husbands or wives (in this case, husbands).

The Nissan Automobile Company case

Another more recent case that raised the same legal issue as the Iwate Bank case was the Nissan Automobile Company case.[14] In this case the company provided that family allowance should be paid to the "substantial" head of household, that is to either the wife or the husband, whichever of the two earned more. The court held that such an application of the head of household criterion was unrelated to sex and that it was a reasonable criterion for deciding which was the real head of household. The court emphasised that, although at the time of the hearing there were more families in the company where the husbands earned more, the application of such a criterion was not unlawful so long as either wife or husband would be eligible for the allowance if they earned more.

The Japan Steel Association case

In the Japan Steel Association case,[15] the claimants (seven women) charged the respondent association with applying different career ladders[16] and wage schedules on the basis of sex; they alleged that this two-track employment structure – standard track for women as assistants to men and management trainee track for men – resulted in wage discrimination against women. The district court held that:

> the existence of wage differentials between male and female employees in this case is caused by sex discrimination in recruitment, hiring, job assignment or promotion under the above separate employment system (in other words, separate career structures). And it is possible to say that such discrimination in recruitment and hiring, etc. is against the principle of "equality under the law" manifested in article 14 of the Japanese Constitution.

However, the court noted, such separate career structures for male and female employees did not seem to be unlawful in the light of the general employment practices of a lot of Japanese companies at the time the claimants were employed (1969-74). On the other hand, the court declared that differentiated calculation of bonuses and annual increments on the basic wage for men and women was against the "public order or good morals" principle established by article 90 of the Civil Code. It therefore ordered back pay for two years.

So far, we have illustrated some typical examples of unlawful wage discrimination on the basis of sex. But discrimination does not always take this form. Illegal wage discrimination "on account of being female" can also be demonstrated where employers consider jobs such as those of nurses, secretaries or receptionists, which are generally done by women, as inferior to jobs generally done by men, and intentionally keep their wages down as a result. In other words, even though the work being performed by women is different in content from that being performed by men, unlawful wage discrimination can be said to occur in so far as it is possible to judge that higher pay would be given if men did these women's jobs.[17] Yet, if this sort of discrimination is to be reduced, the desegregation of jobs must be attempted through the affirmative application of the Equal Employment Opportunity Law.

3. Enforcement arrangements for implementing equal pay policies

3.1 The different methods of enforcement

If the wage differentials between male and female workers do violate the principle of equal pay for equal work, there are two routes by which the victims of discrimination can seek redress, the administrative and the judicial. The former involves administrative agencies, using informal methods such as persuasion or conciliation. The latter involves litigation in the courts.

The LSL also imposes certain legal obligations on employers. For example, employers have an obligation to draw up documents concerning wages, including the amounts of basic wages and allowances paid, the names of employees, their sex, the basic period for calculation of wages, the number of working days, working hours, amount of overtime work and night work, and so on.[18] They also have to keep such documents for at least three years.[19] In addition, they must supply information promptly when the labour inspector asks for it in connection with the enforcement of the LSL.[20]

3.2 Government bodies involved in implementing equal pay

The most important administrative agency as regards remedying unlawful wage discrimination based on sex is the Prefectural Labour Standards Inspection Office, which is part of the national government apparatus. This office is responsible for the enforcement of all provisions of the LSL, including article 4. A certain number of labour inspectors and other general staff are assigned to the office. Labour inspectors are professional executive officers with special powers to enforce the LSL.[21] The directors of the various prefectural offices, and the labour inspectors attached to them, have powers to interrogate, inspect, arbitrate, demand the provision of documents, and so on.[22] Furthermore, they have powers of investigation and arrest similar to those possessed by a judicial police officer.[23]

Article 104 of the LSL also allows workers (both individual employees and the labour union) to notify the Prefectural Labour Standards Inspection Office of violations of the LSL by employers. When this occurs, the Office, usually through an individual labour inspector, undertakes an investigation as to whether the alleged violation has taken place, making use of the powers mentioned above. If a violation is found to have occurred, the Office attempts to correct the situation by making a recommendation to the offending employer. In most cases, such a procedure will result in a settlement, and back pay will be awarded to the aggrieved person or group.

There are also prefectural administrative agencies established by local government. These agencies have several branch offices within each prefecture, generally called labour policy offices or labour centres. All the staff are ordinary civil servants rather than lawyers or labour experts. As a result, they do not have any official powers as regards conciliation, arbitration or settlement of disputes, nor even the power to bring a lawsuit themselves. Their primary responsibilities in their daily work are to maintain the health, safety and welfare of the working people living in cities within the prefecture and to improve their working conditions. Consequently, they have a lot of opportunities to hear grievances, including wage discrimination, and to give the victims advice as to how to proceed. In some cases, they will also give administrative guidance to the allegedly offending employers. Although these methods of providing redress against sex discrimination in employment are completely informal, they do actually contribute to the removal of such discrimination and the achievement of equal treatment for men and women, including the principle of equal pay for equal work.

3.3 Remedies

The judicial remedy for victims of unlawful wage discrimination can take two main forms. First, the practice or system of wage discrimination against female employees can be declared invalid as a violation of article 4 of the LSL, and the victims can be awarded back pay equivalent to the amount of wages they have lost through discrimination. This back pay can be awarded for a maximum of two years.[24] Second, damages can be awarded to the victims by reason of tort violating article 709 of the Civil Code. The former appears to be more advantageous for the victims than the latter. This is because it can actually invalidate the discriminatory practice or system that produced the wage discrimination; the victims will thereafter be paid the appropriate wage without any discrimination. The latter can only make each act of wage discrimination by an employer unlawful; it cannot invalidate the system that causes such discrimination. Consequently, the victims must bring a suit every time an employer discriminates against female employees under such a wage system.

3.4 The burden of proof

One of the most important legal issues in such discrimination cases concerns the burden of proof. Generally, it is the fundamental principle in such actions that the official burden of proof should lie with the claimant, the aggrieved person. In the discrimination suit in which she is alleging violation of article 4 of the LSL by her employer, she must therefore prove that the work she does is equal to that done by male employees; that, despite this fact, there are wage differentials between them; and that such differentials exist only by reason of the claimant "being female". Once the claimant has made her allegation, the employer may defend himself by maintaining that the jobs are not equal, or that the differentials are based not upon the claimant's sex but upon other reasonable causes such as age, seniority or qualifications.

However, as mentioned previously, because the employment and wage structures of many Japanese companies are extremely complicated, it would be very difficult for the claimant to present sufficient evidence to prove the employer's intention to discriminate. For this reason, courts tend to accept a shift in the burden of proof.[25] It thus appears that in many of these discrimination cases the employer has to rebut the claimant's allegations in more positive terms and actually prove that there is no intention to discriminate. If the employer fails in this rebuttal, the court usually allows that intentional discrimination with respect to wages has taken place.

3.5 Experience of equal pay claims

There are few court cases involving wage discrimination based on sex. As already mentioned, one reason is that it is extremely difficult for claimants to prove the existence of discrimination, given that wage systems in Japanese companies tend to be so complicated. Another reason is that obtaining a judicial remedy through litigation on the whole costs too much; it also takes much longer than obtaining an administrative remedy.

Since the Akita Cooperative Bank case, seeking remedy by the administrative route has become gradually more popular, and recently it has obtained good results. Two typical examples are the Sanwa Bank case and the Tateishi Electricity case. The former involved wage differentials stemming from sex discrimination in promotion. In that case, the bank paid about JPY200 million (USD1.6 million) in back pay to female employees in accordance with the recommendation of the Prefectural Labour Standards Inspection Office.[26] The latter case involved sex discrimination as regards initial pay and periodic wage rises, which were differentiated between male and female employees. Here, too, the Office found that unlawful discrimination had taken place and recommended its correction. The company paid JPY600 million (USD4.1 million) in back pay to the female employees who had been discriminated against.

The reason why the administrative remedy has become popular in sex discrimination cases is mainly the fact that it is much more possible for the aggrieved person or group to obtain quick, simple (low-cost) and furthermore flexible redress than by seeking a judicial decision through a civil lawsuit. It therefore seems likely that there will be many more cases in which remedies are sought for in this way.

4. The role of the social partners

Japanese companies generally have a lifetime employment system and seniority-based promotion, and their wage system is closely related to these employment practices. This is broadly known as the seniority-based wage system. The important point here is that all the substantial benefits stemming from such wage systems are available only to male workers. Furthermore, these employment systems not only discriminate against women as regards job assignment, promotion, training and fringe benefits, but they also compel female workers to retire at marriage or at a younger age than men simply because they are female. On the other hand, a great many women are still satisfied with the low-status, low-paying part-time work because they believe that a woman's main role is to marry and take care of her husband and children.[27]

In spite of such a situation, neither workers nor employers (nor their representatives, labour union and employers' association) have been legally required to take positive steps to implement equal pay. Generally speaking, any efforts to abolish wage discrimination and ensure equal pay have arisen from voluntary approaches such as collective bargaining between labour union and employer rather than from any form of legal coercion.

In fact, Japanese labour unions have generally not been willing to involve themselves in dissolving wage differentials between men and women, for several reasons. First, the labour unions have on the whole accepted the stereotype of women workers as assistant and temporary labour and have therefore considered that women's wages should be lower than men's. Second, the labour unions have not been interested in recruiting women workers to the union because of their relatively short years of service compared to men, nor have the women themselves wanted to become members. Under these circumstances, the labour unions have not been concerned with women's terms and conditions of employment, including wages. In any case, female workers work part time and so would be refused membership, since Japanese unions have traditionally included only full-time workers.

Recently, however, the unions' attitudes towards women's issues in the workplace have been changing, and they have begun to take some positive steps towards realising equal pay between men and women. It was mainly after the court decision in the Akita Cooperative Bank case that a number of unions began to participate in implementing equal pay. But such participation is just beginning. Unfortunately, there is no obvious cooperation between workers and employers in establishing criteria for job classification or job evaluation, nor are there any collective agreements that acknowledge the principle of equal pay, let alone provide concrete procedures to implement it.

There are nevertheless strong indications that an increasing number of labour unions now perceive the achievement of equal pay on behalf of women workers as an important goal. Such unions have various courses open to them. The first is to demand the abolition of sexual inequality in initial pay, allowances, increments on the basic wage, and so on. It is also important to outlaw sex discrimination in promotion and wage systems such as the efficiency-oriented wage system, which gives rise to many kinds of sex discrimination. The second is to tackle wage differentials that arise from differences in job content as a result of confining women workers to routine and assistant work. Occupational sex segregation must be ended, and equal opportunities in job assignment, promotion, training and so forth assured. The third course is to work for the abolition of discriminatory wage systems applied to part-time workers or other temporary workers, as the majority of women fall into these categories.[28]

5. Conclusions

Of the many Japanese laws concerning labour relations only one directly prohibits wage discrimination against women in employment, namely article 4 of the

LSL. But this provision is too simple and unspecific in content to be of much significance in regulating unreasonable wage differentials between men and women. More recently, the EEOL was enacted, with the aim of achieving equal opportunity and treatment for women in employment. Unfortunately, this new law nowhere directly prohibits wage discrimination. As far as equal pay is concerned, the legal provisions are thus very poor compared to other countries such as the EC member States or the United States.

However, although the legal framework is so inadequate, considerable progress towards equality in the areas of initial pay and the payment of allowances does seem to have been made since the enactment of the EEOL. Thus, it may be that the EEOL, in conjunction with article 4 of the LSL, can play a really important role in the achievement of equal pay, despite having no provision that refers to equal pay as such.

At the same time, it must be emphasised that a great many conceptual and practical difficulties face those attempting to promote the equal pay principle in Japan. Because article 4 of the LSL does not define the legal concept of "equal work", it is difficult for the victims of wage discrimination to have recourse to the law. In particular, it is almost impossible to determine whether two different jobs are of equal value. The complicated employment and wage structure in many Japanese companies makes this doubly difficult. One obstacle facing any national approach to the promotion of the equal pay principle is that it is very difficult to bring about positive participation in the area of equal pay through legal coercion. Government, employers and labour unions all appear to have a very negative attitude towards any such intervention.

It therefore seems more appropriate to attempt to implement equal pay in the workplace through the voluntary efforts of both labour and management in collective bargaining and the conclusion of collective agreements, and through the intervention of administrative agencies, both national and local. Above all, both labour unions and employers should make all possible efforts to reduce the sex segregation in the workplace which is such a major cause of wage differentials between men and women, and more concretely to achieve equal opportunities for women in such areas as job assignment, promotion, training and fringe benefits.

Notes

1 It is officially entitled the "Law to promote the welfare of female workers by providing for equality of opportunity and treatment in employment for women".

2 The offending employer shall be punished with a period of penal servitude not exceeding six months or a fine not exceeding JPY10,000 (LSL, art. 119).

3 As regards the details of the EEOL, see Loraine Parkinson: "Note, Japan's Equal Employment Opportunity Law: An alternative approach to social change", in *Columbia Law Review*, 1986, Vol. 89, p. 606. For a basic introduction to the law, see "Note, Japan's new Equal Employment Opportunity Law: Real weapon or heirloom sword", in *Brigham Young University Law Review*, 1986, p. 865.

4 Parkinson, op. cit., p. 607.

5 Yasuhiko Matsuda: "Doitsu Rodo, Doitsu Chingin Gensoku to Haiti, Syosin no Kikai Kinto" (the principle of equal pay for equal work and equal opportunity of job assignment and promotion), in *Kikan Rodo Ho*, Autumn, 1985, Vol. 137, pp. 7-8.

6 The United States Equal Pay Act of 1963 affirms that the jobs compared are equal if they require equal skill, effort and responsibility and are performed under similar working conditions (29 USC 206(*d*)(1)). Many Japanese experts support this interpretation. See Yuko Nakashita: "Equal pay for equal work between men and women", in *Labour law and women workers* (Tyuo Keizai Sha, 1988), p. 123.

7 National Public Employees Law, art. 63, para. 1.

[8] The law concerning the salaries of public employees engaged in general affairs (Law 182 of 1953). This law also specifies hours of work. See Kazuo Sugeno: "Kokyo Bumon Rodo ho" (Labour law on the public service), in *Hoso Jiho,* Vol. 35, Nos. 10, 11 and 12, p. 39; Seiichiro Hayakawa and Akira Matsui: *Komuin no chingin (Salaries of public employees)* (Rodo Jyunpo Sha, 1979), p. 71.

[9] Local Government Workers Law, art. 24, para. 6, and art. 25, para. 3. It came into effect on 1 Apr. 1986. It came about as a result of amending the Working Women's Welfare Law (Law No. 113 of 1972).

[10] See Akira Okuyama: "Danjo Chingin Kakusa" (Wage differentials between men and women), in *Rodo Ho no Soten* (Labour law issues), 1979, p. 274.

[11] Since enactment of the EEOL, initial pay is almost the same for male and female employees in many companies. For instance, according to the Basic Wage Statistics Survey for 1986, conducted by the Women's Bureau, Ministry of Labour, the average starting salary for new male university graduates was JPY144,500 per month, an increase of 3.2 per cent over the previous year, while the figure for new female university graduates was JPY138,400, a 3.7 per cent increase. If the average starting salary for male university graduates is indexed at 100, the index for female university graduates was 97 in 1986.

[12] Judgement of 10 Apr. 1975, Akita District Court, 778 Hanrei Jiho 27.

[13] Judgement of 28 Mar. 1985, Morioka District Court, 450 Rodo Hanrei 62.

[14] Judgement of 26 Jan. 1989, Tokyo District Court, 533 Rodo Hanrei 45.

[15] Judgement of 4 Dec. 1986, Tokyo District Court, 1215 Hanrei Jiho 3.

[16] The Association's employment system involved different treatment for female employees in the areas of recruitment, hiring, job assignment and promotion. Traditionally such employment systems were typical of most Japanese companies, where men were expected to be managers while women were hired to peform mainly routine tasks as their assistants.

[17] See Kazuo Sugeno: *Rodo Ho* (Labour Law), 2nd ed. (1988), p. 116.

[18] LSL, art. 108.

[19] LSL, art. 109.

[20] LSL, art. 110.

[21] LSL, art. 99.

[22] e.g. LSL, arts. 19, 33, 85 or 101.

[23] LSL, art. 102.

[24] LSL, art. 115.

[25] The decision in the Akita Cooperative Bank case also supported this tendency; see Kazuo Sugeno: *Rodo Ho,* p. 116.

[26] The awarding of back pay is based upon art. 13 of the LSL. It states that labour contracts that do not satisfy the standards required by the law shall not be totally invalidated but only those parts that actually violate the law. The parts that are invalidated shall be replaced by clauses that do satisfy the standard required by the LSL.

[27] Parkinson, op. cit., p. 627.

[28] See Kensuke Mukui: "Wage discrimination between men and women, and the principle of equal pay for equal work", in Toshio Kuroda et al. (eds.): *Current Women's Labour: Wage and Employment of Women Workers* (1978), pp. 115-116.

7

Equal pay in the Netherlands

*I.P. Asscher-Vonk**

1. Introduction

The problem of the unequal pay of men and women came to the attention of the Government shortly after the Second World War.[1] The government body responsible asked the Foundation of Labour for advice about measures that would improve women's wages. The Foundation only wanted equal pay for specific men's work that was performed by women. As far as wages in general were concerned, they took the view that wages should be related to need.

International moves have been important in the realisation of equal pay in the Netherlands. The Equal Remuneration Convention, 1951 (No. 100), restarted the discussion, albeit without concrete results. The Treaty of Rome, and especially the equal pay provision of Article 119, gave the issue momentum. Nevertheless, as late as 1965 collective agreements were still being approved that were contrary to the equal pay principle.

The individual right to equal pay was embodied in the Minimum Wages Act of 1968[2] and the preceding Minimum Wages Order of 1966. Under the 1966 Order women who usually did the same work as men under similar circumstances were entitled to minimum wages.

The Minimum Wages Act did not distinguish between men and women. Part-timers who worked less than one-third of the usual working week were, however, and still are, excluded from the scope of the Act, an exclusion that especially affects women. The Act also allows for the possibility of the Minister giving an employer dispensation from the obligation to pay minimum wages. This possibility was used for the last time in 1972. The dispensations given were all for women in female-dominated industries: textiles, confectionery, leather, clothing, laundry, baking and sugar manufacturing, and for domestic staff in private households.

Although, thanks to the minimum wages measures, equal pay was for a large part realised in the early 1970s, the situation did not meet the standards set by Convention No. 100. The equal pay principle was not applicable to all employees, and equal pay was limited to pay for equal work, rather than work of equal value. The Equal Pay Directive of 1975[3] obliged EC Member States to take measures to bring about equal

* Professor, Faculty of Law, University of Amsterdam.

pay for equal work or work of equal value. This Directive was implemented by the Equal Pay Act of 1975.[4] For civil servants equal pay was provided for in the Act of 2 July 1980.[5]

Today, the equal pay principle rests largely on the Civil Code and the Equal Treatment Act.

1.1 The legal basis for equality of pay

The Constitution[6] of the Netherlands contains a very general provision on equality that was implemented in 1983, on the occasion of the last amendment to the Constitution. Article 1 of the Constitution reads: "All persons on Dutch territory are treated equally in equal cases. Discrimination on the ground of religion, creed, political faith, race, sex or on any other ground is not permitted", while article 3 reads: "All Dutchmen are equally eligible for public service."

The legal basis for equality of remuneration[7] is article 1637*ij*[8] of the Civil Code and article 1*a*(1) of the Equal Treatment Act.[9] Article 1637*ij* applies to employer-employee relationships generally, article 1*a* of the Equal Treatment Act to civil servants. Article 1637*ij*(1) reads:

> An employer shall not make any distinction between men and women when concluding a contract of employment, providing training for a worker, determining his conditions of employment, deciding on his promotion or terminating his contract of employment. The expression "conditions of employment" does not include benefits or claims under any pension scheme.

A departure from this provision is permitted only where a person's sex constitutes a determining factor, or where women's protection is involved, particularly in relation to pregnancy or maternity, or where the departure is designed to place women in a privileged position in order to remove existing inequalities.

Article 1637*ij* explicitly recognises both direct and indirect distinction between men and women. Direct distinction includes distinction on the grounds of pregnancy, confinement and maternity. Indirect distinction means distinction on the ground of qualities other than sex, for instance marital status or family circumstances, that results in a distinction on the ground of sex. Retaliatory dismissal of a worker who has lodged a complaint under these provisions is expressly forbidden.

Article 1*a* of the Equal Treatment Act makes a very similar provision in relation to civil servants specifically. It should be pointed out here that Article 119 of the Treaty of Rome has had direct effect since 8 April 1976.[10] This means that individuals may claim equal pay even where the national legislation does not provide for it (in occupational social security schemes, for example, which are excluded from the Equal Treatment Act) in so far as the benefit in question is to be considered wages, or where the national law would be contrary to the 1975 Directive. However, no litigation appealing especially to Article 119 has taken place in the Netherlands.

1.2 The definition of pay

Equal pay is defined in articles 7 and 9 of the Equal Treatment Act. When employment conditions are being compared, article 7 states the basis of comparison shall be "the wage which is normally received in the undertaking where the worker on whose behalf the comparison is made is employed, by a worker of the other sex for work of equal value or, in the absence of such work, for work of approximately equal value". Article 9 further states: "The wage received by the worker concerned shall be deemed to be equal to the wage that a worker of the other sex normally receives for work of equal value if it is calculated on the basis of equivalent criteria." According to article 7 "wages" means the remuneration payable by an employer to a worker in return for his job, not including benefits or entitlements under any pension scheme. Article 9 also stipulates that account shall be taken of elements of wages other than cash in accordance with the marketable value that can be assigned to them. This coincides with the concept of wages contained in the Civil Code, where wages are understood to be any remuneration due by the employer to the employee.[11] Tips given by third parties are not wages, nor are expense allowances. It is important whether the payment is actually due. Gifts, given of the employer's free will, are not to be considered wages, but supplements or bonuses are. Social security benefits are not counted as wages.[12] Again, claims or entitlements under a pension scheme are explicitly excluded. This may in a number of cases be contrary to Article 119 of the Treaty of Rome.[13]

Pay for time not worked is counted as wages, since the employer is bound to pay it. Deviation from these provisions, which under certain circumstances is possible, must not be different for men and women: that would be contrary to the equal treatment principle, as laid down in article 1637*ij* of the Civil Code.

Equality is required as regards each element of remuneration. Total remuneration may, however, be unequal, for reasons to be discussed in 2.1 below.

1.3 The definition of "equal work"

According to article 7(1) of the Equal Treatment Act, equal work is defined as "work of equal value or, in the absence of such work, ... work of approximately equal value".

1.4 Scope of the equal pay provisions

The equal pay provisions are inserted in the Civil Code and the Equal Treatment Act. The scope of the Law on the Labour Contract in the Civil Code is limited to those relationships where the employee is personally bound to perform work in the employer's service on payment of wages (article 1637*a*). This definition includes part-time workers, because their labour relationship usually meets these requirements. Article 9(3) of the Equal Treatment Act makes specific provision for the calculation of the wages of part-timers on a pro rata basis. Case law more often than not considers home-based workers and casual workers to be self-employed, either because they are not obliged to perform the task personally, or because they are not in the employer's service, meaning that they do not have to follow his instructions concerning the performance of the task.[14] These people are therefore often outside the scope of the equal pay legislation contained in the Civil Code.

Article 1*b* of the Equal Treatment Act broadens the scope of relationships to situations where an individual, body corporate or public authority lets somebody perform work in his service, not necessarily on a paid basis. As said above, an important group of workers that stays outside the scope of the equal pay legislation contained in the Civil Code does so because they are *not* considered to perform their task in the service of the employer. Article 1*b* seems only to include a slightly wider group (for instance, people who are employed at the same time as receiving a social security benefit) within the scope of the Act. Since home-based workers and casual workers are for a large part women, applicability of the equal treatment legislation to them would be especially important. This group, however, remains outside its scope.

A number of people who are excluded from the scope of the national legislation may nevertheless be able to claim equal pay under Article 119 of the Treaty of Rome or the Equal Pay Directive.[15]

Employees in the public sector – including members of the armed forces – are covered by article 1*a*(1) of the Equal Treatment Act, which confers similar protection to article 1637*ij* of the Civil Code.

2. Procedures for determining "equality"

2.1 Permitted justifications for differences in pay

The Preparatory Documents for the Equal Pay Act[16] state that the principle of equal pay means that the same criteria should be applied for calculating men's and women's wages. The wages actually paid to men and women for work of equal value may differ: the Preparatory Documents mention working overtime and seniority as examples of factors that may cause differentiation in wages that is not contrary to the Equal Pay Act.

The Equal Treatment Committee has treated the question of wage differentiation in a number of advices. Training, age and experience were all considered to be permitted bases for differentiation.[17] The fact that the wages of a man that a woman compared herself with were supplemented up to the level of the wages the man received formerly, which were for a job he was now no longer able to do because of disability, also constituted a valid reason for differentiation.[18] On the other hand, where a man and a woman performed work of equal value, the fact that the man had originally applied for a higher job was not considered a permitted basis for differentiation.[19] In a case where a female lawyer was paid less than all but one of her male colleagues, the employer argued that each lawyer's pay was determined in individual negotiations. Factors taken into account were effort, expectations based on commercial and other qualities, contacts, and so on. The Committee concluded that the same criteria were applied in determining the wages of the men and the woman, in conformity with the law.

In another case[20] not granting a woman an annual salary rise was defended by the employer on the grounds that the woman, a dentist, had an Indonesian diploma, of which the employer could not determine the value, and that in his opinion the woman's performance was inadequate. The Equal Treatment Committee concluded that the woman was entitled to equal pay: the arguments put forward by the employer did not establish a permitted basis for differentiation.

These decisions unfortunately do not yield a clear picture of what circumstances constitute a valid basis for pay differentiation between men and women who perform the same work or work of (nearly) equal value.

The issue of the validity of justifications for unequal pay when jobs are of (nearly) equal value has also come before the courts. In one such case a medical representative, employed for over ten years, found out that she was getting paid less than her male colleague, recently promoted to sales supervisor.[21] The woman's new male colleague also got paid more than she did. According to the Equal Treatment Committee, the jobs of medical representative and sales supervisor were not of equal value, but the Committee made, of its own accord, a comparison with her new colleague. However, this colleague was paid more because of his schooling, age and experience. There was, in the Committee's view, no question of unequal pay. In the procedure before the cantonal judge the employer claimed dissolution of the employment contract. This the judge awarded.

In another case on this issue, the tribunal disagreed with the Committee's view.[22] The collective agreement set out the minimum wages for different jobs in a newspaper firm. It also specified the maximum leeway which the employer had to pay individual employees more than the minimum. Making use of this leeway, the employer paid male canvassers more than female canvassers. The women deemed this difference in pay not to be justified.

The Equal Treatment Committee's view was that the employer did have a certain freedom in the matter, but in using this freedom he should not come in conflict with the Equal Pay Act. In this case there was unequal pay.

But the Central Committee for Clerical Personnel in Newspapers rejected the Equal Treatment Committee's advice: the men's higher pay was based on experience and professional skill. The women could not prove discrimination, and the case was dismissed.

2.2 *The role of job evaluation*

Job evaluation plays a central role in the assessment of work. Article 8 of the Equal Treatment Act prescribes:

> For the purposes of article 7 work shall be assessed in accordance with a reliable system of job evaluation; to this end recourse shall be had as far as possible to the system customary in the undertaking where the worker concerned is employed. In the absence of such a system the work shall be fairly assessed in the light of the available information.

Job evaluation schemes have become widely used in the Netherlands in the years since the Second World War. The guided wages policy, followed till 1968, made the existence of such schemes desirable. Job evaluation schemes are used in almost 40 per cent of enterprises with 20 or more employees.[23] They are usually applied only to lower- and middle-level jobs. In some sectors job evaluation is prescribed by the collective agreement. One such is the Collective Agreement for Hospitals, which refers to the "functieboek" (Book of functions).

Article 8 also prescribes that the job evaluation scheme should be a reliable one: if no job evaluation scheme or an unreliable one is used in an enterprise, the assessment of work has to be made in good faith. The Preparatory Documents[24] state that if no job evaluation scheme or an unreliable one is used, a sounder scheme will be applied. In practice what happens is this: the officers of the LTD (Loontechnische Dienst/Technical Wages Department),[25] when making an inquiry assess the claimant's job and the job of the person she is comparing herself with, using the enterprise's job evaluation scheme or another widely used one. However, the LTD does not as a rule make a job evaluation if from interviews with the employer and the employee it is apparent that they agree about the value of the jobs.[26]

2.3 Sex bias in job evaluation

The application of a job evaluation scheme is no guarantee of non-discriminatory practices. Unequal pay may exist in an enterprise because the job evaluation scheme used is itself discriminatory, or is applied in a discriminatory way.

There is also debate as to when a job evaluation scheme should be regarded as reliable.[27] Smit-Voskuijl[28] examined a number of widely used job evaluation schemes that were generally considered reliable. She stresses that it is necessary to examine both the application of the job evaluation schemes and the schemes themselves. According to Smit-Voskuijl schemes may be found to be discriminatory for different reasons. One of them is the choice of factors to be used as criteria. The question is whether factors that are characteristic of traditionally female jobs are sufficiently valued. The relative weighting of factors is also important.

Urged by Parliament, the LTD was commissioned to examine job evaluation schemes. Its report, issued in 1988[29] concluded that women do not seem to be systematically injured by the *application* of job evaluation schemes. An investigation into the de facto discrimination *within job evaluation schemes themselves* was also promised. However, preliminary investigations suggested that an investigation of job evaluation schemes would not lead to unambiguous, absolute findings, and the Minister of Social Affairs and Employment decided not to go ahead with the investigation.[30]

2.4 The scope of comparison

In the Equal Pay Act 1975, now repealed, article 3(2) allowed the possibility that:

> where no work of equal or approximately equal value is done by a worker of the other sex in the undertaking where the worker concerned is employed, the basis shall be the wage that a worker of the other sex normally receives, in an undertaking of as nearly as possible the same kind in the same sector, for work of equal value or, in the absence of such work, for work of approximately equal value.

This provision was not incorporated in the Equal Treatment Act, as amended in 1989, which means that the equal pay provisions only apply to workers employed by the same employer. This was explained by the fact that the possibility enshrined in article 3(2) had not been made use of.

This seems to me a rather unconvincing argument, given that the use of the Act as a whole was minimal.[31] It seems possible that if more use is made of the Equal Treatment Act in the future, a provision such as that in article 3(2) of the Equal Pay Act will be missed.

3. Enforcement arrangements for implementing equal pay policies

3.1 The different methods of enforcement

Enforcement of the equal pay legislation is predominantly based on complaints. An individual who thinks that the Equal Treatment Act has been violated in her regard may claim equal pay before the cantonal judge or, if she is a civil servant, before the Civil Servants' Tribunal (Ambtenarengerecht).

Article 20*a*(1) of the Equal Treatment Act opens up the possibility of instituting a class action:

> Bodies corporate enjoying full legal capacity whose work includes promoting the interests of persons who would be entitled to lodge a complaint under article 1637*ij* of the Civil Code and the provisions of this Act, may institute proceedings to get declared unlawful any act that is in violation of these provisions, so that that act is prohibited or that an order is issued to undo the consequences of that act.

Article 13 of the Equal Treatment Act institutes the Equal Treatment Committee, and article 14 states that the Committee may, upon receiving a written application or of its own accord, institute an inquiry as to whether an illegal distinction between women and men has been made. A written application can be filed by:

(a) anyone who considers that a distinction covered by the Civil Code or the Equal Treatment Act is being or has been made to their detriment;
(b) any individual, body corporate or competent authority wishing to know whether they are making such a distinction;
(c) a person responsible for determining a dispute concerning such a dis- tinction;
(d) a works council that considers that in the enterprise for which it was established such a distinction is being or has been made (or, in the case of civil servants, a committee established for a particular department);
(e) a body corporate enjoying full legal capacity whose work includes promoting the interests of persons who would be entitled to lodge a complaint under article 1637*ij* of the Civil Code or the Equal Treatment Act.

3.2 Government bodies involved in implementing equal pay

The Equal Treatment Committee is composed of 11 members, including the chair. Each member has a deputy. The members and deputies are appointed and removed from office by the Minister of Social Affairs and Employment, acting in agreement with the Ministers of Internal Affairs, Justice, and Education and Sciences. Before such members are appointed, the Minister must give the employers' and workers' organisations that form part of the Foundation of Labour (Stichting van de Arbeid) an opportunity to submit nominations. Likewise he must ask the Minister of Internal Affairs to consult with representatives of municipalities, provinces and "polder-boards", and with the central organisations of civil servants, and to give them the opportunity to make proposals. In addition, the Minister must consult the Emancipation Council, an advisory body set up by the Government in 1981. The composition of the Committee must reflect the fact that it deals both with private employment relationships and with civil servants.

The members and their deputies hold office for four years at the most, but they can be reappointed immediately. The Minister of Social Affairs and Employment provides secretarial services for the Committee. The Committee may, in the performance of its duties, avail itself of the assistance of civil servants designated by the Minister of Social Affairs and Employment for that purpose.

It may also request any information or documents that, within reason, it regards as necessary for its work. Everybody applied to in this way has to supply the information and documents completely and truthfully – but without prejudice to their right to refuse to answer for reasons of professional confidentiality – and within the time limit put by the Committee. If obtaining this information involves costs, the Committee must obtain the approval of the Minister. On the other hand, if an application to the Committee for an opinion refers to specific people, the Committee is not competent to involve them in the inquiry if they object to this.

The Equal Treatment Committee deals exclusively with matters concerning equal pay for men and women and the equal treatment of men and women in employment. It is an independent committee of experts. "Expert" in this context means having sufficient knowledge and experience of the field covered by the legislation.

The basic aim of the Committee is to prevent the need for judicial procedures. Especially when discrimination has taken place unintentionally, because of unfamiliarity with the law, the Committee's opinion will be followed voluntarily, and court proceedings would in any case be unnecessary.[32]

Article 19 of the Equal Treatment Act states that the Committee shall issue an annual report of its activities and publicise that report. The Committee thus has a means of making more general observations.

The Equal Treatment Committee has no means of enforcing its decisions, nor are its decisions binding on the courts, as is apparent from the various cases in which a court has rejected the Committee's advice.

In one case the Committee gave four separate advices – all to the same effect – and its view was eventually upheld by the Supreme Court. This case involved a female housekeeping assistant who earned less than a male cleaning employee and filed a claim for equal pay.[33] There were historical reasons for the difference in pay: because of different labour market conditions in the past, the employees concerned were employed on a different pay level. The Equal Treatment Committee felt that the jobs concerned were of (nearly) equal value, and should be paid equally, but the cantonal judge considered that the jobs were different. Because of these differences, men were attracted by one job, and women by the other, remuneration apart. Both men and women worked as housekeeping assistants, and the pay was not discriminatory.

In a further advice, the Committee stated again, on the basis of job evaluation, that the work was of (nearly) equal value and that the woman was entitled to equal pay. In its view, this claim was no less valid because the difference in pay was not caused by a difference in sex. The district court then set aside the judgement of the cantonal judge and asked for further advice, and the Committee gave – for the third time – the same advice.

Four more housekeeping assistants, employed by the same employer, sought the Committee's advice and got the same answer. The district court awarded the claim, and the employer appealed to the Supreme Court.

The Hoge Raad (Supreme Court) upheld the district court's judgement, on the following grounds:

(1) The view that, when an employer is bound by a collective agreement, the employees cannot file a claim under the Equal Pay Act, even when their jobs are not mentioned in the collective agreement concerned, is not correct. This view would prejudice the protection aimed at by the equal pay legislation and so cannot be deemed right.

(2) Given that the woman did get less pay than the men she compared herself with, it was beside the point that the reasons for the difference in pay were historical ones. It was also beside the point that both jobs were open to men and women, with women and men being paid equally for doing it.

(3) Considering the specific expertise of the Committee and the importance that is, in view of article 16 of the Equal Pay Act, to be attached to its advices, sound reasoning is necessary to reach a decision at variance with such an advice. The onus is upon the employer to present such reasoning when he has been found in the wrong by the Committee.

This last consideration may, however, have lost some of its force since the recent amendment of the equal pay legislation. Article 16(1) of the Equal Pay Act read as follows: "The employee's claim for equal pay is dismissed, if this employee fails to produce, when filing the claim, an Advice, ... [of the Committee] not exceeding three months of age."

The Equal Pay Act was repealed in 1989, and no such rule is included in the new Equal Treatment Act; seeking the Committee's advice is now a voluntary matter.

In another case the district court felt that the Committee had taken a too limited view of its role.[34] This case involved a female clerical worker, whose pay was lower than that of a male "receiver of incoming goods". The fact that her male colleague loaded and unloaded trucks was not in her view a reason for the difference in pay, so she claimed back pay. It became clear from the LTD's investigation that the jobs of "registrator" and "receiver of incoming goods" were not of (nearly) equal worth, but the jobs of "registrator" and "filler" certainly were. Because the woman's claim was based on a comparison of her job with that of a "receiver of incoming goods", the Equal Treatment Committee could only give advice founded on that comparison, and there was no question of unequal pay.

The district court's view was that the Committee should have made a closer comparison of the claimant's job and that of a "filler", especially as, generally speaking, a claimant cannot be expected to have sufficient expertise to evaluate the jobs to be compared. The court then asked the Committee for further advice. In its judgement of 11 March 1981, the court annuled the judgement of the cantonal judge, who had dismissed the claim on the basis of the Committee's first advice. The court therefore ordered the employer to pay back pay.

This case raises the question of how active the Equal Treatment Committee should be. The district court clearly considered that its task should not have been limited to investigating the job of the claimant and the job she compared herself with, if comparison with another job would clearly have given an answer more favourable to the claimant. But should the Committee conduct an investigation into the value of any number of jobs a claimant's job might be compared with, even when the claimant herself does not make that comparison?

3.3 Legal costs

No costs are involved in the Equal Treatment Committee proceedings. As far as court proceedings are concerned, costs increase according to the level of the court (cantonal, district, regional and the Supreme Court) and the sum being claimed in the proceedings. Legal aid is available to those on a low income,[35] who only have to pay a small contribution.

Apart from court fees, there is the risk that if a claimant fails she will have to pay her opponent's costs, including lawyers' fees, if these were necessary.[36] Whoever loses the case will have to pay the costs. The judge may order each party to pay their own costs if both have been proved partly in the wrong.[37] The risk of having to pay costs may be a serious deterrent to anyone considering starting legal procedures.

3.4 Remedies

There are two remedies available to individual claimants. First, the individual agreement under which discriminatory wages are paid is declared null and void.[38] Second, the employee can claim from the employer wages that are equal to the wages an employee of the other sex normally receives for work of equal value. This provision used to be laid down in the Equal Pay Act (article 2). The Equal Treatment Act, as amended on 1 July 1989, does not contain any provision to this effect, but since it was the intention that this amendment should leave the equal pay legislation virtually unchanged,[39] it may be assumed that anyone who has suffered illegal wage discrimination will be able to claim equal pay.

It can also be assumed that the obligation to pay equal pay is unlimited in so far as the future is concerned. A claim for recovery of pay due has to be made within two years from the moment the payment became due (that is, within two years from the moment when the wage discrimination began).[40] This time-limit is similar to the one prescribed in the Minimum Wage Act.[41] There are no suggestions that these provisions are insufficient. The question of the general effectiveness of the remedies available under the Equal Treatment Act before 1 July 1989 has, however, been raised in the legal literature, and serious doubts have been uttered in that respect.[42]

Article 20*a* of the Equal Treatment Act lays down specific remedies when enforcement of the Equal Treatment Act is sought through a class action. In a class action claimants may institute proceedings to get declared unlawful any action that is in violation of article 1637*ij* of the Civil Code or the provisions of the Equal Treatment Act, so that that action is prohibited or an order is issued to undo the consequences of that action.

3.5 Protection against victimisation

The termination of an employment relationship by an employer because a worker has lodged a complaint, either judicially or extra-judicially, under the provisions of article 1637*ij*(1) of the Civil Code, is prohibited, both by the Civil Code itself and by the Equal Treatment Act. However, the employer will not be liable to pay damages in such cases.

One may doubt whether these measures are sufficient. If we compare them with article 21 of the Works Council Act, which provides protection against reprisals for members, former members and candidates for the works council, two differences are notable. First, the Works Council Act offers protection against reprisals other than termination of the employment relationship: "The employer sees to it that... members of the Works Council... are not injured in their position within the enterprise because of their membership of the works council." Second, the Works Council Act gives a time-limit within which a former member of the works council cannot be dismissed in the usual way; the Equal Treatment Act gives no time-limit within which dismissal is presumed to be the consequence of a complaint under the Equal Treatment Act. If there were a time-limit within which any dismissal following a complaint pursuant to equal treatment would be subject to special regulation, such as needing the permission of a government body or judge, or would be considered null and void, or if there were a rule that when a person is dismissed within a certain time after making a complaint under the equal treatment legislation, the employer has to prove that the dismissal is not because of the complaint, the position of the claimant would be considerably stronger, because she would not be confronted with the difficulty of proving that she has been dismissed because of a complaint. It should be pointed out, however, that the Dutch Law of Proof does permit the judge, on grounds of fairness, to shift the burden of proof to the defendant.

3.6 The burden of proof

The main rule of the Law of Proof, that the party who states something has to prove it, unless any specific rule or requirement of fairness leads to another allocation of the burden of proof, is in principle applicable.[43] However, the Supreme Court ruled in the Binderen/Kaya Case[44] that no rule of law prohibits the judge from considering numerical, statistical differences as sufficient evidence of discrimination, or from considering differences of that kind as prima facie evidence, and on that ground shifting the burden of proof to the party accused of discrimination.

3.7 Access to information on wages

In two cases[45] the Supreme Court has ruled that there may be circumstances that justify alleviating the burden of proof for the claimant, on whom that burden normally rests in accordance with the main rule, by requiring the respondent to provide sufficient data to give the claimant starting points for furnishing possible proof.

Enterprises do not have any duty to submit periodic reports to the Equal Treatment Committee.

3.8 Experience with equal pay claims

Only a very small number of complaints have come before the Equal Treatment Committee.[46] The number of court cases must be even smaller. A few key cases have already been mentioned, and a few more are worth including here.

In the case of *Panhuyzen-De Bruijn* v. *St. Lambertus,*[47] 14 female employees of a hospital filed a complaint with the Equal Treatment Committee. Household department assistants, a kitchen assistant and a laundry assistant all compared their jobs with that of a (male) household assistant; a receptionist and a coffee counter attendant compared themselves with male colleagues who held the same jobs. Most of the women also chose a second person to compare themselves with. All the women earned less than the men.

The Committee's view was that the work of each female employee was of (nearly) equal value with the work of at least one male worker they had compared themselves with. Each woman was therefore entitled to pay equal to that of the man. Three women filed a claim for equal pay. But the district court took the view that the wages for performing a job that has been held by one worker only, and only temporarily at that, does not count as the pay the worker "normally receives". The employer's plea that the women could not in good faith refer to the Committee's advice because this advice was incorrect was dismissed by the court: the judge could come to his own conclusions about the advice. The judge concluded that the work of a household department assistant was not of (nearly) equal value with the work of a male household assistant and that of various other male colleagues, and the claim was dismissed.

In *Lodel* v. *Algemeen Directeur van het Medisch Centrum Alkmaar,*[48] the issue of promotion and its role in raising pay came up. The claimant worked as head of the operating room, location north, of the Medisch Centrum Alkmaar (MCA) with the rank of ward matron. Head of the operating room location south, was a male colleague, who was from 1 January 1979 promoted to the rank of ward master A. This became known to the claimant in October 1982, and she then requested promotion. Her request was turned down, and she filed a complaint with the Equal Treatment Committee.

The Equal Treatment Committee judged that the MCA had acted contrary to article 1(1) of the Equal Treatment Act (Civil Servants) because there was a difference between the claimant's wages and those of a male colleague she compared herself with.

The MCA still defended its decision to promote the man and not the woman. The Centrale Raad van Beroep, the highest court in disputes concerning civil servants, examined whether the MCA could reasonably have reached this decision or whether the decision otherwise contravened any principle of law or general principle of administration.

The court stated that the decision could pass the test: the immediate reason for the man's promotion was that because of his personal qualities – qualities that the claimant did not possess to such a degree – he had become involved in the preparation for integration within the hospital, bearing in mind that he was head of an integrated ward. Moreover, the wage that the claimant did receive was – and the claimant did not contest this – not inadequate in itself.

The court therefore judged that the MCA had reached their decision reasonably.

It should be noted that the Ambtenarenwet (Act concerning civil servants), applicable in a dispute between civil servants and public authorities, allows only a limited test to be applied to the authorities' decision. Even so, the reasoning in this case does not seem very satisfactory. It was not clear that the man's involvement in integration at the time under consideration made the work he did of more value than the work the claimant did.

Indirect discrimination, a notoriously difficult area, was the subject of the following case.[49] According to the HOS System (Herstructurering Onderwijs Salariëring: Note on the restructuring of wages in education and teaching), grading in primary schools of the new type is influenced by the wages last received. Former heads of infant schools, mainly women, are thus graded lower than former heads of primary schools of the old type.

The Equal Treatment Committee considered that the wages-last-paid criterion amounted to prima facie evidence of indirect discrimination. The former level of wages is not relevant to the job so this is not a justifiable distinction. The fact that another aspect of the grading was mainly favourable to women provided no justification.

The district court stated that it was not mainly women that were directly disadvantaged by the HOS system. Of those that were disadvantaged, 43 per cent were female and 57 per cent male. It was not right to choose one relatively small group from these and compare it with another, also relatively small group. The claim was dismissed. The regional court upheld this view, stating that the claimants had not convincingly countered the authorities' defence concerning the weight of management experience of former heads of infants schools in relation to that of former heads of primary schools of the old type. The authorities' defence on this point could serve as an objective justification, so there was no infringement of the Equal Treatment Act.

Another case brought up the issue of employees who are considered to be breadwinners receiving higher wages than other employees.[50] The wages of the other employees could not be raised because the employer was in financial difficulties. The wages could not be averaged out because the wages of the breadwinners would then drop, and this was deemed unjust considering their family circumstances.

The Equal Treatment Committee took the view that the use of the breadwinner concept does involve indirect discrimination, because it is, generally speaking, detrimental to women. The consideration that a basic income should be guaranteed to the family was no longer relevant, as a consequence of a number of measures in the field of secondary income.

The cantonal judge stated that claims for wages came under the Equal Pay Act, article 16 of which required that an employee's claim under the Act must be accompanied by an advice of the Equal Treatment Committee given within the preceding three months. In this case, the Committee's advice was older than three months. The claim was therefore dismissed on procedural grounds.

The cantonal judge based his decision on article 16 of the Equal Pay Act, now lapsed. Even so, the decision seems not to be right. The Equal Pay Act only covered direct discrimination in wages. Indirect discrimination in wages and other conditions of employment was covered by the Equal Treatment Act, which did not contain a provision comparable with article 16 of the Equal Pay Act.

The final case in this section dealt with the relationship between international law and national provisions.[51] The claimants appealed against the deduction of 1.85 per cent from their wages for January and February 1983 under the Act of 12 January 1983.[52] They referred to the right, specified in Article 7 of the International Covenant on Economic, Social and Cultural Rights (New York, December 1969), to equal pay for work of equal value without distinction of any kind.

The tribunal (the Raad van Beroep, the court of first instance in matters concerning civil servants) considered that the provision referred to had direct effect, and could be relied upon by a citizen in a situation where attained equality, based on equal value, was prejudiced, as was happening in this case. The Centrale Raad van Beroep, however, stated that this provision of the Covenant could only have direct effect when the situation in which application of the provision was asked was sufficiently structured and concrete. Moreover, provision could only be presumed to have direct affect in cases of identical or nearly identical work, and not when the work was (only) of equal value. The court considered it very important that the functions with which the claimants compared themselves were not fulfilled under the same authority.

These considerations brought the Centrale Raad to the conclusion that in the present case the situation was not such that Article 7 had direct effect. The claimants could not therefore rely upon it.

4. The role of the social partners

4.1 Union-management involvement in implementing equal pay

Equal pay is one of the social and economic issues that is subject to discussion between trade unions and employers' organisations. These discussions take place at central level, in the Social and Economic Council (SER) and the Foundation of Labour (Stichting van de Arbeid). The principle of equal pay began to be incorporated into collective agreements in the 1970s.[53] One method of involving trade unions and employers' organisations in the implementation of equal pay policies is by seeking their advice as members of the SER or the Foundation of Labour. There is a legal obligation on ministers to ask the advice of the SER about all important measures in the social and economic spheres.

On 12 May 1980 the Foundation of Labour issued a recommendation "to, observing objective job qualifications, give employees of equal value equal chances for work and equal chances within the enterprise, without regard to factors such as age, sex, sexual disposition, marital status, religion, colour, race or ethnic descent, nationality and political choices". This recommendation is now included in a great many collective agreements.[54] In most cases, however, it remains a formulation of intentions rather than affording concrete rights.

The Works Council Act gives the works councils the task of being "on guard against discrimination in the enterprise and especially to promote equal treatment of men and women".[55]

4.2 *Union-management involvement in determining job evaluation criteria*

Article 27(1) of the Works Council Act states that the employer needs the approval of the works council for any decision concerning the establishment, modification or withdrawal of a remuneration and job evaluation scheme. This does not apply if the matter has been dealt with in a collective agreement.

4.3 *Monitoring collective agreements*

Article 4 of the Remuneration Act[56] obliges parties to a collective agreement to inform the Minister of Social Affairs and Employment when a collective agreement is concluded or amended, and to submit a copy of the agreement. A collective agreement takes effect from the date that the Minister sends a Notification of Receipt of the relevant documents.

A provision in a collective agreement contrary to the equal pay principle rule can, in theory, be declared not binding.[57] The Act of 1937 on declaring provisions of collective agreements generally binding or not binding[58] gives the Minister this authority. However, this authority has never been used for the implementation of equal pay.

When the Minister finds that a provision in a collective agreement is contrary to the equal treatment/equal pay principle he uses the Notification of Receipt to point out to the parties to the agreement that the agreement contains a discriminatory provision.[59]

Periodically the Ministry publishes reports on its findings. Up till now these reports have shown that only in one-third of the (not very many) cases where provisions in collective agreements have been found to be discriminatory, have the provisions been amended.

An information leaflet for the parties to collective agreements is to be issued exploring the exigencies of the Equal Treatment Act. One may wonder whether this will be effective, since it is not probable that ignorance of the law is the cause of the limited effect the Minister's remarks on discriminatory provisions in collective agreements have had.

Moreover, the Minister has resolved not to declare generally binding throughout a whole industry provisions in collective agreements that are contrary to the equal pay/equal treatment principle. But the Minister still does not intend to declare provisions in collective agreements unbinding, even for the parties to an agreement, because they are contrary to the equal pay/equal treatment principle.[60]

5. Conclusions

The LTD found that in 1985 about 29 per cent of the enterprises were contravening the equal pay principle.[61] The LTD identified two situations that may cause differences in pay between men and women. The first is where more than one collective agreement is applicable. The second is where labour market forces are influential. The LTD points out that only in 8 per cent of cases of infringement of the equal pay principle was the employer willing to remove the inequality.

On the other hand, in that same year, 1985, only six complaints about unequal pay reached the Equal Treatment Committee.[62] Jaspers and Kleinwee[63] explain the discrepancy between the actual extent of unequal pay and the small number of complaints in terms of a lack of information about the law and the imprecise formulation of the provision. They add that it is sometimes difficult to find a person of the opposite sex to compare one's wages with. Moreover, the protection of claimants against victimisation could be improved, for example, by offering the possibility of compensation[64] and by offering protection against any formal reprisal, not only against dismissal.

The remedies available in cases of unequal pay also seem insufficient. The possibility of penal sanctions, rejected in 1975, should be reconsidered, given the poor observance of the equal pay principle.[65]

The suggestions made here are all to be found in the legal literature prior to the amendment of the Equal Treatment Act of 1 July 1989. However, the amendment of that date embodies only one of the previously suggested improvements, that is, an extension of the possibility of class actions.

Notes

[1] The development of the equal pay principle in the Netherlands is described by W.J.P.M. Fase: *Vijfendertig jaar loonbeleid in Nederland* (Alphen aan den Rijn, 1980), p. 370.

[2] Stb. 1968, 657.

[3] No. 75/117/EEC.

[4] Stb. 1975, 129. Repealed on 1 July 1989.

[5] Stb. 1980, 284.

[6] Constitution of the Kingdom of the Netherlands, 24 Aug. 1815, Stb. 45, last revised 17 Feb. 1983, Stb. 70.

[7] In this text equal pay is read as equal pay for men and women. Art. 7 of the Act on the employment of disabled workers (Stb. 1986, 300) contains a provision concerning equal pay for (partially) disabled workers.

[8] Art. 1637*ij* of the Civil Code was implemented on 1 Mar. 1980, as part of the equal treatment legislation (Stb. 1980, 86), and amended on 1 July 1989, when the Equal Treatment Act was also amended.

9 Act of 1 Mar. 1980, Stb. 1980, 86, as amended 1 July 1989, Stb. 1989, 168.

10 European Court of Justice, 8 Apr. 1976, Defrenne Case.

11 Kamerstukken 13 031, 3, p. 10.

12 Equal Treatment Committee (undated), see A.M. Gerritsen: *Rechtspraak glijke behandeling m/v* NJCM, 1988), p. 114.

13 W.J.P.M. Fase: *Gelijke beloning naar communautaire normen* (SMA, 1982), p. 175.

14 Cf. M.G. Rood and M.J. van de Ven: *Flexibele arbeidsrelaties* (Alphen aan den Rijn, 1988).

15 75/117/EEC.

16 Kamerstukken 13 031.

17 CGB 20 July 1976, Gerritsen, op. cit., p. 107.

18 CGB 19 Mar. 1982, Gerritsen, op. cit., p. 146.

19 CGB 29 Apr. 1982, Gerritsen, op. cit., p. 147.

20 CGB 23 Apr. 1985, Gerritsen, op. cit., p. 161.

21 Kantonrechter (Cantonal Judge), Eindhoven, 11 May 1978.

22 Central Committee for Clerical Personnel in Newspapers, 30 July 1979.

23 Loontechnische Dienst: *Functiewaardering in Nederland* (Ministerie van Sociale Zaken en We kgelegenheid, 1987).

24 13 031, 3, p. 7.

25 Appointed pursuant to art. 17 of the Equal Treatment Act to assist the Equal Treatment Committee in its inquiries.

26 A.Ph. Jaspers and M.T.C. van Kleinwee: *Gelijke behandeling je goed recht?* (Ministerie van Sociale Zaken en Werkgelegenheid, 1985).

27 O.F. Smit-Voskuijl: *Functiewaardering als maatstaf bij de Wet Gelijk Loon* (Sociaal Maandlad Arbeid, 1989), p. 295 ff. Kamerstukken 19 908, 5, pp. 39, 40; 19 908, 6, pp. 13, 37.

28 Smit-Voskuijl, op. cit.

29 Loontechnische Dienst: *Toepassing van bedrijfstakgebonden functiewaarderingsregelingen in Nederland* (Ministerie van Sociale Zaken en Werkgelegenheid, Sep. 1988).

30 Loontechnische Dienst, op. cit., p. 2.

31 See e.g. Annual Report of the Equal Treatment Committee, 1987, p. 84: recently there have been fewer than ten complaints a year.

32 Kamerstukken 19 908, 3, pp. 7-8.

33 HR 13 Nov. 1987, NJ 1989, 689, Gielen/St Bavo.

34 District Court, Amsterdam, 26 Mar. 1980 and 11 Mar. 1981.

35 Act concerning legal aid for poor persons.

36 Code on legal proceedings in civil cases, s. 56.

37 ibid.

38 Civil Code, art. 1637ij(7) and Equal Treatment Act, art. 1*a*(7).

39 19 908, 3, p. 22.

40 19 9088, 3, p. 25; 13 031, 3, p. 10.

41 Stb. 1968, 657.

42 I.P. Asscher-Vonk: *Vorderingen tot naleving van de Wet gelijke behandeling van mannen en vrouwen* (SMA, 1980), p. 503.

43 Wetboek van Burgerlijke Rechtsvordering, art. 177.

44 HR 10 Dec. 1982, NJ 1983, 687.

45 HR 11 Dec. 1987, NJ 1988, 339, and HR 20 Nov. 1987, NJ 1988, 500.

46 The 1987 Annual Report of the Equal Treatment Committee (the last issued) gives a figure of 134 for complaints pursuant to the Equal Pay Act in the years 1980-87. From 1985 to 1987 less than ten complaints per year were filed.

47 Rechtbank (District Court) 's-Hertogenbosch, 2 Mar. 1984 and 2 May 1985, Rolno. 3387/82, 3388/82 and 3389/82.

48 Centrale Raad van Beroep, 29 Dec. 1987, AW 1986, 222.

49 Regional Court 's-Gravenhage, 17 Feb. 1988, Rolno. 86/787.

[50] Kantonrechter (Cantonal Judge) 's-Hertogenbosch, 27 May 1986, Rolno. 2935/85 VT.

[51] Centrale Raad van Beroep, 16 Feb. 1989, NJ/AB 1989, 164, TAR 1989, 77.

[52] Stb. 1983, 1.

[53] Fase: *Vijfendertig jaar loonbeleid in Nederland*, p. 377.

[54] I.P. Asscher-Vonk: *Toegang tot de dienstbetrekking* (Alphen aan den Rijn, 1989), p. 33.

[55] Works Council Act, art. 28(3).

[56] Act of 12 Feb. 1970, Stb. 69.

[57] Fase: *Vijfendertig jaar loonbeleid in Nederland*, p. 379.

[58] Stb. 1937, 801.

[59] *DCA-bevindingen* (Ministerie van Sociale Zaken en Werkgelegenheid, Sep. 1988, p. 98.

[60] Letter from the Minister of 19 May 1988 to the Foundation of Labour.

[61] Loontechnische Dienst: *De naleving van de Wet gelijk loon voor vrouwen en mannen in het Nederlandse bedrijfsleven 1985* (Ministerie van Sociale Zaken en Werkgelegenheid, July 1987).

[62] Annual Report of the Equal Treatment Committee, 1985.

[63] A.Ph. Jaspers and M.T.C. Kleinwee: *Gelijke behandeling je goed recht?*, p. 30.

[64] Cf. I.P. Asscher-Vonk: *Het Voorontwerp van een wet gelijke behandeling: De sanctionering* (NJB, 1982), pp. 390.391.

[65] Cf. ibid., p. 390.

8

Equal pay in Spain

*Teresa Pérez del Río**

1. Introduction

1.1 The legal basis for equality of pay

The legal cornerstone of the equal pay principle in Spain is article 35.1 of the 1978 Constitution, which states: "All Spanish citizens are entitled to adequate remuneration... with the total exclusion of discrimination on grounds of sex."

This article is developed further by article 28 of the 1980 Workers' Statute Act, which provides for the principle in the following terms: "The employer is obliged to pay the same wage for *equal work* with regard to *both the basic wage and wage bonuses* without any discrimination on grounds of sex." In turn, article 17 pronounces null and void "Decrees, collective agreement clauses, individual agreements and unilateral decisions on the part of the employer that contain favourable or adverse discrimination regarding employment, wages, the working day and other working conditions on the grounds of sex".

These two precepts are complemented by two administrative rules which are fundamental as regards wages: Decree 2.380/1973 of 17-VIII (henceforth DOS) and the Ordinance of 22 November 1973 (henceforth 00S).

1.2 The definition of pay

The meaning of "wages" as used in article 28 of the Workers' Statute must be defined. In this respect article 2 of the DOS states: "The earnings of workers in money or in kind for the professional offering of labour services to an employer, in payment for employment, whatever the type of remuneration, or paid rest periods, computed as work, will be legally considered as wages."

Article 4 of the DOS, which regulates pay structure, distinguishes between two elements: the "basic wage" and "wage bonuses". By "basic wage" is understood that part of the worker's pay that is fixed according to work time (for hours, days, weeks or

* Titular Professor of Labour Law, University of Cádiz.

months). If no such rate of pay is specified, the official minimum wage will be taken as the basic wage. Wage bonuses are regulated by article 5 of the DOS, which states that wage bonuses must be one of the following types:

(a) *personal,* for factors such as seniority, qualifications, knowledge of another language or any other special knowledge;

(b) *job-related,* such as increments for difficulty, toxicity, danger, dirtiness, machine operation, flying, sailing, loading, shifts or night-work;

(c) *for quality or quantity of work,* such as bonuses, gratuities, incentives, extra payment for attendance, assiduity or overtime, whether or not these are linked to a system of remuneration based on output;

(d) *those that fall due over periods that exceed a month,* such as irregular gratuities or a share in the profits;

(e) *in kind,* such as board, lodging, house, or any other provisions;

(f) *residential,* such as those for the island provinces or posts in Ceuta and Melillá.

Neither the repayment of expenses incurred by workers in the course of their work nor welfare payments or additional payments made by enterprises voluntarily (voluntary social security programmes) will be considered as part of remuneration.

1.3 The definition of "equal work"

With respect to the concept of "work", article 28 of the Workers' Statute refers to "equal work", not to work that is exactly "the same", nor to "work of equal value". Besides not fulfilling the international regulations in this area, this has given rise to some court decisions which identify the concept of "equal work" with that of "the same work", thus preventing or seriously hindering the fight against indirect discrimination which arises as a result of inadequate job evaluation schemes.

1.4 Scope of the equal pay provisions

In theory, no worker can be excluded from the prohibition of wage discrimination, since the law does not make any distinction, with the obvious exception of self-employed workers, as the Workers' Statute only applies to those who are in someone else's employ. It is a completely different matter whether it can be guaranteed in practice that the principle will be applied to home helps and home-based workers, and casual or part-time workers, who may be the victims of indirect discrimination, which, as will be seen, is difficult to eliminate by means of legal procedures.

2. Procedures for determining "equality"

2.1 Permitted justifications for differences in pay

Both the general state regulations and those concerning collective agreements permit differing basic rates of pay according to age. For example, the official minimum wage fixed by the State by annual decree differentiates between workers under and over 18 whenever, according to court decisions, the former do a job of inferior value to that done by over-18s.

It is also normal to find differentiation in basic rates of pay based on professional categories, which are established according to professional qualifications and specialisation, in short according to the levels of knowledge required to carry out the different jobs included in each professional category and the degree of responsibility involved.

Factors like skill, physical effort, seniority, danger and difficulty are taken into consideration in the fixing of bonuses. We saw that all bonuses must be includable among those listed in article 5 of the DOS. If this is not the case, and if the payment in question is regarded as wages, by elimination it will be considered to be included in the basic wage.[1]

2.2 The role of job evaluation

Systems of objective job evaluation currently play an extremely small part in Spanish employment practices. For some time now, what is known as the Bedaux productivity wage system has been used in some collective agreements. This system frequently alludes to an average performance of 60 Bedaux points. An incentive bonus will be awarded to each worker according to the number of points received. This is on top of the basic time wages and at a rate provided for in the collective agreement. This system obviously cannot be said to be an objective job evaluation scheme in any strict sense. Objective job evaluation is an option that is barely taken advantage of, wages being fixed through collective bargaining, following a system of sheer inertia: a percentage increase is applied annually, based on the level of wages in the previous agreement, which totally avoids making things any more complicated. The effect of this system is to perpetuate traditionally discriminatory practices, which were originally direct and have now become indirect.

2.3 Gender-dominated occupational categories and jobs

Although there are no jobs or occupational categories reserved for women, or where a preference for women is specificed, not even that of "Matron", it is clear that women are in fact concentrated in certain sectors, categories and posts. Given that employers can choose freely whom they wish to employ, one must conclude that employers do prefer to employ women for certain jobs.

Women continue to be concentrated in five of the 36 branches of activity included in the Active Population Survey. In the primary and industrial sectors the ratio of men to women is almost two to one, with one out of two wage-earning women working in the services sector, mostly the public sector, education and the health service being the biggest employers. In the industrial sector a similar number of men and women can be found in chemicals and food, more women in textiles. A great many young women are involved in retail trade.

As far as professional categories are concerned, a greater proportion of male managers are to be found and also a greater proportion (almost double) of women in the position of office clerk. Second-level administrative work continues as always to be performed mainly by women. Most women, whether they go beyond primary education or not, are to be found at the level of office clerks or saleswomen, whilst most men who have completed primary education reach the level of management or middle management. A greater proportion of qualified workers are men, and conversely more women occupy the non-qualified worker categories.

There is no specified proportion of workers of one sex that leads one to consider a certain category or sector as being "gender-dominated" or segregated. One of the employment measures adopted in 1986[2] has as its aim the promotion of the employment of women "in professions where they are under-represented". It does not, however, specify any percentage in order to determine which those professions are.

2.4 The scope of comparison

The comparison of duties in order to evaluate posts, either in the same company or in different companies which come under the same collective agreement, is difficult, given the fact that, in recognising the principle of equal pay, article 28 of the Workers' Statute refers only to the "same work" and not to "work of equal value". A comparison of duties and posts in different companies has never in fact been attempted. Although in theory this comparison would be possible, given that the Workers' Statute does not specifically refer to the place where the "same work" is to be carried out, it is unlikely that a request to compare them would be accpeted by the labour court. It is worth pointing out, however, that there are jurisprudential precedents that accept the comparison of duties and posts between different places of work that are part of the same company and so come under the same collective agreement.

2.5 Examples of indirect discrimination against women

A study recently carried out in Spain (1989), commissioned by the Institute of Women, has revealed the following facts: the average wage of Spanish working women is 18-19 index points below that of men. The relationship between women's wages and men's shows an overall index of discrimination of 81.5 per cent, without taking into account other factors. If we examine wage payments for men and women according to occupational categories, we can see that the differences in income increase with occupational status, becoming greatest among top and middle management. The variable that seems most to influence income level is "experience", in the case of both men and women, and the greatest wage discrimination is related not to years of schooling but to years of work experience. It seems that men's professional experience is valued more highly than women's, as there is a great difference in their earnings when they both have the same experience.

A series of recent cases concerning the regulation of wages by collective agreement also suggests that, when basic wages are fixed, the sex of the workers who have traditionally held the different positions belonging to the various professional categories is frequently taken into account. In other words, although there are few collective agreements nowadays that actually fix different basic wages according to the sex of the workers, and "direct discrimination" has almost completely disappeared, posts traditionally held by women continue to be undervalued.

Paradigmatic cases here are those of the national footwear collective agreement, Artes Gráficas (Graphic Arts), and Gullon and Fontaneda Biscuits from the food sector. Until 1984 the nationwide footwear collective agreement included different wage schemes for men and women, in spite of the fact that they belonged to the same professional categories and worked in the same manufacturing department, the women's wages always being lower. A distinction was thus made for the same skill and job between male workers, Skilled Workman 1st, earning ESP1,825 a day, and female workers, Skilled Workwoman 1st, earning ESP1,722 a day. Faced with a claim of discrimination by the union, the labour court ruled null and void those clauses of the agreement that brought about differentiation on grounds of sex. As a result, a new agreement was negotiated according to which the posts in the manufacturing department were divided into groups: Group I included all the posts that had previously been filled by men alone and Group II those that had been filled by women. The posts in Group I were immediately evaluated higher than those in Group II so that, for example, a Skilled Worker 1st belonging to Group I (who is always male) will earn a higher wage than a Skilled Worker 1st belonging to Group II (who is always female), although, from the definition of the duties corresponding to these posts, it can be readily concluded that they are "similar". In short, direct formal discrimination was eliminated, but the real discriminatory situation remained, since the *basic rates of pay* were fixed lower for the categories and posts filled by women, without an objective evaluation of the jobs. As the principle of non-discrimination on the grounds of sex is formally respected (since theoretically all the workers belonging to Group I are entitled to earn the same wage, be they men or women), and furthermore as men and women never do exactly the same work (since all the former belong to Group I and the latter to Group II), this situation does not constitute a violation of article 28 of the Workers' Statute, which mentions "equal jobs" and not jobs of "equal value". Any move to eliminate this practice of indirect discrimination thus becomes unviable. Moreoever, if a male worker who has held a Group I post is temporarily or permanently assigned to a Group II post, he continues to earn the wage corresponding to the post for which he was originally employed. It is therefore quite normal for a male Skilled Worker 1st in Group II to earn a higher wage than a female Skilled Worker 1st in the same group.

Something similar occurred in the case of Artes Gráficas: until 1984 the collective agreement contained a scale known as Female Complementary Posts. The removal of this clause from the agreement by the competent jurisdiction led to the negotiation of a new agreement in which the word "female" disappeared from the system of classification, but the group or scale of Complementary Posts remained the same. These positions, which are filled almost exclusively by women, are evaluated in such a way that, for example, a Skilled Worker 1st belonging to this mainly female group earns the same as a Skilled Worker 3rd belonging to any other predominantly male group, without any objective job evaluation whatsoever. It is therefore noteworthy that article 6.2 of the same collective agreement includes the principle of non-discrimination on the grounds of sex.

In the Gullon and Fontaneda collective agreements, the workers in Group IV are divided into three subgroups: *(a)* production personnel, *(b)* auxiliary posts (both traditionally carried out by men), and *(c)* packing, wrapping and end-product personnel (mainly women). The latter subgroup's basic wage is fixed lower than that of the other two, who receive the same wage. No objective job evaluation exercise has been carried out, but the need for one is clear, since from the very names of the subgroups it can be deduced that greater specialisation and responsibility are required for posts in subgroup *(c)* than for those in subgroup *(b)*.

Wage discrimination frequently occurs in relation to wage bonuses too. The list of allowable bonuses contained in article 5 of the DOS includes traditional criteria of risk in jobs considered to be "male", especially in Spain where even today courts deem heavy, dangerous, unhealthy, night-time jobs unsuitable for women.

Consequently, the majority of collective agreements include bonuses that are basically applicable to male posts, and none based on criteria such as attention, speed and precision, all attributes that are commonly required for female jobs. Apart from being a breach of the Jurisprudence of the Community Court of Justice,[3] this seems to be a clear case of indirect discrimination.

One of the most blatant recent cases of discrimination in relation to wage bonuses was that of Jaeger Ibérica from the metal sector, part of the multinational group Fiat Matra. In February 1985 the workers' committee contested the implementation of the collective agreement, which contained what was known as an "assiduity bonus", whose express aim was to "respect the pay differences that existed among different workers of the company when the agreement came into effect". This clearly has nothing to do with attendance or non-attendance at work, as was implied by the name. For men this bonus was fixed at about ESP9,000, while for women it was less than ESP2,000. The obvious discriminatory nature of the bonus was recognised by a court decision and ratified on appeal by the Central Labour Court.[4] In both decisions the discriminatory nature of the assiduity bonus was emphasised; both courts found it invalid and ordered the company to pay the same bonus to men and women. The company repeatedly refused to abide by the decision, and the case was not resolved until May 1989 after almost a month's strike, which ended with a commitment on the part of the company to put into effect pay equality between men and women and not to enter into any more delaying tactics.

Another recent discrimination case with not such a happy ending, which had major repercussions on public opinion, involved the company Avon Cosmetics SA. In every department of this company there are professional categories reserved exclusively for men and others reserved exclusively for women. Subgroup B of Workers' Group IV (Industry Professionals) has the following categories: *(a)* Skilled Worker 1st, *(b)* Skilled Worker 2nd, and *(c)* Specialist and Unskilled Assistants. Obviously the skilled posts belong to a higher category and so command a higher basic wage. However, Avon also pays its employees an "Avon Personal Bonus", and the sum paid to those holding posts in the third subgroup, which is occupied exclusively by men, is notably higher than that paid to the other two categories, which are occupied exclusively by women, even though it is recognised that the women's jobs are considerably more complicated and uncomfortable than the men's and require greater concentration and responsibility. Avon has not undertaken any job evaluation, and the Avon Personal Bonus makes up

75 per cent of the total wages that the workers earn, since the periodic pay increments are almost exclusively based on that bonus, as recognised in the court decision. The Avon Personal Bonus is not assigned on the grounds of seniority in the company or the professional category of the workers. All the Specialist and Unskilled Assistants received a larger bonus than the female employees, even though the latter had been employed longer. The men's jobs could be said to require greater physical effort, but they are performed in the area of the end-products department in collaboration with, or in support of, the female skilled workers who are responsible for making the orders, monitoring the goods, packaging the products, identifying their destinations, and dispatching them.

The conclusion reached by the judge was that the women's jobs were at least "equal" or of "equal value" to those performed by the men (notice the identification of the two concepts), and the company was ordered to "restore the damaged right and to implant a fair wage system". This meant that the female Skilled Worker 2nd should receive the same Avon Personal Bonus as the Unskilled Assistants, while the female Skilled Worker 1st should receive the same as the Specialist Assistants. These payments were to be backdated to the moment the contested agreement came into force.

In fact there was an appeal against this judgement before the Central Labour Court which revoked it and acquitted the company on what seem to me to be debatable procedural grounds.

The cases of indirect discrimination that have been examined are not the most frequent type, but they are the most flagrant. The sole adoption of risk criteria characteristic of "male" posts (like the need to exert physical effort) when fixing wage bonuses, and "forgetting" to evaluate adequately the attributes required for posts regarded as "female" (speed, continuous attention, precision), leads to a discriminatory situation which cannot be eliminated by traditional procedures. If discrimination is to be eliminated, objective criteria for job evaluation must be adopted, which are relevant to the current characteristics of production processes.

3. Enforcement arrangements for implementing equal pay policies

3.1 The different methods of enforcement

The procedures provided for in the current legislation for the enforcement of equal pay policies are based, on the one hand, on individual or collective claims (individual or collective conflict procedures) and, on the other, on the procedure for monitoring the legality of collective agreements, established in article 90.5 of the Workers' Statute (see 4.3 below).

3.2 Government bodies involved in implementing equal pay

There is no organisation whose sole function is to make sure that the principle of non-discrimination in pay is applied. The Institute of Women, created in October 1983 as part of the Ministry of Social Affairs, has been conferred with the sole responsibility of fighting sex discrimination and promoting equal opportunity policies for women, in employment and working conditions, among other areas. It has worked out a three-year plan of action (1988-90), which includes studying and analysing the wage situation of women. The aim is to be able to propose effective measures for the elimination of discrimination once its causes have been analysed. As already mentioned, this study was published in February 1989.

Over the past few months the unions have shown a special interest in the issue of equal pay, in particular the Union Confederate Office for Working Women *(Secretarías Confederales para la Mujer)* of Workers' Committees *(Comisiones Obreras)* and the General Workers' Union *(Unión General de Trabajadores)* who, by means of research work and the publicising of discriminatory practices, alert public opinion and urge the competent official bodies to initiate the appropriate proceedings.

None of these organisations has the power to receive or initiate claims or complaints concerning gender-based pay discrimination, and they have even less power of a jurisdictional, arbitrational or conciliatory nature. The only thing they can do, and they are doing, is to investigate and publicise cases of discrimination and propose measures for its eradication.

The only exceptions here are the committees of workers' representatives and staff delegates. Article 64 of the Workers' Statute entrusts these representative bodies with the general responsibility of making sure that the relevant labour regulations (including those relating to equal pay), agreements, working conditions and prevailing customs in the company are adhered to, and gives them the power to take suitable legal action in the event of non-fulfilment.

3.3 Legal costs

Neither the individual nor the collective conflict procedure involves any costs for the workers who make use of them. In practice, the only possible cost to be faced is the lawyer's fees, and this depends on whether the claimant is a member of a union or not and whether the procedure used is the individual one. Most unions offer legal advice and defence free, or at least at a low cost, to their members. In any case, a "legal aid" lawyer can be requested,[5] though this might not be appropriate given the complexity of this type of action.

If the procedure followed is that for collective conflict, the cost for the claimants is low and normally paid by the unions.

3.4 Remedies

The effects of a decision in favour of the aggrieved claimants will depend yet again on the type of procedure used. In the collective conflict procedure a favourable decision will bring about the annulment of the contested clause of the agreement,[6] and the right of the claimant will be recognised to receive a wage at least the same as that for the posts (usually male) with which comparison was requested in order to demonstrate discrimination. This will be backdated to the moment when the contested agreement was signed or came into effect, with a maximum limit of one year before the first proceedings were initiated.[7]

If the individual procedure is followed, the decision will only affect the claimants, and the discriminatory clause in the agreement cannot be annulled. This proceeding, denominated "indirect contestation", brings about the non-application, in the case of an individual, of a certain clause of an agreement that has been deemed discriminatory. The right of the aggrieved worker not to be discriminated against is thus recognised, and also therefore her right to earn an adequate wage and to receive the due back pay under the same terms as stated for the collective conflict procedure.

It is a different question whether, later, the jurisdictional acceptance of the individual claim will lead indirectly to a collective claim, as would happen if the rest of the aggrieved workers started *a posteriori*, through their representatives, the process of "direct contestation", or the collective conflict procedure, as a result of which the disputed clause could be annulled. The ordinary individual conflict procedure is clearly defective from the point of view of obtaining effective judicial remedy. The collective conflict procedure is more effective from all points of view: effectiveness of the remedy, protection against possible reprisals against the claimants, and obtaining adequate publicity, and the resulting support of public opinion for the workers.

One problem with the collective conflict procedure is that it must be initiated by the legal or union representatives of the workers, who may well be precisely the same ones who signed the agreement to be contested, and may therefore not be enthusiastic about going back on their own actions. At present, the elimination of discriminatory practices does not appear to be at the top of the list of Spanish union claims.

3.5 Protection against victimisation

Spanish legislation provides no protection against "retaliatory dismissals". An employer who is found to have dismissed a worker without cause (insufficiently justified) is obliged to pay compensation but has no obligation to reinstate the worker who has been unfairly dismissed. Only where the dismissal qualifies as "radically invalid" (occurring in violation of fundamental rights such as union freedom) is there any obligation to re-employ, making it impossible to substitute compensation. In other words, unless the retaliatory dismissal qualifies as "radically invalid" (and to date we have no evidence that it ever has been), the dismissed worker will only be entitled to receive modest compensation.

Given the high level of unemployment among women in Spain (almost 28 per cent), the possibility of dismissal, even with compensation, discourages many women from defending their rights using the individual conflict procedure. As already stated, this danger does not arise when the collective conflict procedure is used.

3.6 The burden of proof

The burden of proof usually lies with the claimant. However, a decision of the Constitutional Defence Tribunal[8] modified this principle in cases where a claim is made against discriminatory dismissal (in general, not only on grounds of sex). Here it falls on the person against whom the claim is made, once a case of discrimination has been shown to exist, by means of a preliminary presentation of factual evidence.

Under Basis 19 of the new 1989 Bases of Labour Procedure Act, this reversal of the burden of proof will apply in all cases where discrimination is alleged, not just in relation to dismissal:

> in those proceedings in which the plaintiff alleges sex discrimination it is always the person against whom the claim is made who must give objective, reasonable justification for the measures adopted and for their proportionality by means of the kind of proof that he deems suitable.

3.7 Access to information on wages

With respect to information and monitoring as regards wages, article 64.1.3 of the Workers' Statute stipulates that the workers' legal representatives in the company must issue a report before the employer can implement decisions in such areas as the recommendations of time and motion studies, the introduction of bonuses or incentive payments, and job evaluation. However, the contents of the report are in no way binding on the enterprise.

The employer has no obligation to make information on wages available to any other social or administrative body, with a view to monitoring compliance with equal pay policies. Theoretically, it is the Labour Inspectorate that acts in this area, either on its own initiative or as a result of complaints presented by workers. But this body is already proving inadequate as regards its basic function, which is to ensure that safety and hygiene requirements at work are met, and to supervise the regulation of job promotion and welfare payments.

Companies have to fill in a questionnaire which is sent periodically by the National Institute of Statistics for the compiling of the wage survey, but the purpose of this is merely informative. Incidentally, the questionnaire ceased to include the variable "sex" in 1977 for no apparent reason, thereby making it difficult, if not impossible, to study wage differences between men and women and to analyse their causes.

Bearing in mind that this indicator is used in all OECD countries, and that information on this subject is constantly being requested in questionnaires sent by the EC and the ILO with a view to monitoring compliance with the international regulation in this area, the Institute of Women, in its Equal Opportunity Plan for 1988-90,[9] includes the following aim:

> The revision of the questionnaire sent to companies so as to introduce the variable "sex" in the different professional categories, branches of economic activity and other areas treated in the said questionnaire, analysing and publishing the results broken down between men and women.

3.8 Experience with equal pay claims

The most flagrant cases of wage discrimination in recent years have already been presented in section 2.5. These are by no means the only cases, but they are the most significant. The women's claims have met with varied success, and some have yet to be resolved definitively.

In the case of Jaeger Ibérica (clear discrimination over the assiduity bonus), the Central Labour Court pronounced in favour of the aggrieved worker.[10] In the case of Avon Cosmetics, on the other hand, the same Central Labour Court acquitted the company on procedural grounds, although judgement had first been pronounced in favour of the claimants.[11] The proceedings which had been initiated were suddenly not deemed to be appropriate, and the employer was acquitted without any deeper consideration of the matter.

The other cases expounded are still pending final resolution, and some others have been resolved by means of industrial action. In *Sociedad Espanola de Metales Preciosos SA* (Precious Metals Public Association), for example, technological innovation affected various jobs and made a new evaluation of those jobs necessary. Among these was the position classified as "Service Secretary", which includes a great many of the women employed in the company. Following the new evaluation, this was situated at 4 on an evaluation scale from 1 to 12.

The discriminatory nature of this evaluation was obvious from the outset, since the definition of duties that the evaluation was based on did not include all the tasks that were actually carried out, such as commercial work performed over the telephone or attending to clients in direct sales. Only the administrative work was recognised, and scarcely any value was given to the knowledge of languages that was necessary for the work as intermediaries in direct sales. All these duties and knowledge were valued, on the other hand, for the exclusively male post known as "Commercial Traveller", which was given an evaluation level of 7. The only actual difference between the two posts is that the latter make business trips (which are paid for by means of expense allowances) while the former do not.

On repeated occasions different women applied for the post of "Commercial Traveller" and the company turned them down on the sole grounds that the post was reserved for men. In July 1987 the workers' committee was presented with a demand that the evaluation of the post "Service Secretary", affecting 15 women, be revised. The aggrieved workers based their claim on the greater degree of responsibility involved in the tasks that they were gradually being given, without corresponding financial remuneration.

Faced with the company's refusal to revise the evaluation, the aggrieved workers decided to come out on strike. After three months during which they had to fight, almost without help, not only against the company but also against their own colleagues who were not at all sympathetic towards their stand, they won their claims, which consisted of: *(a)* a change of name of the post to "Commercial Officer", thus opening up the possibility of men entering this job; *(b)* an increase of two levels (from 4 to 6) in the evaluation scale; and *(c)* an increase in wages, making them comparable with those of male workers in the post of "Commercial Traveller".

It is worth emphasising, however, that at the moment no woman in the company occupies a management post or position of responsibility, and access to positions like "Commercial Traveller" or "Customs Dispatcher", which are obviously better paid, continues to be denied them.

There is no precise up-to-date information with respect to the amount of use that is made of the legal procedures provided for in the Spanish legal code for protection against violation of the equal pay principle. What is clear is that not many cases are presented or solutions reached, especially compared with the level of wage discrimination that is revealed by the statistics.

There appear to be various different reasons for this. On the one hand, as already stated, there is the inadequacy of the ordinary individual conflict procedure for dealing with cases of discrimination: the parties in this procedure, and therefore the remedies, are exclusively individual, and furthermore there is no specific protection against retaliatory dismissal. As a result the only really effective procedure is the collective conflict procedure.

The problem here is that the competence to initiate this procedure lies with the same workers' representatives who signed the collective agreement containing discriminatory clauses, especially when this agreement is a company one. Another factor here is that the workers' committees at company level are becoming increasingly unionised, i.e. their members are affiliated to unions, and the unions obviously give priority to defending the interests of their members. Given the low level of female membership of unions, the fight against discrimination cannot be a basic strategic priority for the unions at present.

With regard to judicial procedures initiated by individuals, bodies specialised in detecting and eliminating discrimination should be able to act on behalf of the individual victims. Moreover, it is crucial to provide effective protection against retaliatory measures by employers against workers who assert their right to equality. It also seems important that the judicial decisions in such cases should be able to go beyond the direct conflict between the parties. If it were possible to prove that a particular instance of wage discrimination was the result of managerial discriminatory policy, it would then be possible to oblige the employer to modify it. An "indirect contestation" could then result in the removal of the contested discriminatory clause.

Finally, it is crucial that the public authorities, social partners and citizens in general should become aware of discrimination, and that its eradication should be seen as a priority objective. If this is not the case, it is unlikely that the measures adopted will be sufficiently effective.

4. The role of the social partners

4.1 Union-management involvement in implementing equal pay

Article 28 of the Workers' Statute, which, as mentioned above, imposes on employers the obligation to pay the same wage for "equal" work, is the only legal provision that can be taken as a point of reference with regard to a policy of equal pay. There is no normative provision that requires the social partners to take positive steps to ensure pay equality, although, as already mentioned, article 64 of the Workers' Statute does impose upon the workers' representative bodies a general responsibility to ensure that the company adheres to the relevant labour regulations and collective agreements. The social partners, especially the unions, are however beginning to recognise the need to put an end to the discriminatory situation faced by women in employment, but this recognition is, for the moment, of limited significance.

With respect to "informal" or non-legal procedures to solve conflicts over pay, all the collective agreements must establish as part of the "necessary content" of the agreement what are known as "Parity Commissions" (joint commissions of employers and employees) to deal with "whatever matters are referred to them" about the collective agreement itself.[12] These matters are usually related to the interpretation of the agreement. Most often the commissions are granted the role of mediating and arbitrating in individual or collective conflicts, without damaging the right of the workers to "effective jurisdictional protection" recognised in the Constitution and asserted in many court decisions. These commissions can, therefore, if the collective agreement confers that responsibility on them, intervene in individual or collective conflicts over the application of the equal pay principle without prejudicing the right of victims to have recourse, when necessary, to "formal legal procedures".

4.2 Union-management involvement in determining job evaluation criteria

There is also a tendency for union and management to negotiate systems of job evaluation that are more relevant to the issue of discrimination than those used up until now. The legislation does not lay down at what bargaining level job classifications have to be determined (branch, local or plant). Normally, except in the case of large companies, the job classifications are contained in agreements with a wider scope than just one company. In fact, we believe that it will be necessary to adopt provisions in this area at levels higher than that of the collective agreement, possibly even at an international level. The social partners could then take these as a point of reference when introducing and implementing such systems.

The most common practice at present is unfortunately to take the path of sheer inertia: the two sides in collective bargaining continue to take as their point of reference, when determining annual pay rises, previous agreements or even completely out-of-date labour ordinances whose job evaluation criteria are usually directly or indirectly discriminatory. Clear examples of this are provided by the national footwear collective agreement and *Artes Gráficas:* not only were the job evaluation schemes themselves discriminatory, as was recognised by the courts, but discriminatory professional classifications were used as a basis for the evaluations.

As already noted, article 64.1.3 of the Workers' Statute obliges the employer to obtain a report from the workers' representative bodies in the company before implementing any decisions in respect of job evaluation. They can therefore "inform" the employer, when an evaluation of posts is carried out, that the evaluation is directly or indirectly discriminatory and, as a result, does not comply with the prevailing labour regulations (i.e. article 28 of the Workers' Statute). If the employer does not modify the evaluation, the workers' representatives can take legal action.

4.3 Monitoring collective agreements

Article 90.5 of the Workers' Statute establishes a procedure for monitoring the legality of collective agreements. In Spain, agreements must be presented to the competent labour authority (the competent department of the Ministry of Employment) for registration. If, at this stage, the labour authority deems that any agreement infringes the law or seriously harms the interests of a third party, it will, on its own initiative, approach the competent jurisdiction, which will take measures to rectify the supposed anomalies, after hearing both sides and following the procedure laid down in article 136 of the Labour Procedure Act. This procedure has proved inadequate from the point of view of the effective judicial protection of the right to equal pay, especially the elimination of indirect discrimination. Collective agreements continue to contain an appreciable number of clauses that are illegal or of debatable legality, and not only concerning sex discrimination.

The reason for this is, in our opinion, the inadequate staffing of the labour authorities concerned. Another reason is that the staff are inadequately specialised. The solution could lie in making more money available and above all in making sure that staff responsible for monitoring agreements are sufficiently knowledgeable. Ideally, specialised bodies with sufficient experience to detect indirect discrimination and considerable knowledge of job evalualtion should be made responsible for monitoring adherence to the equality principle.

There is no time-limit within which the social partners have to reach an agreement concerning wages or any other matter, apart from the exception included in article 10 of the 1977 Labour Relations Decree Law which regulates collective conflicts, where it is stated that "the government, at the proposal of the Ministry of Labour, taking into account the duration or the consequences of a strike, the positions of the parties and the serious harm that it might bring to national industry, may decide on compulsory arbitration".

5. Conclusions

Despite the number of years that have passed since Spain in 1968 ratified the ILO's Equal Remuneration Convention, 1951 (No. 100), which enshrines the equal pay principle, it is clear that Spanish women continue to experience serious discrimination in this area. Although one can detect a certain reluctant tendency on the part of public authorities and unions to fight this situation more effectively, the procedures provided for in current legislation are inadequate and inappropriate, and therefore do not conform with the principle of "effective judicial protection of rights" laid down in article 24 of the Spanish Constitution.

There have also been attempts to introduce objective job evaluation schemes and, above all, to diversify female work, which is considered to be a vital condition for the eradication of discrimination in working conditions, including pay. When men and women occupy the same jobs without distinction, discrimination, if it does exist, will be "direct", which makes it possible for it to be eradicated even by traditional procedures. The segregation of jobs by sex, on the other hand, makes "indirect" discrimination possible, and this is much more difficult to detect. The traditional procedures have proved ineffective in eliminating this type of discrimination.

As emphasised by the survey on wage discrimination carried out by the Institute of Women, an improvement can be detected in the pay of younger women when compared with that of men in the same age range. There seems to be a correlation between the age of the workers and pay differences (the older the workers, the greater the differences in pay between men and women). This could indicate a tendency towards greater equality in wages or, with the general improvement in educational standards among the younger generation, a tendency for the differences and discrimination between men and women to decrease in the medium to long term. In the medium to short term, on the other hand, the analysis shows that the income differences in favour of men increase with occupational status, reaching their highest level among management and middle management. The greatest differences appear among workers with over 14 years' schooling.

However, the variable that most influences the level of wage income for both men and women is experience: the greatest pay jumps occur as a result of this variable. Within this context, male experience is valued higher than female experience, starting from an average level of education and becoming more pronounced at higher educational levels.

All this demonstrates that to insist solely on, or give top priority to, problems of professional skills in the Equal Opportunity Plans is not going to be sufficient, or even essential, to eliminate wage discrimination because it will generate "discouragement" among the female workforce. Increased access to employment and diversification of jobs are vital. The fight against sexual segregation is a top priority, as is the strengthening of procedures to provide protection against discrimination.

The equal pay legislation in force in Spain is ineffective basically for the following reasons:

(1) The legislation refers not to "work of equal value" but simply to "equal work", which makes it difficult, if not impossible, to detect and eradicate "indirect" discrimination.

(2) The procedures provided for victims of wage discrimination to seek redress are totally inadequate: they do not include the procedural instruments that have been shown to be effective in this area and in the fight against discrimination in general (the possibility of social groups initiating the procedure; decisions having effect beyond the mere conflict between the parties; totally effective protection for aggrieved workers faced with possible reprisals by the employer, etc.).

Notes

1 OOS, art. 10.

2 Ministerial Order 21-2-1986, arts. 14 and 15.

3 Decision 1-VII-1986, case 237/85, *Rummler* v. *Dato Druck*, among others.

4 s. 22-VII-1986.

5 Labour Procedure Act, art 3.

[6] Workers' Statute, art. 17.
[7] Workers' Statute, art. 59.2.
[8] No. 119/1981 of 23-XI.
[9] Part III: "Employment and working conditions".
[10] s. 10-V-1989.
[11] s. 19-IV-1989.
[12] Workers' Statute, art. 85.2.

9

Equal pay in the United Kingdom

*Christopher McCrudden**

1. Introduction

1.1 The legal basis for equality of pay

The main legislative provision requiring equality of pay between men and women in Great Britain is the Equal Pay Act 1970, which came into force in 1975. This Act has been amended by a number of other pieces of national legislation, in particular the Sex Discrimination Act 1975, the Equal Pay (Amendment) Regulations 1983 and the Sex Discrimination Act 1986. In Northern Ireland, the main provision is the Equal Pay Act (Northern Ireland) 1971, as amended by the Sex Discrimination (Northern Ireland) Order 1976, the Equal Pay (Amendment) Regulations (Northern Ireland) 1984, the Sex Discrimination (Northern Ireland) Order 1976, and the Sex Discrimination (Northern Ireland) Order 1987.[1]

The main European Community (EC) provisions which bind the United Kingdom so far as equal pay is concerned are Article 119 of the Treaty of Rome and Council Directive 75/117/EEC (the Equal Pay Directive).

1.2 The definition of pay

The Equal Pay Act applies to terms and conditions of employment generally and not just "pay" or "remuneration" (as in the Equal Pay Directive). Equality is required, in the circumstances to be considered subsequently, in the terms of the man's and the woman's contract of employment. This includes pay, but goes beyond it.

If any term in the woman's contract is less favourable than a term of a similar kind in the man's contract, the term of the woman's contract is treated as modified so as to make it not less favourable, irrespective of whether she is as favourably treated as the man when the whole of his contract and the whole of her contract are considered.[2]

What is included in the terms of a contract will depend in any particular situation on the construction of the contract. The following have, for example, been

* Lincoln College, Oxford.

held to be included as terms of a contract: basic pay, benefits in kind such as the use of a car, cash bonuses and sickness benefits.[3]

The Equal Pay Act excludes pension schemes from the application of the Act. It provides that the Act shall not operate in relation to terms of the contract of employment "related to death or retirement, or to any provision made in connection with death or retirement other than a term or provision which, in relation to retirement, affords access to opportunities for promotion, transfer or training or provides for a woman's dismissal or demotion".[4]

These restrictions in the Equal Pay Act have led to claimants relying on the provisions of the Treaty of Rome. There has thus been considerable interpretation of the meaning of "pay" for the purposes of Article 119 in references from British courts to the European Court of Justice. The European Court of Justice has held that "pay" includes: the conditions for admission to an occupational pension scheme, where the benefits paid to employees constitute consideration received by the worker from the employer in respect of employment,[5] contributions paid by an employer in the name of the employees to a retirement benefits scheme, where the contributions are included in the calculation of employees' gross salary and directly determine the calculation of other advantages linked to salary;[6] and travel facilities accorded to employees after retirement.[7]

1.3 The definition of "equal work"

In the British statutory scheme, there are three grounds on which a person ("the applicant") may claim that she is doing work which may be compared with another person of another sex ("the comparator"): that she is doing "like work" to that person, that she is doing work which has been "rated as equivalent", or that she is doing work which is of "equal value" to that other person.

Section 1(4) of the Equal Pay Act provides that the determination as to whether a woman is employed on "like work" with men should be approached in two stages. First, is the work she does "of the same or broadly similar nature"? This has been interpreted as requiring consideration of the type of work involved and the skill and knowledge required to do it.[8] A broad judgement ought to be adopted. Second, if it is work of a broadly similar nature, are any differences between the things she does and the things the men do "of practical importance in relation to terms and conditions of employment"? This second limb of the test has been interpreted as meaning that only differences of a kind which the industrial tribunal would expect to find reflected in the terms and conditions of employment should be seen as "of practical importance" sufficient to defeat a claim. Trivial differences, or differences not likely to be reflected in the terms and conditions of employment, should be ignored.[9] In comparing her work with theirs, "regard shall be had to the frequency or otherwise with which any such differences occur in practice as well as to the nature and extent of the differences".

The Equal Pay Act also provides that a woman may claim equal pay where she is employed on work rated as equivalent with that of a man. This is the case if her job and his job have been given an equal value, "in terms of the demand made on a worker under various headings (for instance effort, skill, decision), in a study undertaken with a view to evaluating in those terms the jobs to be done by all or any of the employees in an undertaking or group of undertakings, or would have been given an equal value but for the evaluation being made on a system setting different values for men and women on the same demand under any heading".[10] The job evaluation exercise must be "analytical" in order to comply with these provisions, that is, the jobs of each worker covered by the exercise must have been valued in terms of the demands made on the worker under various headings.[11] Once a job evaluation exercise has been undertaken and has resulted in a conclusion that the woman's job is of equal value with the man's, it is not necessary for the pay structure to have been adjusted as a result of the job evaluation exercise for the woman to be able to proceed under this head.[12]

Unlike with "work rated as equivalent", where the employer is required to implement the findings of a job evaluation exercise which has been (in legal terms) voluntarily introduced by him, the third head of "equal value" provides that a woman may claim to be doing work of equal value to a man, and ensure that their jobs are evaluated, even where the employer has not voluntarily carried out a job evaluation exercise. Except where the particular man with whom the woman seeks to compare herself is employed on like work, or work rated as equivalent,[13] the woman may call in aid the legal process to *require* that a job evaluation exercise be carried out evaluating her job and the job she is arguing is of (at least)[14] equal value with hers, in terms of the demands made on her. The Act specifies that the demands are to be assessed "for instance under such headings as effort, skill and decision".[15] This provision was introduced after the European Court of Justice decided that the United Kingdom was in breach of the Equal Pay Directive.[16]

1.4 Scope of the equal pay provisions

The Equal Pay Act applies only in the case of contracts under which a woman is employed at an establishment in Great Britain. A comparison of the work of the applicant and that of a comparator is valid only when the applicant is employed in the "same employment"[17] as the comparator. This is regarded as being the case in four circumstances:

- where the applicant is employed by the same employer as the comparator in the same establishment;
- where the applicant is employed at the same establishment as the comparator though by a different employer, provided the employers are associated;
- where the applicant is employed by the same employer as the comparator though in another establishment, provided common terms and conditions of employment are observed either generally or for employees of the relevant classes;[18]
- where the applicant and the comparator are employed by different employers in different establishments, provided common terms and conditions are observed either generally or for employees of the relevant classes, and the employers are associated.

Two of these terms have a special meaning. For the purposes of the Equal Pay Act, "employed" has an extended meaning in comparison with general British labour law. It means "employed under a contract of service or of apprenticeship or a contract personally to execute any work or labour". Employers are "associated" if one is a company of which the other (directly or indirectly) has control or if both are companies of which a third person (directly or indirectly) has control.[19]

Homeworkers, part-time workers and casual workers are covered by the Act if they fall within the definitions and if they are able to find a relevant male comparator. The position with regard to homeworkers is further clarified explicitly by a provision in the Act that "where work is not done at an establishment it shall be treated for the relevant purposes as done at the establishment from which it is done or (where it is not done from any establishment) at the establishment with which it has the closest connection.[20]

The Equal Pay Act covers the public sector in much the same way that it covers the private sector, with the exception of the armed forces, which are excluded from the coverage of the Act.[21] The Act provides, however, that neither the Secretary of State nor the Defence Council shall make or recommend the making of "any instrument relating to the terms and conditions of service of members of the naval, military or air forces of the Crown, if the instrument has the effect of making a distinction, as regards pay, allowances or leave, between men and women who are members of those forces, not being a distinction fairly attributable to differences between the obligations undertaken by men and those undertaken by women".[22] Unlike the other provisions of the Act, this prohibition is not enforceable by an individual through the judicial process. Instead, either the Secretary of State or the Defence Council may refer to the Central Arbitration Committee for their advice on any question as to whether a provision made or proposed should be regarded as making an impermissible distinction.

There is no requirement that an establishment be of any particular size before it is included in the coverage of the legislation. As seen above, however, the applicant must be employed at an establishment in Great Britain. Precisely what constitutes employment at an establishment in Great Britain is set out in detail in the Sex Discrimination Act 1975.[23]

The Act does not operate in relation to terms which afford special treatment to women in connection with pregnancy or childbirth.[24] Nor, with two exceptions, does it operate in relation to terms in a contract of employment related to death or retirement, or any provision made in connection with death or retirement.[25] The first exception relates to terms in respect of access to membership of an occupational pensions scheme within the meaning of the Social Security Pensions Act 1975.[26] The second relates to discrimination as regards retirement age between men and women. This was established for the public sector by the European Court of Justice in *Marshall* v. *Southampton and South West Area Health Authority*.[27] The principle established in *Marshall* was extended to the private sector by the Sex Discrimination Act 1986.

The Act does not operate in relation to terms in the contract of employment affected by compliance with any laws regulating the employment of women.[28]

2. Procedures for determining "equality"

2.1 Permitted justifications for differences in pay

The British legislation provides that employers will succeed in justifying pay differences if they can show where a woman has established "like work" or "work rated as equivalent", that there is a "genuine material difference" between the woman's case and the man's "which is not the difference of sex". Where the woman has established "work of equal value", the employer must show that there is a "genuine material factor which is not the difference of sex".[29]

Employers have in the past raised a wide range of defences. Some have argued that they receive different average profits from the work done by men and the work done by women, and arguments have long been put that women are statistically more likely to miss work, and that they cost more to employ. Employers are not permitted to put forward these assertions as defences. However, other defences raised by employers have given rise to more legal controversy.

To succeed in a defence the employer must show that the variation in the women's pay is genuinely due to the difference or factor. Thus where a difference or factor has in the past contributed to the variation but no longer does so, the variation is no longer justified.[30]

The courts have been careful to scrutinise the employer's justification. If the court finds that the personal difference alleged is merely a pretext for intentional discrimination, or that intentional discrimination was a causal element in the variation, the employer will not succeed. In particular, employers have not been permitted to rely on material differences that have their roots in direct discrimination in the past.

Today perhaps the most difficult issue in the implementation of equal pay legislation arises when an employer attempts to justify unequal pay by relying on factors that, though on the surface neutral, actually have a disparate impact on women. The resolution of this issue is vital in determining how effective the equal pay legislation will be. Though the courts in Britain have considered defences that involve a disparate impact, no common approach has yet emerged.

In a number of cases, the courts have allowed an employer to justify lower pay for women in terms of factors personal to the particular men or women being compared, such as a different performance rating, where the rating is based on a system of performance appraisals; seniority, where employees receive periodic pay increases based on their tenure with the employer; and "red circling", a procedure whereby the position of an employee is re-evaluated and, as a result the employee is downgraded, but their wages are temporarily fixed until the wages appropriate to the downgraded position are equivalent to their current wages.[31]

The House of Lords also held that differences in working hours and length of holidays may constitute a justification for a variation in pay.[32] In *National Coal Board v. Sherwin*[33] the employer argued that the fact that the men were employed on night work, while the women were not, constituted a genuine material difference. While the Employment Appeal Tribunal accepted that the fact that the men and women worked at different times could constitute a material difference, it was considered that in the circumstances of the case the variation between the men's and the women's pay was greater than could be justified by the fact that the men worked permanently on the night shift.

In one case, a female part-time worker sought pay equal to that received by male full-time workers.[34] The Employment Appeal Tribunal held that any difference in pay must be "objectively justified".[35] The tribunal therefore held that to show a "material difference", an employer must show that the lower pay for part-time workers is reasonably necessary to achieve some justifiable objective other than a gender-related objective – for example, greater efficiency. It would not be enough to show that the employer intended to achieve this legitimate objective; the employer would have to show that the objective was actually achieved.

Since then the European Court of Justice's important decision in *Bilka-Kaufhaus GmbH* v. *Weber von Harz*[36] has clarified the appropriate test even further, both in the context of part-time workers and more generally. The European Court of Justice laid down that the relevant test is:

(a) whether there are objective grounds justifying the difference;

(b) whether the practice is "necessary"; and

(c) whether the difference claimed to be justified is proportionate to the objective pursued.

Employers have also pointed to market forces as reasons for differences in pay. Some have argued that it is necessary to maintain a balance between the internal and the external wage structure. Here the employer is, in effect, claiming that external job-for-job comparison should be used to limit internal factor comparison, which would otherwise lead to the conclusion that two "different" jobs, generally compensated differently, should instead be paid equal wages.

Interpreting the "material difference" defence, Lord Denning[37] confined the defence to the "personal equation of the woman as compared to that of the man",[38] such as longer length of service, superior skills or qualifications, greater output or productivity, or "red circling". The court would not, however, consider any *extrinsic* forces that led to the man being paid more. An employer could not avoid his obligation under the Act by saying, "I paid him more because he asked for more", or "I paid her less because she was willing to work for less". If any such excuses were permitted, Lord Denning held, "the Act would be a dead letter. Those are the very reasons why there was unequal pay before the statute. They are the very circumstances in which the statute was intended to operate".[39]

Since that case, however, the authority of this rejection of the "market forces" argument has been weakened, even in the context of "material difference" claims. In a more recent case,[40] the House of Lords upheld an employer's market forces defence. A Health Board argued that the almost £3,000 difference between a male prosthetist and a woman applicant was justified because she had been recruited directly to the National Health Service, whereas he had been transferred in at the higher rate that he had previously enjoyed in the private sector. Although all the prosthetists on the higher rate were men, and all but one on the lower rate were women, the majority of the court upheld the differential because it was essential to recruit from the private sector at higher rates in order to staff the service.

Another subject of considerable debate in Britain, at the time of writing, is the extent to which, and under what circumstances, the fact that the relevant men and women are in different collective bargaining units or separate pay structures may constitute a justification for a variation in pay between them.[41] In one case,[42] an industrial tribunal accepted an employer's justification based on these grounds, while in another[43] a differently constituted industrial tribunal rejected an employer's argument based on similar grounds.

2.2 The role of job evaluation

Job evaluation plays a major role in determining whether or not work is "equal". We can consider the role of job evaluation in at least three different contexts.

First, as already mentioned, one of the three grounds on which a person may base a claim for equal pay is that she is doing work which has been "rated as equivalent" under an analytical job evaluation scheme. Second, a tribunal is required[44] to discontinue hearing a case to determine whether two jobs are of equal value where an existing non-discriminatory job evaluation scheme has given the applicant's job a value different from that of her male comparator. Third, where a claim is referred to an independent expert, the expert is required to draw up a report, using a non-discriminatory, analytical job evaluation scheme to determine whether the applicant and the comparator are doing work of equal value.

2.3 Sex bias in job evaluation

The concern that job evaluation schemes may be sexually biased is thus explicitly taken into account with respect to job evaluation exercises. What "discrimination" in such a situation means has been the subject of some litigation. In one case,[45] an industrial tribunal held that there was no presumption that a voluntary scheme discriminated on the grounds of sex. The burden of proof, the tribunal asserted, lay with the employees to show that there were reasonable grounds for believing that it did discriminate. The tribunal adopted a particularly narrow test for determining whether discrimination could be inferred: whether there is good reason to suppose that any comparative value set by the system on any demand or characteristic would be given a more favourable value if those determining values were not consciously or subconsciously influenced by consideration of the sex of those on whom the demands would chiefly be made. The tribunal added that there would be sufficient reason for such a supposition if it had found that a traditionally female attribute was undervalued.[46]

In another case[47] the applicants argued that the respondent employer could not show that the benchmark job ranking order was not based on intentional or unintentional discrimination. In particular, it was argued that an inference should be drawn from statistical evidence which established the preponderance of female ancillary workers in the employment of the respondent in the bottom three grades. However, the tribunal was not prepared to make an inference of discrimination. Three factors seem to have contributed to this decision:

(a) the statistical evidence could be explained in ways other than discrimination being at work;

(b) those carrying out the job evaluation exercise, in the person of the employer's expert, impressed the tribunal; and

(c) the job evaluation scheme had proven "acceptable".

The failure (as found by the tribunal, at least) of the unions concerned to press the question of discrimination in negotiations at national level enabled the respondent to argue successfully that the scheme was broadly acceptable.

2.4 Gender-dominated occupational categories and jobs

The relevance of whether an occupational category or job is gender-dominated is not explicitly considered in the legislation. However, there are a number of circumstances in which it would appear to be relevant; first, as seen above, in providing evidence from which an inference may be drawn as to the operation of a discriminatory job evaluation scheme; second, in providing evidence from which an inference may be drawn that a material factor is tainted with discrimination. In a third situation, it has been determined to be irrelevant. There is no requirement, however, for the occupational category or job to be dominated by women in order for a woman employed in that category or job to be able to succeed in establishing that she is doing work of equal value with a male comparator in a different category or job. Nor is there any requirement for the category or job in which the male comparator is employed to be male dominated. In *Pickstone* v. *Freemans plc*[48] the House of Lords held that the claim of a woman applicant seeking to establish that she was doing work of equal value with a male comparator doing different work could proceed despite the fact that another male was employed in the same job as the woman claimant.

2.5 The scope of comparison

We have already considered the basic scope of comparison, that is, that the man and the woman must be in the "same employment". This section will discuss some remaining issues relevant to the scope of comparison.

The choice of the relevant comparator is that of the applicant not the employer or the tribunal.[49] There is no requirement that the comparator selected by the applicant should be representative of a group.[50]

Under EC law, as applied in the United Kingdom, the principle of equal pay is not confined to situations in which men and women are contemporaneously doing equal work. It therefore applies where it is established that a woman receives less pay than a man who was employed prior to her and did equal work for the employer[51] However, a change in an employer's trading position leading to reduced profitability can constitute a defence against a woman's claim for equal pay with her male predecessor, provided the employer can show that he was not taking advantage of the applicant's sex to get the work done at a rate less than that for which a man would have worked.[52] Comparisons are, however, confined to parallels that may be drawn on the basis of concrete appraisals of work actually performed by employees of different sex in the "same employment" (see 4.1).

There is no provision for either intra-industry or cross-industry comparisons under British law, though the position under EC law is uncertain.

3. Enforcement arrangements for implementing equal pay policies

3.1 The different methods of enforcement

Equal pay matters may be referred to an industrial tribunal by various different parties. An employee may complain that a term of her contract contravenes an equality clause. An employer may apply to a tribunal for an order determining the rights of employer and employees where a dispute arises in relation to the effect of an equality clause. The Secretary of State may refer to a tribunal any question concerning whether a woman's employer is contravening an equality clause, if it is not reasonable to expect her to take steps herself to have the question determined. The Equal Opportunites Commission (in Northern Ireland, the Equal Opportunities Commission for Northern Ireland) may take preliminary action in the industrial tribunal before taking injunction proceedings in the county court against a discriminator.

The Equal Opportunities Commissions also have the power to mount a formal investigation without first having received a complaint. Investigations may be of two types: an investigation into a named person in which the Commissions investigates whether the employer is contravening an equality clause, and a general investigation in which there is no specific allegation by the Commissions of a breach of an equality clause. The first type of investigation may lead to recommendations or a non-discrimination notice or both. The second type may lead only to recommendations. Since 1976, there has only been one equal pay investigation of the first type, into Electrolux.

Enforcement of EC law is provided for in two ways. First, the Commission of the European Communities may initiate proceedings directly against a Member State in the European Court of Justice, alleging that the State is not complying with its obligations under the Treaty of Rome or a Directive.[53] In addition, where the requirements of the Treaty or a Directive are directly effective in the Member State, an individual may make use of them directly in domestic legal proceedings, even where there is no such provision in the national legislation. If a national court is faced in this way with a question of EC law, it may, and in some circumstances must, refer the issue to the European Court of Justice for a preliminary decision.[54] The remainder of this paper will consider in more detail enforcement of national legislation.

3.2 Tribunal procedures

The Equal Pay Act provides only that no claim shall be "referred" to an industrial tribunal if the applicant has not been employed by a particular employer within the six months preceding the date of the reference.[55] The Employment Appeal Tribunal has held, however, that this provision does not preclude a tribunal from hearing an equal pay complaint (other than one made by the Secretary of State for Employment) lodged more than six months after the applicant's employment with the employer ended.[56] The six months' time-limit only applies, it held, where there has been a "reference", and this refers only to a claim made by the Secretary of State, not one made by an ordinary applicant. It is uncertain whether this decision will stand.

A person who wishes to claim under the heads of "like work" and "work rated as equivalent" must send a completed form to the Central Office of Industrial Tribunals in either Scotland, England and Wales, or Northern Ireland. The Equal Opportunities Commissions are empowered to grant advice and assistance to those taking equal pay cases. A conciliation officer from the Advisory, Conciliation and Arbitration Service (ACAS) (in Northern Ireland, the Labour Relations Agency) will then attempt conciliation. Unless this is successful, or either party withdraws, the case will proceed to a tribunal hearing. At the hearing the applicant first attempts to prove her case; the respondent then attempts to rebut her case or to establish a defence or justification.

In "equal value" cases the procedure is different in a number of significant respects. The first major difference is that there are three preliminary stages unique to equal value cases. First, a tribunal is required, before proceeding to hear the parties on the claim, to invite them to apply for an adjournment for the purpose of seeking to reach a settlement. Second, a preliminary stage may take place involving consideration of the defence of genuine material factor. On the application of either party, a tribunal may hear evidence and permit the parties to address it on this issue. Third, a tribunal is required to discontinue hearing a case where an existing non-discriminatory job evalauation scheme has given the applicant's job a value different from that of her male comparator.

Unless the applicant's case falls at one of the preliminary stages, the tribunal is required to refer the question of equal value to an independent expert and adjourn the hearing pending receipt of the expert's report.

When the tribunal receives this report, the hearing is reconvened to consider it. The expert's report will be admitted as evidence in the case unless the tribunal decides not to admit it.[57] If the report is not admitted, another report must be commissioned. If it is admitted, the tribunal must then decide whether to accept the independent expert's assessment of equal value, and whether any defence has been established by the employer.

3.3 Government bodies involved in implementing equal pay

Apart from the Equal Opportunties Commissions, there are three main government bodies involved in the process of adjudicating equal pay claims before the industrial tribunals, namely the industrial tribunals themselves, the independent experts (in so far as equal value cases are concerned), and the Advisory, Conciliation and Arbitration Service (ACAS; in Northern Ireland, the Labour Relations Agency – LRA), which has the role of conciliation. The Central Arbitration Committee (in Northern Ireland, the Industrial Court) used to have an important role, but this has now been very largely abolished. The Secretary of State for Employment also has powers to refer cases on his own initiative to the industrial tribunals, but this power has never been exercised.

The equal pay jurisdiction is merely one of a number of jurisdictions which have been given to industrial tribunals since they were first established in the 1960s. An industrial tribunal is composed of three members: a legally qualified chairman, a panel member appointed from a panel representative of employers, and a panel member chosen from a panel of representative of employees. In all sex discrimination cases, including equal pay cases, there is a convention that at least one of the panel members will be a woman. In Great Britain, appeals from industrial tribunals are heard by the Employment Appeal Tribunal, in Northern Ireland by the Court of Appeal.

In equal value cases, the procedure is different from that in other equal pay cases. In these cases the tribunal is required, unless a preliminary hearing has determined that the applicant cannot proceed, to select an independent expert to draw up a report as to whether the applicant and the comparator are doing work of equal value. Independent experts are appointed by ACAS or LRA on a part-time basis. The criteria for appointment are experience in job evaluation, an understanding of the legislation, industrial experience, and the necessary time to undertake cases.

ACAS and LRA have two main roles under the legislation. The first is the appointment of independent experts. The second, much more time-consuming fuction is conciliation. In all equal pay cases ACAS and LRA have the role of attempting to conciliate between the two parties. If this is successful, then the agreement is registered officially with the industrial tribunal.

Until the passing of the Sex Discrimination Act 1986, the Central Arbitration Committee (the Industrial Court in Northern Ireland) had the jurisdiction to receive complaints from either party to a collective agreement alleging that the agreement was overtly discriminatory between men and women, and could amend the agreement to remove the discrimination. The 1986 Act, however, removed this jurisdiction. Instead, it provided that discriminatory provisions in collective agreements are rendered void, but no mechanism was provided whereby this voidness could be established without the need for an individual complaint being made before an industrial tribunal.

3.4 Legal costs

The rules relating to legal costs in industrial tribunals differ from those applicable to ordinary courts. In tribunals each side is normally responsible for their own costs. There is provision for the losing side to pay the costs of the other side, but this is limited to cases where the tribunal decides that it was unreasonable for the losing party to proceed, and this relatively infrequently happens. A major source of funding for individuals taking equal pay cases before tribunals is either the Equal Opportunities Commissions, or a trade union. Full legal aid is not available for appearances before industrial tribunals; this only becomes available at the stage of appeal before the Employment Appeal Tribunal and beyond.

3.5 Remedies

Where an applicant has been successful in establishing her claim, the tribunal may award three types of remedy: a declaration as to the rights of the parties, an order for back pay, or an order of damages. Back pay may be awarded where the breach of the equality clause relates to pay. Damages may be ordered where the breach concerns other terms in the contract of employment. In the case of back pay and damages the Act stipulates that the tribunal may not make an award relating to the contravention of an equality clause earlier than two years before the claim was commenced.

3.6 Protection from victimisation

The Sex Discrimination Act 1975 provides that it is unlawful to victimise a person for bringing proceedings under the Equal Pay Act, or for giving evidence or information in connection with such proceedings, or for otherwise doing anything under or by reference to the Act, or for alleging that a person has committed an act which would amount to a contravention of the Act.[58]

3.7 The burden of proof

The burden of proving like work, or work rated as equivalent, or work of equal value lies ultimately with the applicant, though the burden of establishing the defence of genuine material factor or genuine material differences lies with the employer.[59]

3.8 Access to information on wages

The ordinary rules relating to getting further and better particulars and the discovery and inspection of documents apply in equal pay cases before industrial tribunals as they apply in other cases before tribunals. Within the constraints of relevance, most information can be required by either side from the other, though confidentiality will sometimes successfully be used to prevent disclosure of otherwise relevant evidence.

There are special rules relating to access to information by the independent expert. The expert has no authority to require any information to be produced, but may apply to the tribunal for an order to require any person to furnish relevant information. The expert cannot, however, obtain an order requiring a person to give oral evidence. Nor does there appear to be any power to order an employer to permit the independent expert access to the place of work.

Under general labour law provisions, employers are obliged to disclose to any independent trade union recognised by them information without which the union representatives would be impeded to a material extent in carrying out collective bargaining, and which it would be in accordance with good industrial relations practice for the employer to disclose.[60] This may include information required in order for the union to bargain over equal opportunity issues, including pay.[61]

3.9 Experience with equal pay claims

Before the new equal value provision was introduced in 1983, litigation under the Equal Pay Act had fallen to virtually nothing. After 1983 there was a resurgence of interest and many more claims were lodged. The most recent figures available show that in 1988, 552 cases were received by ACAS for conciliation, 108 were settled, 1,131 were withdrawn, and 291 went to an industrial tribunal.[62] Of the 552 received, 120 were specifically equal *value* cases. Discounting a large multiple application concerning a particular public service issue, the 1988 caseload was 64 per cent down on 1987, and was "unexpectedly low".[63] One reason suggested was uncertainty about how the law was to be interpreted.

The other main forum in which equal pay issues tend to be considered is collective bargaining. ACAS noted in its 1988 Annual Report that "it appeared that trade unions were continuing to prefer negotiated solutions to tribunal complaints wherever possible. The widespread and close interest in equal pay for work of equal value was certainly not to be measured by the number of formal complaints being made".[64]

4. The role of the social partners

4.1 Union-mangement involvement in implementing equal pay

Although little systematic research has been completed recently, it would appear that the issue of equal pay, in particular equal pay for work of equal value, is beginning to be given a degree of priority in the bargaining agenda between unions and employers of a kind that it has not had for at least ten years. This is at least partly due to the general growth of interest in equal pay for work of equal value, and the publicity which continues to surround the issue. It has also been observed that union interest in the issue may have been stimulated in part by a desire to attract more women members, at a time of generally declining membership. In some cases, it appears to have been an important consideration that trade unions as such have no direct access to industrial tribunals, whereas collective bargaining is a forum that is open to them. Handling the issue through collective bargaining therefore has on occasion been seen as allowing the union greater control than supporting an applicant's case in an industrial tribunal.

Where unions are taking an interest in the issue, different strategic considerations appear to affect the type of approach that is taken. In this context, it may be important to distinguish public sector and larger private sector employers from small to medium-size private sector firms, the former being more likely to have a common national agreement, a more developed personnel function, and a more recently updated job evaluation scheme. In the public sector and larger private sector firms, unions are more likely to decide to adopt a comprehensive and integrated strategy nationally, with responsibility for the issue being allocated to a senior official. In small and medium-sized private sector firms, the tendency has been to establish a support structure at national level, but to leave the regions and branches to pursue claims. Whatever the size and characteristics of the employer, the appropriate strategy seems increasingly to be decided upon pragmatically, with a mix of both collective bargaining and litigation being considered and decisions being reached on which is appropriate in particular circumstances.

The relationship between voluntary collective agreements and compulsory equal pay standards has particular poignancy in the area of equality between men and women at work. On the one hand, collective bargaining and union representation are likely to be the most effective avenues by which real change will be brought about, for the tribunals simply cannot take over wage determination in every industry. On the other hand, an important part of the structure of pay inequality between men and women is derived from, or is encapsulated in, previous arrangements (for example, job evaluation criteria) agreed by these very unions.

4.2 Monitoring collective agreements

There is no automatic monitoring by government of collective agreements to ensure that they are not discriminatory, though the Equal Opportunities Commissions consider particular agreements from time to time.

There are a number of sources of advice for trade unions and employers. Some, for example the Equal Opportunities Commissions, ACAS and LRA, advise both sides of industry. In addition, the Trades Union Congress has recently established an Equal Rights Department which advises unions on recent developments, and the Confederation of British Industry has issued advice to employers with regard to equal pay.

5. Conclusions

Both macroeconomic analysis of changes in the levels of earnings of women relative to men and case-studies in particular organisations appear to show that the Equal Pay Act has had, in the words of one authority, "a significant, if limited impact" in Britain.[65] This seems to have been due in part to the eradication (at least overtly) of the "woman's rate" in collective agreements, in part to the encouragement which the Act gives to the use of voluntary job evaluation schemes, and in part to changes brought about by the threat of disruption. To the extent that the changes were due to the impact of the legislation, it appears to have had most effect in eradicating the relatively crude forms of discrimination.

Women's gross hourly earnings have nevertheless remained at below 75 per cent of men's since 1977. The reasons for this disparity are complex, arising in part from the more subtle indirect forms of discrimination that continue to exist:

Occupational segregation, and the discriminatory recruitment and promotion practices which maintain it, places many women in lower-paid, lower status jobs. Inadequate provision for workers with caring responsibilities means that women generally cannot compete equally with men in the workplace. The growth in part-time working, while enabling many women to enter paid employment, has been accompanied by... a lower standard of employment protection for those workers.[66]

It is too early to say whether the equal value principle will result in changes as significant as those which appear to have resulted from the original Act.

The legislation as it stands does present certain difficulties. One concerns the meaning and extent of the material difference/factor defence, which is so unclear as to cause considerable uncertainty, particularly to employers and their advisers. It is by no means clear in what circumstances a particular factor may, or may not, constitute a justification.

The job evaluation defence is also problematic in that the special status accorded to existing job evaluation schemes operates as an unjustified barrier to a woman seeking to pursue an equal value claim. There should be the possibility of independent assessment of the relevant jobs.

The limitations of the "same employment" criterion, even as expanded in the statutory definition, constrain the scope of comparison unduly. An alternative approach was that adopted under Dutch law, which provided:

Where no work of equal or approximately equal value is done by a worker of the other sex in the undertaking where the worker concerned is employed, the basis shall be the wage that a worker of the other sex normally receives, in an undertaking of as nearly as possible the same kind in the same section [of industry].[67]

The existing legislation provides no remedy for a situation where a man and a woman are doing work which is neither like work nor work of equal value, but where the variation in pay between the man and the woman is due to discrimination. Nor does it provide any clear mechanism by which discriminatory terms in collective agreements may be amended by judicial process.

Finally, tribunals can only prescribe remedies to benefit the individual claimant. They should be empowered to order relevant remedial action in respect of the grade or organisations more generally, for example, by requiring that discriminatory practices by discontinued.

There is also room for improvement as regards the procedures for implementing the equal pay legislation. Two undesirable features of the present situation are the plethora of preliminary stages before tribunal meetings, and the extent to which multiple hearings are now the norm in equal value cases. It would be a great improvement if the number of preliminary hearings could be reduced and if both the issue of equal value and the employer's defences could be dealt with at one hearing, as is the case with other equal pay and sex discrimination cases.

The delay in reaching final decisions, particularly in equal value cases, is now a significant barrier to justice for many applicants. These delays appear to result in part from the succession of preliminary hearings, but also in part from delays in reporting by the independent experts, who are taking considerably longer than the 42 days to report, set out in the legislation.

Costs are another major problem for applicants. In more complex cases, an applicant is more likely than not to need a job evalaution expert, especially where there is an existing job evaluation scheme. Experience thus far appears to show that they must not only be expert, but be able to convince any later tribunal that they are expert, sensible, and a match for both the independent expert and the expert on the other side. In complex cases, legal advice also needs to be available to applicants, as early as possible in the process. Funding also needs to be secured on the assumption that issues may need to be taken to appeal.

The effect of these considerations is that the cost of taking a complex equal value case to a tribunal is potentially very high, and well beyond the pocket of any likely applicant. The absence of legal aid has meant that applicants are dependent on either the Equal Opportunities Commissions or their trade union for the funding of cases, yet so far such funding has been available to few applicants.

The role of the independent expert is unsatisfactory in two major respects. First, a desirable consistency in approach between different experts appears not yet to have been achieved; no guidelines on the difficult questions which such experts are expected to tackle have yet been produced. Second, there is considerable uncertainty as to the status of the expert vis-à-vis the industrial tribunal, particularly as to the weight to be attached to the expert's reports.

Finally, there is the problem of victimisation. Once an application has been made to the industrial tribunal, it has proved necessary to institute protection against the possibility of victimisation of those named as applicants, for example by letting it be known that harassment will be treated as a collective grievance, and that proceedings for victimisation will be instituted at the first sign of harassment. Unfortunately this has not prevented applicants from withdrawing in part because of such harassment.

Notes

1 For the purposes of this commentary, the provisions of the relevant legislation in Great Britain will be discussed. The provisions of the Northern Ireland legislation may be regarded as the equivalent except where a specific difference is noted.

2 *Hayward* v. *Cammell Laird Shipbuilders Ltd.* (1988) IRLR 257 (HL).

3 ibid.

4 Equal Pay Act, s. 6(1A).

5 *Bilka-Kaufhaus GmbH* v. *Weber von Hartz* (1986) IRLR 317 (ECJ).

6 *Worringham* v. *Lloyds Bank Ltd.* (1981) IRLR 178 (ECJ).

7 *Garland* v. *British Rail Engineering Ltd.* (1982) IRLR 111 (ECJ).

8 *Capper Pass Ltd.* v. *Lawton* (1976) IRLR 366 (EAT).

9 ibid.

10 Equal Pay Act, s. 1(5).

11 *Bromley* v. *H. & J. Quick Ltd.* (1988) IRLR 249 (CA).

12 *O'Brien* v. *Sim-Chem Ltd.* (1980) IRLR 373 (HL).

13 *Pickstone* v. *Freemans plc* (1988) IRLR 357 (HL).

14 *Murphy* v. *An Bord Telecom Eireann* (1988) IRLR 267 (ECJ).

15 Equal Pay Act, s. 1(2)*(c)*.

16 *Commission of the European Communities* v. *United Kingdom* (1982) IRLR 333 (ECJ).

17 s. 1(6)*(c)*.

18 *Leverton* v. *Clwyd County Council* (1989) IRLR 28 (HL).

19 Equal Pay Act, s. 1(6)*(c)*.

20 Sex Discrimination Act 1975, s. 10(4).

21 Equal Pay Act, s. 1(9).

22 Equal Pay Act, s. 7(1).

23 ss. 10(1) and 10(5). See also Sex Discrimination and Equal Pay (Offshore Employment) Order 1987.

24 Equal Pay Act, s. 6(1)*(b)*.

25 Equal Pay Act, s. 6(1A)*(b)*.

26 Equal Pay Act, s. 6(1A)*(a)*.

27 (1986) IRLR 140 (ECJ).

28 Equal Pay Act, s. 6(1)*(a)*.

29 Equal pay Act, s. 1(3).

30 *Beneviste* v. *University of Southampton* (1989) IRLR 122 (CA).

31 See, e.g. *Snoxell* v. *Vauxhall Motors Ltd.* (1978) IQB 11; *Sun Alliance Ltd.* v. *Dudman* (1978) ICR 551; *Shields* v. *E. Coomes (Holdings) Ltd.* (1978) ICR 1159.

32 *Leverton* v. *Clwyd County Council* (1989) IRLR 28 (HL).

33 (1978) IRLR 122 (EAT).

34 The Employment Appeal Tribunal (EAT) initially referred the issue to the European Court of Justice, which replied somewhat ambiguously. See *Jenkins* v. *Kingsgate (Clothing Productions) Ltd.* (1981) ECR 911 (Preliminary Ruling). When the ECJ judgement was considered by the EAT, the EAT decided that it was possible for British law to confer greater rights on the woman then European law could confer. It thus applied a more restrictive test as to whether the employer could use, as a defence, the fact that a woman worked part time than the ECJ was prepared to do. (1981) ICR 715.

35 (1980) ICR 6.

36 (1986) IRLR 317 (ECJ).

37 *Clay Cross* v. *Fletcher* (1979) 1 A11 ER 474.

38 ibid., at 477.

39 ibid.

40 *Rainey* v. *Greater Glasgow Health Board* (1987) IRLR 26 (HL).

41 *Reed Packaging Ltd.* v. *Boozer and Everhurst* (1988) IRLR 333.

42 *Clark* v. *Bexley Health Authority and Secretary of State; Enderby* v. *Frenchay Health Authority and Secretary of State for Health*, 24 EOR 42 (IT).

43 *Webster* v. *Hoover plc* (unreported).

44 Equal Pay Act, s. 2A(2).

45 *Neil* v. *Ford Motor Co.* (1984) IRLR 339.

46 ibid., p. 402. The dispute continued after the decision, erupting into industrial protests which in turn led to the appointment of an independent job evaluation panel by the company with the agreement of the unions. The panel found the work of the women sewing machinists to be undervalued by the company's job evaluation scheme in eight out of 28 characteristics that the panel recommended regarding. The panel's conclusions were accepted by the company.

47 *McAuley et al.* v. *Eastern Health and Social Services Board* (IT, unreported).

48 (1988) IRLR 357.

49 *Ainsworth* v. *Glass Tubes & Components Ltd.* (1977) IRLR 74.

50 *Thomas* v. *National Coal Board* (1987) IRLR 451.

51 *Macarthys Ltd.* v. *Smith* (1980) IRLR 210 (ECJ).

52 *Albion Shipping Agency* v. *Arnold* (1981) IRLR 525 (EAT).

53 Treaty of Rome, Art. 169.

54 Treaty of Rome, Art. 177.

55 Equal Pay Act, s. 2(4).

56 *British Railways Board* v. *Paul* (1988) IRLR 20.

[57] *Tenant Textile Colours Ltd.* v. *Todd* (1989) IRLR 3 (NICA).

[58] Sex Discrimination Act 1975.

[59] See, e.g. *National Vulcan Engineering Insurance Group Ltd.* v. *Wade* (1978) IRLR 225.

[60] Employment Protection Act 1975, ss. 17-21.

[61] ACAS, Code of Practice No. 2 (Disclosure of information to trade unions for collective bargaining purposes).

[62] ACAS, *1988 Annual Report,* table 11.

[63] ibid., p. 31.

[64] ibid.

[65] P.L. Davies: "European equality legislation, UK legislative policy and industrial relations", in C. McCrudden (ed.): *Women, employment and European equality law* (Eclipse Publications, 1987), p. 42.

[66] EOC: "Equal pay: Making it work" (EOC, 1989).

[67] Netherlands Equal Pay Act, s. 3(2). The 1979 Report of the Commission of the European Communities on the implementation of the principle of equal pay argued that the 1975 Directive required a wider comparison than that of just the "same establishment". Rather, "the 'value of work' of the two posts or duties which are to be compared must therefore be established, where there is in the undertaking or undertakings in question no appropriate system for reevaluating jobs, simply 'on an equitable basis' having regard to the available data", and in accordance with the terms used in the Dutch law. See generally C.A. Crisham: "The equal pay principle: Some recent decisions of the European Court of Justice", in *Common Market Law Review,* 1981, 18, p. 601; R. Plender: "Equal pay for men and women: Two recent decisions of the European Court", in *American Journal of Comparative Law,* 1982, 30, p. 627.

10

Equal pay in the United States

*Janice R. Bellace**

1. Introduction

Except for wartime periods, the issue of equality of pay between men and women did not receive government attention in the United States until after the Second World War. In the first phase of the national discussion, attention focused on the specific issue of equal pay between men and women performing essentially similar tasks. The federal Equal Pay Act of 1963 was a product of this period.[1]

During the late 1960s and the early 1970s, the public's attention turned to the broader issue of equal opportunity in employment, prompted by a recognition of the barriers Black people confronted in employment. The response of the United States Congress to the 1960s civil rights movement was Title VII of the Civil Rights Act of 1964.[2] Title VII is a broad anti-discrimination statute that prohibits employers from treating people less favourably in employment on a number of grounds, one of which is sex. Because of the legislature's concerns, early enforcement efforts concentrated on the issue of equal access to jobs. In the first wave of sex discrimination cases, around 1970, plaintiffs complainted about lack of access to specific jobs as a result of discriminatory hiring, training and promotion practices. Remuneration complaints under Title VII were rare prior to 1975.

In the late 1970s, the issue of pay equity was raised once again. Many had assumed that once women had equal access to jobs, equal pay would be achieved. The continuing wage disparity between men and women caused supporters of women's equality to explore further the causes of unequal pay. In this phase, the national debate moved to the issue of "comparable worth"; that is, the question of why women are paid less for what many think is work of similar value to more highly paid men's work. Cases were filed under Title VII. The judicial response has been mixed, as explained below. During the 1980s, the response of the executive branch of the federal Government to comparable worth was hostile. Lacking a favourable climate in the federal regulatory sphere, supporters of comparable worth have directed their efforts at state level. A handful of the 50 states have enacted comparable worth legislation, but only for public sector employees.

* Associate Professor of Legal Studies and Management, the Wharton School, University of Pennsylvania.

The United States is not a signatory to the Equal Remuneration Convention, 1951 (No. 100). Because of this, one cannot speak in terms of the United States responding to specific standards set forth in that Convention. None the less, any country that seeks to implement a guarantee of equal pay will encounter certain key issues. The United States is no exception. Because of the strong legislative and judicial backing given to the general principle of equality in employment, claims based on a notion of comparable worth have been raised in lawsuits. Those who raise a comparable worth claim cannot, however, rely on any explicit guarantee of equal pay for work of equal value.

1.1 The legal basis for equality of pay

Historically, progress towards the goal of equal pay has not originated in the private sector. The Governmment, through various forms of intervention and regulation, has been the main initiator of change. In both the First and Second World Wars, because women were assigned to traditionally male jobs to which they previously had not had access, equal pay issues arose. Although the work of the National War Labor Boards did not result in any legislative pronouncements, their wage-setting principles had a profound impact on wage structures in industry. During the First World War, for instance, the National War Labor Board applied the principle of equal pay in its awards, stating: "If it shall become necessary to employ women on work ordinarily performed by men, they must be allowed equal pay for equal work."[3] The Second World War Labor Board, in particular, vigorously promoted the concept of job evaluation as a means of achieving wage equity. In applying job evaluation techniques, it followed the principle that on jobs performed by women "which differ only inconsequently, and not in measurable job content, from jobs performed by men", women were to receive equal pay with men.[4]

At the end of the Second World War, millions of American women left the labour force. Equal pay was no longer a priority item on the national legislative agenda, although the issue was still pressed at the state level.[5] In 1963, Congress enacted the Equal Pay Act.[6] This statute gave legislative force to the ideas promoted by the National War Labor Boards, but it did nothing to broaden their scope. Essentially, the Equal Pay Act of 1963 contains an equal pay for equal (same or substantially similar) work[7] guarantee. Where women seek to compare themselves to men working on dissimilar jobs, they must file under Title VII.

One difficulty in discussing employment rights in the United States lies in the relationship between the federal and state Goverments. The federal Government does not have the sole ability to act in labour and employment law matters. As a result, if Congress does not act, the states are free to do so. If Congress does act, federal regulation may coexist with state regulation (concurrent jurisdiction), or it may displace state regulation (exclusive jurisdiction). Generally, if the United States Congress enacts legislation, Congress chooses whether it will displace state regulation. If it does not, the states may introduce legislation in the same area but the state legislation may not undercut federal standards. In the area of anti-discrimination law, Congress has chosen to permit the states to legislate alongside federal legislation. Congress has not enacted legislation expressly guaranteeing equal pay for work of equal value, but a few states have ventured into this area for state employees. These state initiatives are discussed at the end of this chapter. Unless otherwise noted, the discussion in this chapter refers to federal law and practice.

1.2 The definition of pay

The statutory language of the Equal Pay Act of 1963 refers specifically to wages and wage rates. In nearly all cases brought under that statute, the plaintiff has complained that men working on the same or very similar jobs were paid more than women. The Equal Pay Act can, however, reach elements of remuneration outside the wage packet. In one case, female stewardesses of an airline sought equal pay with male pursers.[8] Apart from the wage differential, the stewardesses challenged the monetary allowance the pursers received to cover the cost of cleaning their uniforms, since the stewardesses were expected to wash and iron their own uniforms.

In most Equal Pay Act cases, the plaintiff has pointed to the basic hourly wage rate.[9] The courts have required that the "pay" being compared be broken down into its component parts: that is, the basic rate must be separated from shift differentials, weekend premiums, merit system bonuses and basic rate gradations related to length of service. Since the two jobs being compared in Equal Pay Act cases have necessarily been fairly similar, the same fringe benefit and pension arrangements would typically have applied to both jobs.

The non-wage elements of remuneration that have been challenged in equal pay lawsuits in some countries, such as pensions, have been challenged under Title VII in the United States. This is often done because even though some of the female claimants may work on the same or substantially similar jobs with some men in the company, the claimants cut across many job titles. As a result, if the employer applies the same sickness and disability plan to all employees, regardless of job title, and all female employees are treated differently from all male employees under the plan, the claim is appropriately brought under Title VII.[10] Title VII prohibits employers from treating women less favourably in employment than men because of their sex. Title VII can thus reach any compensation practice of an employer.[11] It should be noted that social security payments under a state scheme are not within the scope of Title VII, because Title VII is directed at employers.

The Supreme Court has held that employers may not require female employees to make larger monthly contributions to a pension fund than that of comparable males in order to receive the same monthly pension payment upon retirement.[12] Similarly, in *Norris* the Supreme Court held that employers violate Title VII when they utilise a private pension plan whereby male and female employees contribute the same amount to their retirement annuity plan, but at the pay-out stage women receive lower monthly benefits than men who have paid the same amount into the scheme.[13] In *Norris,* the challenged annuity plan was not operated by the employer; rather, private companies contracted with the employer, agreeing to enrol employees in specific plans. The private companies used sex-based actuarial tables, which was standard practice throughout the life insurance and pension fund industries. Despite this, the Supreme Court held that the employer could not rely on this actuarial practice as a defence because Title VII prohibits employers from treating women less favourably than men in employment.

1.3 The definition of "equal work"

The scope of the 1963 Equal Pay Act is narrow. Section 3 of the Act states that no employer shall pay women less than men in any establishment "for equal work on jobs the performance of which requires equal skill, effort, and responsibility, and which are performed under similar working conditions". As interpreted by the courts, this statutory phrase amounts to a requirement that a woman be employed on the same or substantially similar work with a man, and that they must be working at the same geographical location. The Equal Pay Act guarantee does not extend to dissimilar work. Nor does it extend to situations where women in one establishment perform the same job as men in another establishment belonging to the same company and the men are better paid.

The courts have accepted that the Equal Pay Act guarantee applies where the woman's job and the man's job are not identical, but are substantially similar.[14] The courts are required to determine whether the differences between the two jobs are significant: that is, whether the wage differential compensates for an appreciable variation in skill, effort or responsibility between otherwise comparable work activities.

Here it should be emphasised that the practical difficulties presented by female protective legislation had ceased to be a problem by 1970.[15] Prior to that time, many states had legislation that prevented women from working at night, or from lifting weights in excess of 30 pounds. Thus, the male and female jobs might be very similar, but the men might occasionally lift heavy weights. In some cases, the night shift job was very similar to the day shift job, but some additional tasks were required. The men's job usually had a different job title, and a higher wage rate. Even before 1970, courts would ask whether the size of the wage differential accurately reflected the difference in time and effort expended on the additional task. By 1970, most female protective legislation had been repealed as a violation of Title VII's prohibition against sex discrimination. Thus, employers could assign women to the same work as men. In this period, many gender-linked job titles, such as "maid" and "janitor", disappeared in favour of unisex job titles.

The scope of the equal pay guarantee under Title VII of the 1964 Civil Rights Act is very unclear. When Congress enacted Title VII, it did not consider sex-based wage discrimination. Notwithstanding this, the broad language of Title VII obviously catches pay discrimination within its sweep. Section 703*(a)* states that it shall be an unlawful employment practice for an employer to "discriminate against any individual with respect to his compensation, terms, conditions, or privileges of employment, because of such individual's... sex". Title VII was enacted almost as the Equal Pay Act of 1963 was coming into force. Because sex was not included as a ground for unlawful discrimination until the very last stages of legislative consideration, scant notice was taken of any potential overlap between the Equal Pay Act and Title VII. Section 703*(h)* of Title VII, the Bennett Amendment, states that it does not violate Title VII for employers "to differentiate upon the basis of sex in determining the amount of the wages or compensation paid... if such differentiation is authorised by the provisions" of the Equal Pay Act.

In the 1970s some courts interpreted the Bennett Amendment to mean that a woman could not bring a wage discrimination claim under Title VII unless she could also bring that claim under the Equal Pay Act. These courts took the view that Congress, in passing the Bennett Amendment, intended that employers should only be required to pay women the same as men when the women and men were doing the same or substantially similar work. In 1978, the United States Supreme Court resolved the dispute over the interpretation of the Bennett Amendment in the *Gunther* case.[16] The Supreme Court held that the Bennett Amendment merely incorporates the four defences listed in the Equal Pay Act into Title VII.

In *Gunther,* the Supreme Court thus held that the Bennett Amendment does not restrict Title VII's prohibition of sex-based wage discrimination to claims for equal pay where men perform the same or substantially similar work. Beyond this narrow statement, its thinking in the *Gunther* case is not clear, with even the Court cautioning that it was not deciding "in this case the precise contours of lawsuits challenging sex discrimination in compensation under Title VII".[17] Although nearly a decade has passed since the *Gunther* case, no other comparable worth case has been heard by the Supreme Court. Hence, there is no further clarification of its thinking on the parameters of Title VII's equal pay guarantee.

Although the Supreme Court in *Gunther* did not expressly exclude the possibility of a plaintiff in a comparable worth case succeeding by arguing disparate impact (indirect) discrimination, the majority opinion strongly implies that the Court is extremely reluctant to venture into the area of unintentional or indirect discrimination.[18] The lower federal courts have read *Gunther* as limiting comparable worth claims under Title VII to cases where the plaintiff can prove disparate treatment discrimination: that is, where it is shown that the employer deliberately underpaid women because the holders of the job were women.[19]

The difficulties in proving intentional discrimination are illustrated by the widely-publicised *AFSCME* case.[20] In *AFSCME,* the employer (the State of Washington) continued paying less for certain traditionally female jobs than for male jobs, even after the employer's own job evaluation consultant concluded that the female jobs were of comparable worth to the male jobs, because the wage differentials reflected prevailing market rates. The federal appellate court held that the employer had not deliberately discriminated against women. Since *Gunther,* some lower federal courts have even expressed the view that comparable worth claims are not cognisable under Title VII.[21]

1.4 Scope of the equal pay provisions

The Equal Pay Act applies to employers who are covered by the Fair Labor Standards Act. Although there are numerous exceptions to the Fair Labor Standards Act, they are not of importance with regard to the issue of women's work. Title VII applies to employers who have 15 or more employees. Both statutes apply to most federal, state and local government employees, in addition to employees in the private sector.

Although there are provisions banning industrial home work in certain industries, modern home-based work is treated like any other work. Likewise, part-time, temporary and casual workers are protected by the legislation.

2. Procedures for determining "equality"

2.1 Permitted justifications for differences in pay

In a complaint brought under the Equal Pay Act, the employer may rebut the employee's claim that her job is the same as or substantially similar to that of a man in the same establishment. The language of the statutory guarantee requires that the two jobs be compared in terms of skill, effort and responsibility, and in view of the conditions under which the man and the woman work. The statute expressly lists four defences available to the employer: an employer may explain the pay discrepancy by pointing to a seniority system, a merit system, a system that measures earnings by quantity or quality of production (piece-work), or "any factor other than sex".

In an Equal Pay Act case, there is no market rate defence. If the plaintiff can show that the woman's job and the man's job are the same or substantially similar, the fact that women can be hired for lower wages than men is not a valid defence (under the "factor other than sex" defence).[22] In one case, the employer related starting salaries to the newly hired person's salary in the last job, with the result that women doing the same job as men had lower basic salaries. This was held to violate the Equal Pay Act.[23] The courts have also found that the higher cost of employing women resulting from higher insurance premiums (unemployment compensation, workers' compensation, health and life insurance) is not a valid defence under the Equal Pay Act.

Several cases involving retail salespersons have produced the opposite result.[24] In these cases, salesmen were typically assigned to a department selling high-priced items and saleswomen to a department selling lower-priced items. There was a higher profit margin on the more expensive items. Courts have upheld the employer's defence that the men were paid more because the employer reaped a higher profit from the men's department, even though there was no attributable difference in the men and women's skill, effort or responsibility.

Since the 1981 *Gunther* decision of the Supreme Court, there have been few comparable worth cases decided under Title VII. The federal courts have held that if an employer uses market forces to set pay rates or follows industry practice in establishing job ladders, that employer is not deliberately discriminating against women. All defences available to an employer under the Equal Pay Act are also available in a Title VII lawsuit, but Title VII does not list any other employer defences. As a result, case law must be examined to determine what defences have been upheld.

2.2 The role of job evaluation

Neither the Equal Pay Act nor Title VII stipulates that any particular method should be used by the courts to determine whether work is "equal". There is no procedural device whereby a judge can, during the fact-finding process, issue an order directing a neutral expert to make recommendations based on a job evaluation exercise undertaken by the expert. Job evaluation is not required at any time.[25] Its use in litigation by either party is entirely optional. In most cases brought under the Equal Pay Act, the man's job and the woman's job have been the same or very similar. As such, the courts have tended simply to compare them in a non-analytic way. In Title VII litigation, where job evaluation has been used, the courts have not drawn any distinction between qualitative systems, such as job classification,[26] and quantitative systems, such as points rating systems.

In cases brought under Title VII where the woman's job was dissimilar to the man's job, more sophisticated means of comparing the value of the two jobs have been required. It is common practice in the United States for the parties in a lawsuit to call expert witnesses to testify as to the validity of the defendant's policies and practices. In comparable worth cases, the parties have often called management consultants as expert witnesses. In some cases, the employer had used a formal job evaluation scheme in conjunction with a wage survey as a basis for determining the company's wage rates.[27] In other cases, no formal job evaluation scheme had been used; the consultants merely gave their opinion of the employer's wage hierarchy. In these cases, consultants typically explained how a job hierarchy was constructed, and how wage rates were attached to each job. Not surprisingly, the employee's expert usually disagreed with the employer's expert.

It must be emphasised, however, that in Title VII cases the issue is not sex bias in job evaluation: the issue is whether the employer deliberately discriminated against women in setting wages. If the employer followed some understandable method of setting wages, other than by placing employees into sex-linked categories,[28] then the employer has not violated Title VII.

2.3 Sex bias in job evaluation

Although the issue of inherent sex bias in job evaluation schemes has been raised in the academic literature, the issue has not yet surfaced in litigation. This may be due to the fact that most proprietary job evaluation schemes seek to mirror the market. Although job evaluation is promoted as a means of identifying worth based on job content, it serves in practice as a link between market rates and job content.[29] Thus, if the market values the lifting of heavy weights more than manual dexterity, the scheme should weight these factors accordingly. If an employer used this job evaluation scheme, he would not be deliberately discriminating against women. Because, at the present time, the federal courts are only considering disparate treatment (direct or intentional) discrimination in comparable worth cases, the issue of sex bias in conventional job evaluation schemes is irrelevant as a matter of law.

2.4 Gender-dominated occupational categories and jobs

In cases under the Equal Pay Act, the woman's job and the man's job must be in the same establishment, in terms of both employer identity and physical location. Because the level of intra-firm occupational sex segregation is high,[30] the gender composition of the male job and the female job has not been an issue in Equal Pay Act cases. Although proof of independent discriminatory conduct is not needed in an Equal Pay Act case, the issue has arisen where the employer defends by alleging that some factor "other than sex" explains the wage differential. Evidence that an employer directly or indirectly did not assign women to certain jobs has been deemed to be relevant.

In comparable worth cases under Title VII, the plaintiff typically argues that job classes that are traditionally and predominantly female are paid less than job classes that are traditionally and predominantly male. Occupational sex segregation tends to be greater in lower-paid jobs. As a result, most of the cases where this issue has arisen have involved higher-paid jobs requiring college degrees, for example, registered nurses (female) and pharmacists (male). The courts have generally accepted that if 70 per cent of the incumbents of a job title are of one sex, that job can be deemed gender-dominated.

2.5 The scope of comparison

Under the Equal Pay Act, because the two jobs must be the same or substantially similar, it is highly unlikely that a woman would seek to compare her job to a male job in a very different occupational category. In comparable worth cases under Title VII, women have compared themselves to men in very different occupational categories. To take one example, secretaries have compared themselves to tree trimmers. In nearly all such cases, the employer has successfully defended by arguing that the men's jobs and the women's jobs are in different labour markets, with different prevailing rates.

Both the Equal Pay Act and Title VII prohibit the employer from discriminating. Because of this, the plaintiff as a rule cannot make a comparison with someone employed by a different company.

3. Enforcement arrangements for implementing equal pay policies

3.1 The different methods of enforcement

Originally, the Equal Pay Act of 1963 was enforced by the Wage and Hour Division of the Department of Labor. This occurred naturally because the Equal Pay Act forms part of the Fair Labor Standards Act, and the Wage and Hour Division enforces many of the Fair Labor Standards Act's provisions, such as the minimum wage. In 1964, in enacting Title VII, Congress established an independent federal agency, the

Equal Employment Opportunity Commission (EEOC) to enforce Title VII. In 1977, during President Carter's Administration, a reorganisation of the federal Government occurred. At that time, the authority to enforce the Equal Pay Act was transferred to the EEOC.

The EEOC does not conduct routine compliance reviews with regard to pay matters. It can, however, act on its own initiative to investigate suspected acts of wage discrimination. None the less, in nearly all instances, a case begins when an individual files a complaint with the district office of the EEOC.

There is no positive obligation placed on employers or unions to promote equal pay. Only employers can violate the Equal Pay Act. Title VII prohibits both employers and unions from acting in ways that discriminate against women.

Unions have been sued under Title VII on the grounds that collectively bargained agreements raised discriminatory barriers to certain jobs, but most such lawsuits have been based on race. There has been no case where women have argued that a union negotiated a wage structure designed to discriminate against women. In practice, several major unions have been prominent supporters of the notion of comparable worth and have used litigation as one means of attempting to secure higher wage rates for women's jobs.

3.2 *Filing an equal pay charge*

A woman with a pay complaint usually consults with a lawyer or goes directly to a regulatory agency. She may go to a state or local fair employment practices agency or to the EEOC. The federal agency, the EEOC, is generally better known to the general public, so it often happens that the woman goes there.

Inquiries (telephone, written or in person) concerning the filing of charges are referred to an intake unit in the EEOC's district office for assistance and evaluation. An EEOC employee attempts to arrange an office interview with anyone raising what is apparently a Title VII or Equal Pay Act matter. If that is not possible, a telephone interview is conducted. The initial interview consists of pre-charge counselling and an in-depth discussion regarding the nature of the charging party's problem; it includes a determination of the basis of the charge and a definition of the issues and the scope. If the charging party insists, the EEOC will allow a charge to be filed even where there is no apparent legal basis for it.

In an Equal Pay Act case, either the EEOC or the aggrieved employee may file suit. In actual practice, the plaintiff in many Equal Pay Act cases has been the agency (the EEOC or, formerly, the Secretary of Labor).

When Congress enacted Title VII, it did not intend the EEOC to displace the efforts of state and local fair employment practices agencies. As such, section 706 of Title VII requires that the EEOC defer filing a charge for 60 days to allow the applicable state or local agency to act in the matter, unless the state or local agency has waived its right to act. This 60-day deferral policy does not apply to Equal Pay Act charges.

Once a charge is filed, the EEOC begins to investigate the matter. At the conclusion of the investigation, the EEOC makes a decision as to whether there is reasonable cause to believe that the claim has sufficient merit to warrant litigation if the matter cannot be conciliated. (Private attorneys who are approached by charging parties concerning the claim usually pay close attention to the EEOC's reasonable cause determination.)

In the case of a Title VII charge, the EEOC must engage in conciliation in the hope that the parties will reach a settlement between themselves. This is not required in Equal Pay Act cases. This sort of settlement is most frequently sought in cases where a fact-finding conference is held, usually shortly after the charge is filed.

Section 706 of Title VII provides that if a charge has not been resolved within 180 days of filing, the EEOC must notify the charging party, who may then file a civil action in the federal district court within 90 days of receipt of the "right to sue" letter. Because of its very substantial workload the EEOC is usually not in a position to file suit within 180 days of the filing of the charge. It is required to issue the "right to sue" letter, and many charging parties elect to file their own lawsuit once they receive this. In actual practice, all comparable worth cases under Title VII have been litigated by private plaintiffs.

3.3 The Equal Employment Opportunity Commission

Title VII created the Equal Employment Opportunity Commission (EEOC), which consists of five Commissioners, appointed by the President and confirmed by the Senate. The EEOC's General Council is also appointed by the President and confirmed by the Senate. The EEOC has its headquarters in Washington, DC, and district offices throughout the United States. It is dedicated solely to enforcing Title VII, the Equal Pay Act, and the Age Discrimination in Employment Act.

Although the EEOC deals with matters other than equal pay, its sole focus is thus discrimination in employment. As a result, it is sensitive to the key themes that pervade the notion of discrimination. Furthermore, the scope of its work brings to its attention interlocking discriminatory practices, for example, initial assignment to different job ladders, and the wage differentials between jobs on different ladders. The EEOC also has advisory and research functions. Its Office of Policy Implementation, in particular, is responsible for determining how the purposes of the statutes can be effected.

The EEOC has rule-making powers, as accorded to many federal agencies in the United States. It can issue substantive regulations, or "guidelines", that interpret the statute's meaning with respect to specific employer practices. Employers can challenge an EEOC guideline as an incorrect interpretation of the statute. Generally, the courts accord great deference to the agency's guidelines. Its guidelines on sex discrimination are widely acknowledged to have had a very significant impact on employment practices in the United States.

As far as its enforcement powers are concerned, the EEOC can conciliate a charge, or it can seek a negotiated settlement. It may file suit, as a plaintiff, in a "pattern of practice" suit whereby it asserts that the defendant employer acts in a discriminatory manner in the regular course of business. It may also intervene in a lawsuit filed by a private plaintiff. In discrimination lawsuits, the EEOC has often been instrumental in negotiating a consent decree settlement with a defendant employer whereby the employer commits himself to undertaking widespread changes in his employment practices.

The EEOC also has broad investigatory powers. It has the right to have access to and to copy all evidence, to require the attendance and testimony of witnesses, and to issue subpoenas in support thereof. It may require people to respond to written interrogatories, or to testify in person at a deposition. The discovery phase of a lawsuit is extremely important. Both the EEOC and private plaintiffs have the right to require the employer to disclose all information relevant to the case.

3.4 Legal costs

In the unlikely event of the EEOC deciding to take up a case itself, there is no cost to the aggrieved person herself. If she has to secure the services of a private attorney, however, the costs can be substantial. Besides the attorney's fees, there will be all the costs of the discovery stage of the lawsuit. If the plaintiff in a Title VII or Equal Pay Act case prevails, the court has the discretion to grant her attorney's fees. If it were not for this provision, few attorneys would ever accept the case of an individual woman against a company. Even with this provision, the attorney must consider the extremely substantial expenses that will be incurred in litigating the case, and the very substantial length of time, perhaps years, before a judgement may be given. As a result, most attorneys in private practice will not accept a case unless they believe it has a very good chance of success.

In view of the fact that it is extremely difficult for plaintiffs to succeed in a comparable worth case at the present time, it is not surprising that few cases are being litigated and that most of these are being brought by unions and professional associations.

3.5 Remedies

Back pay is available in lawsuits under both the Equal Pay Act and Title VII. Liability for back pay cannot extend further back than two years prior to the date that the charge was filed with the EEOC.

In an Equal Pay Act case, the employer would be ordered to adjust the wage rate for the woman's job to that of the comparable man's job. In a pay case under Title VII, the court may order such affirmative action as it finds appropriate. A court would typically direct the employer to draft a revised wage schedule. If the plaintiff found this wage schedule acceptable, the court would probably approve it and incorporate it as part of the court's order. If the plaintiff did not accept the revised schedule, the court would order a hearing on the remedy, and then make a decision as to appropriate relief.

There has been no indication that plaintiffs in the United States are dissatisfied with the relief available under the statutes.

3.6 Protection from victimisation

Section 704(*a*) of Title VII states that it shall be an unlawful employment practice for an employer to discriminate against any individual because that person has opposed any unlawful employment practice of the employer, or because that person has made a charge, testified, assisted, or participated in any manner in an investigation, proceeding or hearing under Title VII. Similar protection applies in Equal Pay Act cases. This section has been deemed to have exceptionally broad coverage, and has been interpreted liberally.

3.7 The burden of proof

In an Equal Pay Act case, the plaintiff must prove that the woman's job is the same as or substantially equal to the man's job in terms of skill, effort and responsibility. If the plaintiff is able to make a prima facie case, the employer may rebut her evidence, or assert one of the four statutory defences. Generally, the burden of proof lies with the plaintiff.

Because of a dearth of cases and the pronounced reluctance of the Supreme Court in the one comparable worth case it has considered to address this issue, it is extremely unclear what a plaintiff in a comparable worth case under Title VII must prove. It can only be said with certainty that the plaintiff must prove that the employer intentionally paid people doing predominantly female jobs less than those doing predominantly male jobs because women were the incumbents of the jobs. There is no burden on the employer to prove that the company followed non-discriminatory compensation policies, or even generally accepted compensation policies. In practice, most employers have not been required to buttress their reliance on prevailing market rates with specific, detailed evidence on local labour market conditions.

3.8 Access to information on wages

Employers are not required to submit periodic information on their wage rates to the EEOC or to any other federal agency. Under the Fair Labor Standards Act and the Equal Pay Act, employers must, however, make available their wage data for inspection by the Government.

Once the EEOC begins to investigate an equal pay complaint, it does have the right of access to relevant company wage data. Private plaintiffs, during the discovery phase of litigation, can also gain access to this information.

3.9 Experience of equal pay claims

Claims brought under the Equal Pay Act have met with success in the courts. The courts have been sensitive to wage differentials that cannot be justified by the actual difference in the content of the man's job and the woman's job. The Equal Pay Act guarantees, however, extends only to cases where the man's job and the woman's job are the same or substantially similar.

The attempt by women to narrow the wage gap through comparable worth litigation under Title VII has been notably unsuccessful. In the 1980s, the EEOC was very reluctant to litigate in these cases. The few cases that were brought, usually by unions and nurses' associations, were not successful. The major hurdle has been the stipulation that relief is available only where employers deliberately pay the female incumbents of a job less than they would have paid if the same job were held by men. The courts have expressly voiced their profound reluctance to intervene in the wage-setting practices of employers when different jobs are being compared. Moreover, many judges have stated strongly that they would not want to upset market forces, at least without a very clear indication from Congress that they should do so.

A decision of the United States Supreme Court could conceivably make a significant difference. The Court could, for instance, allow disparate impact (indirect discrimination) claims in comparable worth cases, on the grounds that disparate impact claims are allowed in all other Title VII cases. In view of the composition of the Supreme Court, such decisions are highly unlikely in the foreseeable future. As a result, without an expansion of the statutory guarantee of equal pays to equal pay for work of equal value, it is unlikely that any significant progress will be made in the courts.

4. The role of the social partners

Unions in the United States represent less than 20 per cent of the labour force. The 1980s witnessed a sharp decline in the influence of unions on the national political scene. Because of this and because of traditional American views on the role of unions, their ability to further the cause of pay equity is confined for the most part to collective bargaining, supporting litigations and lobbying for equal pay legislation.

American unions are aware of the appeal of pay equity to their female members, and to potential members, and several major American unions have been prominent supporters of pay equity. The International Union of Electrical Workers (IUEW) has brought equal pay complaints since the 1940s. The American Federation of State, County and Municipal Employees has been active in lobbying state legislatures to review the pay structures for public sector workers.

American unions have traditionally negotiated not only on wage rates, but on how jobs should be slotted into wage grades based on notions of value. There are prominent examples of unions forcing the rearrangement of jobs in a hierarchy, even when no women were involved.[31] This tradition has served union negotiators well, enabling them to focus on pay equity concerns, especially in clerical units and in the public sector. In a highly publicised union organising campaign in the late 1980s among clerical employees of Yale University, comparable worth issues were prominent. Once the union had won representation rights, it attempted to address those concerns in collective bargaining. The union responded to an unsatisfactory offer from the employer with a strike, and the parties were then able for the first time to negotiate a collective agreement that dealt with comparable worth issues.

5. State government action

In the late 1970s, during the Administration of President Carter, the EEOC, under its chairperson Eleanor Holmes Norton, expressed a strong interest in the comparable worth issue. In the 1980s, during President Reagan's Administration, the comparable worth issue languished. With virtually no prospect of federal regulatory action on comparable worth, supporters of the comparable worth principle turned their attention to state legislatures. California, Hawaii, Iowa, Massachusetts, Minnesota, Montana, Oregon and Washington have all enacted legislation in the comparable worth area.

Generally, in the first phase of state government action, the legislature recognises the prevalence of pay inequities between female-dominated and male-dominated job classes, and calls for a study of state (public sector) employees. In the next phase, some action is directed. Most of the states listed above are still in the first phase. Iowa and Minnesota have moved to the next phase where specific job reclassifications, which will recognise comparable worth, must be devised. This may be an extended phase, since implementing comparable worth often carries a higher price tag than contemplated by state legislators. In Washington State there was significant backsliding on the State's commitment to comparable worth once the full financial ramifications became apparent.

Although state action on comparable worth is important, it must be kept in perspective. No state legislature has enacted legislation that applies to the private sector. In a sense, the states that have enacted legislation are acting as employers: that is, they are reviewing the pay structures they have for their own employees. There does not yet seem to be any spillover effect on the practices of private sector employers, nor on other state governments.

6. Conclusions

The implementation of the equal pay for equal work guarantee has been relatively successful in the United States. On the other hand, the movement towards the realisation of an equal pay for work of equal value guarantee has only taken its first steps, and its forward momentum has been halted by a non-receptive judiciary and an inactive federal executive and legislative branch.

Without further legislation, the federal courts could develop the scope of Title VII's equal pay provisions by allowing plaintiffs to make a disparate impact claim in a case of alleged sex-based wage discrimination.[32] The courts have been loathe to do this, on the grounds that this would disrupt market forces. Yet, in other areas of Title VII law, the courts have been willing to go against the market, if that meant opening up opportunities for previously excluded groups. It may be that courts do not yet have a sufficient understanding of how employers set wages, how job evaluation schemes relate to market forces, and how internal labour markets work. They may therefore be reluctant to entertain challenges to an employer's wage hierarchy because they are all too well aware that they will have difficulty in evaluating the arguments.

If courts would allow plaintiffs to put forward disparate impact arguments, this would lead to the development of valid employer defences. This, in itself, would be beneficial as it would force into the arena of public discussion the legitimacy of various factors used in wage-setting.

At present, however, there seems to be lacking a strong national consensus that the persistent wage gap between men and women[33] is the result of less favourable treatment of women. Unless a consensus develops, it is unlikely that the understanding of the meaning of the principle of equal pay will change significantly in the United States.

Notes

[1] The Equal Pay Act of 1963 amends the Fair Labor Standards Act (FLSA), by adding section 206*(d)* to the FLSA.

[2] The Act provides in part: "It shall be an unlawful employment practice for an employer: (1) to fail or refuse to hire or to discharge any individual, or otherwise to discriminate against any individual with respect to his compensation, terms, conditions, or privileges of employment, because of such individual's race, color, religion, sex, or national origin; or (2) to limit, segregate, or classify his employees or applicants for employment in any way which would deprive or tend to deprive any individual of employment opportunities or otherwise adversely affect his status as an employee, because of such individual's race, color, religion, sex, or national origin."

[3] *Report of the Secretary of the National War Labor Board to the Secretary of Labor, for the twelve months ending May 31, 1919* (US Government Printing Office, 1920), pp. 69-71.

[4] *National War Labor Board, Termination Report* (US Government Printing Office, 1945), pp. 296-297.

[5] Equal pay bills were introduced into Congress during the Second World War, but were not enacted. The State of New York enacted an equal pay law in 1945. Between 1945 and 1963, 22 states enacted equal pay legislation. Karen Shallcross Koziara: "Women and work: The evolving policy", in K. Kosziara et al. (eds.): *Working women: Past, present, future* (Washington, DC, Bureau of National Affairs, 1987), p. 379.

[6] 29 USC s. 206*(d)*(1).

[7] The original equal pay bill of 1962 would have required equal pay for work of "comparable character". The term "comparable character" was later replaced by "equal work". The intent behind this amendment was to narrow the scope of the equal pay guarantee. Koziara, op. cit., p. 379.

[8] *Laffey* v. *Northwest Airlines,* 572 F.Supp. 354 (DDC 1983), *aff'd in part and remanded in part,* 746 F.2d 4 (D.C.Cir. 1984), *cert. denied,* 472 US 1021 (1985).

[9] One study found that the average wage differential between the man's job and the woman's job in equal pay cases is 15 per cent. Elizabeth A. Cooper and Gerald V. Barrett: "Equal pay and gender: Implications of court cases for personnel practices", in *Academy of Management Review,* Jan. 1984, 9, pp. 84-94, at p. 84.

[10] A major case where this occurred is *General Electric* v. *Gilbert,* 429 US 125 (1976).

[11] Title VII protects employees from discrimination. The Supreme Court has indicated that the protection of Title VII would not be applicable among partners, e.g. if the partners, who were mostly male, in a law firm decided to divide the firm's profits among the partners in a way that discriminated against female partners. *Hishon* v. *King & Spalding,* 467 US 69 (1984) (Justice Powell concurring).

[12] *City of Los Angeles Department of Water & Power* v. *Manhart,* 435 US 702 (1978). As there has been no difference in the United States in the retirement ages for men and women under pension plans, this was not an issue in the case.

[13] *Arizona Governing Committee for Tax Deferred Annuity & Deferred Compensation Plans* v. *Norris,* 463 US 1073 (1983).

[14] The leading case is *Shultz* v. *Wheaton Glass Co.,* 421 F.2d 259 (3d Cir.), *cert. denied,* 398 US 905 (1970).

[15] S. 709 of Title VII states that compliance with state law is not an admissible excuse for violating Title VII's anti-discrimination requirements. In 1969, the Equal Employment Opportunity Commission revised its Guidelines on Sex Discrimination to specify that Title VII superseded state protective legislation that barred women, as a class, from jobs.

16 *County of Washington, Oregon* v. *Gunther,* 452 US 161 (1981).

17 ibid., at 181.

18 The Supreme Court has described disparate impact discrimination claims as those which "involve employment practices that are facially neutral in their treatment of different groups but that in fact fall more harshly on one group than another and cannot be justified by business necessity". *International Brotherhood of Teamsters* v. *United States,* 431 US 324, 336 n.15 (1977).

19 An early and typical case is *Spaulding* v. *University of Washington,* 740 F.2d 686 (9th Cir. 1984). In this case, professors at the University's school of nursing claimed that they were paid less than the faculty of any other school. All other schools had a predominantly male faculty; the nursing school's faculty was overwhelmingly female.

20 *American Federation of State, County & Municipal Employees* v. *Washington,* 770 F.2d 1401 (9th Cir. 1985). The women had been successful at the trial level. This short-lived victory is the only significant comparable victory in the courts since 1981.

21 *American Nurses Association* v. *Illinois,* 606 F.Supp. 1313 (N.D.I11. 1985).

22 *Corning Glass Works* v. *Brennan,* 417 US 188 (1974).

23 *Kouba* v. *Allstate Insurance Co.,* 523 F.Supp. 148 (E.D.Cal. 1981).

24 See e.g. *Hodgson* v. *Robert Hall Clothes, Inc.,* 473 F.2d 589 (3d Cir.), *cert. denied,* 414 US 866 (1973).

25 Employers are not required to use job evaluation as part of their wage-setting policies nor for monitoring the impact of these policies.

26 The United States Government, and many state and local government units, use job classification as the basis for slotting jobs into wage grades.

27 For example, in *Vuyanich* v. *Republic National Bank,* 24 Fair Empl. Prac. Cas. (BNA) 128 (N.D.Tex. 1980), the employer had used the Hay system. A representative of Hay Associates testified on the application of the job evaluation scheme.

28 An example of where an employer lacked a rational wage structure is *Taylor* v. *Charley Brothers Co.,* 25 Fair Empl. Prac. Cas. (BNA) 602 (W.D.Pa. 1981). The employer basically placed all the men in grade 1 and all the women in grade 2, regardless of their job titles and what tasks they actually performed.

29 See Donald Schwab: "Job evaluation and pay setting: Concepts and practices", in E. Robert Livernash (ed.): *Comparable worth: Issues and alternatives* (Washington, DC, Equal Employment Advisory Council, 1980) pp. 51-77, at p. 49.

30 For a general discussion of the American situation, see Barbara F. Reskin (ed.): *Sex segregation in the workplace: Trends, explanations, remedies* (Washington, DC, National Academy Press, 1984).

31 An example would be the work the United Steelworkers of America did in the basic steel industry in the late 1930s and early 1940s.

32 After the *Gunther* decision, this was a possibility. For a discussion of how cases might be argued, see J. Bellace: "Comparable worth: Proving sex-based wage discrimination", in *Iowa Law Review,* 1984, 69/3, pp. 655-704. No federal court case in the last five years has indicated that the disparate impact claim is a valid line of argument.

33 In the 1950s, before the enactment of equal pay legislation, women earned about 59 per cent of what men earned. This figure remained in the 59-63 per cent range for approximately 30 years. In the 1980s, the gap narrowed somewhat. If one compares full-time, year-round workers, women earn about 70 per cent of what men earn.